BUSINESS/SCIENCE/TECHNOLOGY DIVISION
CHICAGO PUBLIC LIBRARY
400 SOUTH STATE STREET
CHICAGO, IL 60605

REF
HD
5812.2
.A7
H35
2000

HWBI

Constructing Boundaries

SUNY Series in Israeli Studies
Russell Stone, editor

Constructing Boundaries
Jewish and Arab Workers
in Mandatory Palestine

Deborah S. Bernstein

STATE UNIVERSITY OF NEW YORK PRESS

Published by
State University of New York Press, Albany

© 2000 State University of New York

All rights reserved

Printed in the United States of America

No part of this book may be used or reproduced in any manner whatsoever
without written permission. No part of this book may be stored in a retrieval
system or transmitted in any form or by any means including electronic,
electrostatic, magnetic tape, mechanical, photcopying, recording, or otherwise
without the prior permission in writing of the publisher.

For information, address State University of New York Press,
State University Plaza, Albany, N.Y., 12246

Production by Michael Haggett
Marketing by Patrick Durocher

Library of Congress Cataloging-in-Publication Data
Bernstein, Deborah.
    Constructing boundaries : Jewish and Arab workers in mandatory
Palestine / Deborah S. Bernstein.
        p.   cm.
    Includes bibliographical references (p.   ) and index.
    ISBN 0–7914–4539–9 (hardcover : alk. paper). — ISBN 0–7914–4540–2
(pbk. : alk. paper)
    1. Labor market—Israel—Haifa—History—20th century.   2. Haifa
(Israel)—Economic conditions.   3. Jews—Israel—Haifa—Economic
conditions.   4. Palestinian Arabs—Employment—Israel—Haifa.
5. Labor movement—Palestine—History—20th century.   6. Haifa
(Israel)—Ethnic relations.   I. Title.
HD5812.2.A7H35   2000
331.12'095694'6—dc21   99–37759
                                                                  CIP

BUSINESS/SCIENCE/TECHNOLOGY DIVISION
CHICAGO PUBLIC LIBRARY
400 SOUTH STATE STREET
CHICAGO, IL 60605

R0171956021

To my father, Herbert Bernstein,
and in memory of my mother, Sylvia Levinthal Bernstein,
from both of whom I learned to respect all people.

BUSINESS

Contents

Part II
In the Labor Market

Tables

Illustrations

Preface

This book has been in the making for quite a few years, but never in a vacuum. No writing of history takes place in a vacuum, and certainly not in Israel / Palestine. New questions have emerged, new perspectives, new insights, as circumstances have constantly changed. Even the words have taken on different meanings. I began this study at the height of the *Intifada*, and continued it as the peace accord between the State of Israel and the Palestine Liberation Organization was signed in 1993. It was a period of hope and expectation for far-reaching, though probably not immediate, change. My study of the past, of the pre-state Mandatory period, increased my awareness of the radical change taking place. For the first time in the long Arab-Jewish / Israeli conflict, the recognized Jewish / Israeli leadership negotiated directly and openly with the Palestinian leadership, chosen and recognized by its people. The complex of rejection-recognition-cooptation-manipulation, which was woven into the relations I studied, appeared to be changing, and a tentative, precarious move toward mutual acceptance could be felt. But not for long. Yitzhak Rabin, who symbolized both the shift and its precariousness, was murdered. Negotiations continued, but lost so much of their deeper significance.

During this long and complex period we, Israeli Jews, have been faced with questions, doubts, and dilemmas. We questioned the legitimacy of our present position in Israel / Palestine as a land, and toward the Palestinians as a people, thus leading to our questioning and querying the legitimacy of our past. Were new alternatives being offered? Had there been alternatives in the formative past? Were there courses that could have been taken? These questions instructed much of my work. At times, as I "roamed" through the past among the archive files, attempting to hear-decipher-reconstruct voices of the various actors, I sensed an uncanny familiarity. And in turn, much around me appeared to reproduce patterns and relations of the past. The construction of boundaries, which I study in this book, left a deep legacy, riveted with tension and contradiction, that, ideally, we will be able to face in the coming years.

Friends and colleagues followed my work with interest and encouragement. Many of my colleagues read chapters of the manuscript at various stages of writing. I would especially like to thank Nurit Bird-David, Yoram Carmeli, Gad Gilbar, Gustavo Mesch, Uri Ram, Paul Ritterband, Henry Rosenfeld, Yossi Shavit, Zvi Sobel, Michael Saltman, Ilan Talmud, and Yuval Yonay. I benefited from their comments and insight. The Department of Sociology and Anthropology of the University of Haifa offered much support and help when necessary, as did the Faculty of Social Science and the Research Authority of the University of Haifa. I would also like to thank the students who assisted me, most especially Nehama Offir, Fadi Nahas, Nuha Rouhana, and Dana Weiss. I would like to extend thanks to the workers of the many archives where I carried out my research, and especially to Yael Tadmor and Ilan Gal-Peer of the Labor Archive of the Lavon Institute in Tel Aviv. I would also like to thank Judy Hill for her careful, caring, and conscientious editing of the manuscript. And finally, I would like to thank the Israel Foundation Trustees for the grant that enabled the research for this book, and the Research Authority of the University of Haifa for the additional financial support.

Figure 1. View of Haifa from Mount Carmel, circa 1930.

Constructing Boundaries

Introduction

Ya'acov Davidon arrived in Haifa, a port town in the north of Palestine, on the 2nd of November, 1921.[1] He had come by train from Jaffa, and made his way through the narrow streets of the Arab *suq*, heading toward the wooden huts that his friends, of the builders' collective, had constructed on the lower slopes of Mount Carmel. The streets were almost empty and the few people about seemed sullen and frightened. He was soon to learn that the Arabs had staged a demonstration that day, the anniversary of the Balfour Declaration. The police had dispersed it and badly wounded two of the demonstrators. Riots had broken out, and many Jews had been hurt. Davidon continued determinedly on his way. He walked by ominous looking Arab men, but soon left the main path, preferring to creep over the rocks through thorny bushes, till scratched and weary, he reached Herzl Street, the main thoroughfare of the new Hebrew neighborhood of Hadar Hacarmel. He was joyfully greeted by Jewish workers who were on guard duty. He was safe—once again in an all-Jewish environment. The following morning, he set out, together with members of the collective, for one of the many construction sites in the neighborhood. It would soon be the heart of the new Jewish community of Haifa.

His life, over the next few years, evolved within this newly established community: He dwelt, with friends, in the camp of tents that the Haifa Labor Council (HLC) constructed for the hundreds of new immigrant workers. He usually ate in the HLC workers' kitchen, where meals were cheap, and then crossed the street to join other Jewish workers at the Lebanon Café. He enjoyed the improvised theater where the immigrants staged Hebrew plays. At times, he courted young women from among the dwellers of the tent camp in the gardens of the Technion, the new institution for higher technological education. He worked on the construction sites of the Chelanov Buildings, on Herzl Street. They were the first buildings to be constructed of bricks manufactured by Jewish immigrants in Tel Aviv, rather than of stone, as was the custom of the Arab masons. On occasion he and his friends would see a silent film, at "the Coliseum," a large hall built by two Jewish partners. Khalil, "the king of advertising," would march around town, dragging one leg, ringing his bell, with scores of children of all religions running after him, and would announce the event of that evening. On Friday nights, all the young men and women of the new Jewish community would congregate at the small shop of Mustafa al-Hajj, by the old Arab market. There al-Hajj would preside over containers of cool drinks, with strange tastes, colors, and names—the *tamarhindi*, the sweet juice made of dates, the *barad* full of ice flakes, and the *buza*, sweeter than honey.

The life that Davidon describes is self-contained within the Jewish community, but not isolated from the general milieu. This semi-separate world was typical of the Jewish immigrant experience. The immigrants arrived at the ports of Jaffa and Haifa and found themselves thrust into the hustle and bustle of a Middle Eastern Mediterranean port. From the port they most likely moved into a homogeneous Jewish environment—a collective agricultural settlement or a Jewish urban neighborhood. They would probably have been employed by a Jewish employer. They would, most probably, have affiliated with the large Jewish labor organization, the General Federation of Jewish Labor—the Histadrut— and the local Jewish workers' council. Some would join one of the many political parties active in the Jewish settlement. Yet at the same time, they could not but be aware that they were in the Middle East—in Palestine—among a large Arab population. As they traveled from place to place, they passed by numerous Arab villages. The call of the *Muazin* must have been part of the daily sounds for many of the Jewish settlers. Both Arabs and Jews used public transport. Many of the immigrants, living in the mixed towns of Haifa or Jaffa, Jerusalem, Safad, or Tiberias, might have had Arab neighbors or landlords. Most of the Jewish settlers bought fresh vegetables from the Arab *suq*, where prices were low, and they might have hired a young Arab boy to carry their purchases in a large basket on his back to their homes. Many families employed an Arab woman to do the weekly washing or an Arab plumber to repair the piping if, as happened frequently, no Jewish plumber was available. On occasion, they might hire an Arab cart driver to transfer a heavy load. Some of the Jewish workers might be employed together with

Arab workers in a government office or possibly in a small printing shop, while others might compete with Arab workers over work in construction or porterage. How much was the daily life of the Jews in the towns affected by the presence of the large Arab population and how much did it affect their collective, communal life? To understand the development of the Jewish community, we must locate it within the context of Palestine with its Arab majority and examine the forces impinging on and affecting it, and in turn, being affected by it.

In this study of the interrelations of Jewish and Arab labor in the labor market of Mandatory Haifa, I argue that the Jewish settlement cannot be understood as an isolated autonomous entity, self-explanatory in terms of its own internal development. The Jewish settlement as a whole, as well as the collectives and individuals within it, existed and functioned in a mixed environment in which Jews and Arabs were interrelated. They constantly impacted and impinged on one another. This was part of their everyday reality, whether or not they acknowledged it. The patterns of Jewish and Arab responses to each other's presence will be the major concern of this study.

CURRENT APPROACHES AND NEW DIRECTIONS

The dominant approach of historiographers of the Jewish settlement has been quite different from the approach that I follow. The Zionist-oriented historiography that developed within the Jewish community, and later within the State of Israel, focused on itself, and itself alone. It portrayed the Jewish community as isolated, even insulated from its Arab neighbors in a manner that located it in a contextual vacuum. Similarly, even in the historiography that dealt with the pre-Zionist Jewish immigrations to Palestine, the focus was solely on the Jewish community. Ben-Zion Dinur, the important early Zionist historian, stated this focus explicitly in his explanation of the term the *"Yishuv,"* which he coined:

> The name *Yishuv* [Settlement—D.B.] is a special term for the Jewish population and for it alone, and it is short for the term *Yishuv Eretz Yisrael,* [the settlement of the Land of Israel]. It refers to the Jewish population in the Land of Israel, at times when the Jews do not govern it. For, regardless of the size of the Jewish population, it has a unique image, special to the Jews in this land.[2]

For the early Zionist historians, as Barnai demonstrates, the almost exclusive focus on the Jewish community was part of an explicit denial that the Land of Israel and the people living in and on it had any significant history other than its Jewish history.[3] This symbolic and substantive exclusivity remained a central feature of the historiography of the Jewish settlement in Palestine, even as it moved away from a manifestly ideological portrayal of the Jewish community. The work of Anita Shapira represents the acme of academic historiography as it attempted to relieve Zionist historiography of "the burden of hagiography."[4] "There was, of course," she writes, "general awareness that all historians are products of their time and place, burdened with the preconceptions inculcated in them by their education, society and personal biography." But the attempt was to transcend these "human limitations."

> Placing oneself in the shoes of history makers necessitated understanding their spiritual world, listening to the slightest nuances in their words, comparing their public stances with what they said in private, following the dynamics of social and political relations, distinguishing between central and marginal issues, between slips of the tongue and actual intent, between what had an impact and what remained empty talk and, in effect, setting their words against their deeds.[5]

Such "thick" historical reconstruction, and its sensitive tuning in, kept the limelight firmly focused on, and in, the Jewish *Yishuv*, as a separate, autonomous, and isolated entity. Such isolation was indeed the goal of most of the vast majority of the Jewish community, and of its leadership, and it reflected the way they perceived themselves. Scholars reflected these perceptions by zooming in on the internal dynamics of the Jewish community. The issues they studied, their terminology, and the causal factors to which they pointed in their analyses, all reinforced the image of a social entity, largely unaffected by its immediate social, political, and economic environment. When such "external" factors were included, they seemed to appear out of nowhere, and remained in the background. Thus there was no attempt to ground them in anything like the historical understanding granted the Jewish community. As early as 1979, Shlomo Swirsky noted that S. N. Eisenstadt, by far the dominant Israeli sociologist, focused almost exclusively on internal developments within the Jewish settlement. Swirsky argued that he ignored developments outside of the Jewish community, even those of the Jewish diaspora. He also ignored issues concerning British policy and the Arab population of Palestine that were crucial to the Jewish settlement. Swirsky went on to claim that Dan Horowitz and Moshe Lissak, the leading sociologists of the pre-state period, who recognized these factors, treated them as "external systems," as part of a "dual" environment in which the "center" (i.e., the leadership of the *Yishuv*) functioned. Swirsky contended that, having acknowledged these factors, they continued to focus their analysis almost exclusively on internal developments within the Jewish settlement.[6] Avishai Ehrlich, in his important article "Israel: Conflict, War and Social Change,"[7] contends that the Arab-Israeli conflict, so central a phenomenon to Israeli society, has been ignored by Israeli sociology—and sociologists:

> A survey of existing literature shows a paucity of research on the connection between aspects of the conflict and major spheres of Israeli social structure; economics and stratification, politics, culture and values, socialization and the family. Even fewer are the researches which deal with consequences of the conflict on Israeli structure from a macro-societal point of view, using historical-comparative methods or trying to establish connections between the dynamics of the conflict and processes of social change in Israel.[8]

Recently, a new theoretical approach has been developed that adopts a perspective distant from that of the Zionist actors. It studies the Jewish-Zionist settlement in Palestine within the framework of colonial settlers' societies. As Uri Ram states, "It depicts Israel as a settler-colonial society driven by the needs of territorial acquisition and pressures of the labor market, and it regards the Israeli-Arab conflict as the most crucial determinant in the shaping of Israeli society."[9] It thus focuses attention on the wider context of settlement and on the conditions in the land. It attributes importance to the existing population, the Arab population in Palestine—its demographic, social, economic, and political features. Furthermore, it identifies levels of contact between the Arab society and the Jewish settlement and notes their impact on one another. In the late 1970s, Kimmerling, an early pioneer of this perspective, identified the central foci of conflict between Jews and Arabs as ownership of land, monopoly over labor, and the demographic balance between the two national groups. He discussed the Arab position and the evolving British policy as part of the Jewish-Arab conflict. He did not stop there, but examined the impact of these positions on the process of "Jewish nation building." Kimmerling argued that the need to come to terms with Arab opposition and British compromises significantly determined many of the structural and institutional features that developed within the Jewish community.[10] His later work continues along similar lines.[11] Gershon Shafir has developed the "colonial perspective" more explicitly.[12] He identifies the nature of the Jewish settlement movement in terms of types of colonial movements, defining each type in terms of the relations between the settling movement and the local population vis-à-vis demography, land, and labor. He argues that the central features of the Jewish settlement—its self-segregation from the Arab population and its cooperative-collective institutions, both of which had already emerged in the late Ottoman period—were not a result of ideology, as the mainstream approach contends, but of strategic responses to the detrimental impact of Arab labor. Shalev follows a similar approach in his detailed study of Jewish organized labor during the British Mandatory period and into statehood.[13] He analyzes the policies of the Histadrut—the General Federation of Jewish Labor—in terms of its response to the threat that Arab labor posed to Jewish labor. Again, what was seen as the internal dynamics of the Jewish settlement, by most students of the Yishuv, was understood as strategic structural choices in response to impinging and intervening forces, in the context of a colonial immigrant-settlers' movement. The works of Kimmerling, Shafir, and Shalev are part of a much larger, ongoing, controversy in Israeli historiography, which has become known as "The New, versus the Old Historians" or the post-Zionist historiography.[14] This controversy has become a major focus of intellectual and public debate, touching on the most essential themes of Israeli self-image and self-legitimization. This controversy has been invaluable in challenging prevailing concepts, shaking the taken-for-granted assumptions of Israeli-Zionist understanding, highlighting ideological preconceptions, and raising many new and probing questions.[15] And yet, after three to four years of debate, at times extremely heated and polemical, the controversy over Israeli historiography seems to me to have become self-perpetuating, a goal in itself rather than a stimulus for new research and analysis.[16] I, therefore, choose to acknowledge this stimulating controversy from which I benefited greatly, to indicate my basic historiographic orientation, and to move on to my own study and analysis, without delving into heated polemics and partisan affiliation.

     This study of the interrelation of Jewish and Arab labor in the urban labor market of Haifa shares much of the perspective of Kimmerling, Shafir, and Shalev. It expands this perspective and develops it along new lines and into new spheres. I argue that the Jewish settlement cannot be understood as an isolated autonomous entity, but rather as an evolving entity, affected by, and responding to, the conditions and the population within which it developed. This does not necessarily boil down to arguments about direct interaction between Jews and Arabs or about joint action between them. On the contrary, separation and segregation were often the case, though not at all times and under all conditions. But separation is itself a kind of interaction, a dynamic process of response to challenge and threat. It is a process in flux, dynamically responding to specific and changing circumstances. Furthermore, separation might be one form of response, but other forms might emerge as well, complementing or contradicting one another. The one study that has attempted to break down the distinctions between the Jewish and Arab communities is Zakary Lockman's recent work on Jewish and Arab workers.[17] Lockman's study is an important contribution to the historiography of Palestine. He presents (or represents) Jewish and Arab workers as active social agents, to be taken seriously and granted respect, as few students have done so far, be they historians or sociologists, "new" or "old." And yet, by confining himself to those cases of direct interaction and cooperation between Jews and Arabs, he seems, much of the time, to ignore the separation between them, so pervasive in the lives of both. By focusing on attitudes, perceptions, and discourse, Lockman tends to "release" his actors from the full force of the national, political, and economic context in which they interacted and impinged on each other.

I contend that the Arabs of Palestine cannot be portrayed as an "external" factor that, once having been introduced, can be left out of the discussion of further processes and developments. This, however, is the case, in large measure with the works of Shafir and Shalev, despite their critique of such an approach by earlier sociologists. They do, indeed, treat the historical condition of the Arabs in Palestine in detail, and acknowledge their essential impact on the developments within the Jewish community, but, having done so, they proceed to focus their analysis on the Jewish community. I shall attempt to demonstrate that the Arab population not only affected the Jewish settlement, but was actively interrelated with it. It placed severe constraints on the Jewish settlement and was constrained by it. It elicited reactions on the part of the Jewish settlers and actively responded to them.

The dominant response of the Jewish settlement to the threat posed by the Arab population was self-segregation and the erection of boundaries, while the dominant response of the Arab population was strong opposition to Zionist immigration. Nevertheless, both of these responses were dynamic, and they shifted in shape and form, depending on the overall political and economic conditions, as well as on the specific social location of various actors. The closer the actors were to the grass roots, the greater was their tendency to give priority to their immediate class interests and this included cooperating with each other in the same workplace. The closer they were to the organizational leadership, the greater the tendency to give priority to national-political considerations, even to the extent of jeopardizing joint action with co-workers.

I was motivated to embark on this study by the anticipation of far more direct contact and interaction between Jews and Arabs than the conventional model led us to expect. I assumed that such interaction would most likely develop in a mixed town. Haifa, one of a number of mixed towns, was chosen as the most suitable case study. A major proportion of Haifa's population, among both Jews and Arabs, were recent arrivals. Thus the relations that evolved and that I will analyze in this study, were an outcome of the period of large-scale Zionist immigration and settlement, and had few roots in the earlier pre-Zionist period. I further expected the economy, and especially the labor market, to be an arena most susceptible to interpenetration. Resources of capital, commodities, and labor would be likely to move between Jewish and Arab economic ventures and lead to various forms of interaction, cooperation, and competition. Here too, Haifa was the most appropriate place to examine this assumption, because it was the main center of economic development in Palestine for the Jewish economic sector, the Arab sector, and for government economic enterprises. Haifa's strategic location along the coast, together with a its deep-water harbor and easy overland access to the east, Trans-Jordan, Iraq, and potentially on to India, lent it its vital importance to the British government. Large Jewish industry concentrated in Haifa for similar reasons, even before the First World War, and even more so once the government contributed to the development of the town and its infrastructure. Arab entrepreneurs were attracted to Haifa in response to its rapid development and the promise it seemed to hold for the future. As a result, the town became the focus of a large-scale influx of rural Arabs in search of work and of Jewish immigrants in search of a place to settle down that might provide stable employment. The abundance of workers triggered the development of workers' organizations, and Haifa became the most cohesively organized concentration of Jewish urban workers, as well as the center of the major Arab workers' organization—the Palestine Arab Workers' Society. Thus, the varied economy, the plentiful supply of workers, and the generally high level of organization made Haifa a suitable arena for the study of relations between Jewish and Arab labor. These considerations were reinforced by a prevailing image, in Jewish sources, of Mandatory Haifa as a place in which relatively close relations existed between Jews and Arabs, especially among the circles of organized Jewish labor, led by the Haifa Labor Council and its powerful secretary Aba Houshi.

As I delved deeper into the evidence of the period, of the time and place, I became increasingly aware that my expectations for the discovery of direct contact and interaction might not be confirmed. Instead, I found myself a witness, or rather an active reconstructor, of a process of segregation and boundary building on the part of organized Jewish labor. As I acknowledged the centrality and dominance of this process, I also became increasingly aware of the diverging voices. These voices, from within the ranks of Jewish labor, emphasized common class interests and searched for forms of cooperation that would transcend national perspectives so as to improve the common lot of Jewish and Arab workers, even if on an ad hoc, piecemeal basis. At the same time, and despite the fact that most of my source material came from the archives of Jewish institutions, Arab labor began to make its own appearance. Through the daily Arab press of the period, through leaflets of protest of Arab labor organizations, through minutes of conventions of Arab labor, through minutes of joint meetings of Arab and Jewish labor activists, and through letters and memoranda sent by Arab labor organizations to government officials, the position of Arab labor began to emerge. At times, it was almost as if two loudspeakers were directed at me, from opposite sides, each proclaiming, at the very same time, a different, almost symmetrically opposite, message. Beshara Doumani has discussed a similar divergence between the historiographic interpretation of Israeli, Zionist-oriented, and Palestinian popular writers and scholars.

> As with all forms of intellectual production, the writing of history is organically linked to and affected by the ideological environment and historical context of the author, often shedding more light on the times of the writer than on the intended subject. The historiography of Palestine is a classic example of this phenomenon. As a land of great symbolic significance to adherents of the world's three monotheistic religions, and as the common objective of two competing national movements, its past has been subjected to multiple and, at least on the surface, contradictory traditions of historical interpretation. Throughout this century, the interplay between power and knowledge has produced a series of tunnel visions, each of which questions the legitimacy of the other.[18]

I do not claim to be able to present both groups with as much detail, or with anything like as much sensitivity. I do not know if anyone can. But I do hope that I am able to move away from the "Jewish 'internal'–Arab 'external'" model, that has explicitly, and implicitly, guided previous studies.

The units of analysis in this study were determined by the overall perspective previously presented. The Jewish community was not distinguished, a priori, from the Arab community, for separate analysis and presentation. On the contrary, encompassing arenas were chosen, in which Jews and Arabs were undergoing different processes, which were an outcome of their previous history. These processes had a reciprocal effect on both groups. The most general level of analysis is that of Palestine as a whole, with its colonial government, Arab majority, and growing Jewish minority. The more focused level of analysis is that of the town of Haifa, in which both Arab and Jewish communities evolved and consolidated. And the most detailed level of analysis is that of specific industries within Haifa, in which both Jews and Arabs were employed. It was within these arenas that both Arabs and Jews worked out their different courses of development, usually veering away from each other, at times competing and conflicting, and yet at others times, they did find common causes.

THE SPLIT LABOR MARKET THEORY
AND ITS HISTORICAL GROUNDING

The theoretical model of the Split Labor Market (SLM) as developed by Edna Bonacich[19] has provided me with a theoretical starting point for the study of the dynamics of this labor market. In her theory she posits a situation in which two groups of labor, belonging to different ethnic / national origins, meet in the same labor market. The more advantaged ethnic group is able, due to its past history and its more advantaged position within world capitalist development, to ensure a higher value for its labor. It is threatened by the presence of the less advantaged groups, whose labor has lower value, and is thus more attractive to employers intent on maximizing profits. The theory then develops the different ways in which cheaper labor might serve to displace and substitute for the higher-priced labor, and the strategies of the higher-priced labor group to maintain its relative advantage. To quote one of Bonacich's formulations of the gist of the split labor market theory:

> This approach places labor competition at the center of racist-nationalist movements . . . Uneven development of capitalism on a world scale, exacerbated by imperialist domination, generates "backwardness" or "under-development" for certain "nationalities." Workers of these nations, unable to defend themselves against exploitation of the severest kind, became "cheap labor". The availability of cheap labor leads dominant workers to be displaced or threatened with dis-

placement, since employers would prefer to hire cheaper labor. . . . Dominant group workers react to the threat of displacement by trying to prevent or limit capital's access to cheap labor, through efforts to exclude members of "cheap labor" groups from full participation in the labor market. That these exclusionary efforts have a "nationalist" or "racist" character is a product of historical accident which produced a correlation between ethnicity and the price of labor.[20]

Thus, in the absence of a split labor market, we would not expect the emergence of nationalist movements and the confrontations between them. Bonacich states her conclusion clearly:

I would like to reemphasize that "race" is not the only line along which a division in the working class, based on price of labor differences, is drawn. Sex and nationality mark other important instances. The dynamic is a class dynamic. Race, sex, nationality become the symbolism in which the conflict is expressed, but they are not in themselves the cause. . . . When there is no split in the labor market along these lines, I would predict a decline in racism, sexism, etc. and the emergence of a united proletariat. "Race" is important only so long as it is rooted in class processes.[21]

The SLM theory has been applied to the study of Jewish labor in Palestine by Shafir and Shalev.[22] Both studies accepted the SLM theory as developed by Bonacich, and applied it, as a major explanatory model, supplemented by additional theoretical concepts, to the issues with which they were concerned. My own approach differs. The theoretical model of the SLM serves primarily as an insightful guideline, to help understand and highlight the story of Jewish and Arab labor in Mandatory Haifa. But the story, its actors and dynamic development, has an impetus of its own. Thus the relation between theory and "story" is far looser, more complex, and interactive. The theory informs the case; it serves as an implicit organizing guideline, but, at the same time, it is informed by the dynamics that appear to me to emerge from the evidence. As this process of reciprocal negotiation between theory and evidence consolidated, I became increasingly aware of some basic limitations of the SLM theory. The relations between Jewish and Arab labor in the labor market of Haifa, in construction and in manufacturing, in the Haifa port and in the Palestine Railways reveal a more complex and dynamic interrelation and interaction than the SLM model would have led us to expect. Thus the historical grounding of the theory has led me to conclusions concerning the SLM theory that may be of importance for its theoretical elaboration and future use.

Bonacich's theory strives to explain ethnic or national conflict in terms of class relations. As I attempted to apply it to the dynamic relations between Jewish and Arab labor, it became clear to me that a far more varied and complex setting would have to be taken into account. It is not enough to mechanically register the ways in which cheap labor might substitute for more expensive labor, and the strategies the more expensive labor latter might pursue in response. If we are to understand which modes of action were actually pursued and by whom and, as important, which possible modes were avoided or overlooked, if we wish to gain insight into why some courses of action succeeded while others did not, we must locate our actors in their historical setting. This historical setting motivates them by more than just economic factors. In turn, these economic factors, certainly not to be underestimated, are themselves dynamically shaped by additional factors that do not necessarily overpower or overdetermine the economic ones, but they do powerfully interact with them.

Groups of workers of different ethnic or national origins are motivated, in many cases, not only by the desire for employment and for maximal wages, and employers are not always motivated only by the desire to maximize profits. Nationalism, and the creation, consolidation, and advancement of national entities are an additional, powerful force effecting relations between groups whose interests, in these respects, might pull in different directions. I contend that nationalism is relevant for the dynamics of the split labor market because it actively intervenes in it. National aspirations and national interests in themselves help determine the initial split and the various ways the different parties react in the SLM context. At times, it is in the context of national movements that the split is formed in the first place, and it is in the context of national conflict that the strategies of both the more expensive and cheaper labor are shaped and played out. Nationalism cannot be considered merely a facade for conflicts of labor market interests and be expected to disappear when the labor conflicts disappear. Nor is it a force that determines all else, so that labor market contradictions are merely playing out national conflicts. In cases of conflicting national groups within a split labor market, we can expect the competition between the two groups of workers to sharpen the national boundaries. At the same time, the differing national interests will effect the strategies pursued within the SLM.

The case of Palestine is a good example of such intricate relations. Both Jewish nationalism—Zionism—and Palestinian nationalism were in the process of being formed, and as part of that process they responded to one another on numerous fronts, among them the restricted and split labor market of Palestine. I do not intend to enter the interesting recent debate over the nature of nationalism and national communal identities. A number of leading scholars, among them Ernest Gellner, Anthony Smith, Benedict Anderson, and Eric Hobsbawm, have emphasized the nature of nationalism as a recent creation of the modern, capitalist world. They all claim nationalism to be a new creation rather than a recreation of, or a continuity with, the distant past, as many nationalist ideologies claim. Yet some of the scholars consider nationalism to be totally new and unrelated to the past, as in B. Anderson's concept of "imagined communities," while others, most prominently Anthony Smith, claim that modern nationalism links itself, culturally, to a distant common ethnic basis.[23] Recent Israeli scholars have attempted to analyze Zionism in the context of this wider debate of the imagined and/or reconstructed nature of national identities. The main aim of their analysis has been to relate to Zionism as part of a much larger phenomenon—that of nationalist movements and identities—and to consider it as a newly constructed, or even "imagined" identity, rather than as a revival of ancient days, myths, and identities.[24] Yet, as intriguing as this debate is, for the purpose of the present study we should note that by the end of the First World War both Jewish and Palestinian nationalist identities were firm enough to be driving forces for both communities, far stronger than any rival identities. Thus the conflict that developed between the Arab and Jewish communities, discussed so far in terms of SLM hostility, was far more than that. It was an overall national conflict that concerned all aspects of life. It was a conflict over land, over the relative share of the population, and over sovereignty, as well as over the share of employment.[25] It was first and foremost a conflict between two national communities and national movements. The commitment to the national cause was expressed at the ideological level in both communities. But it was not only an abstract ideological commitment. Nationalism shaped everyday life and practice to the most concrete and minute degree. Who was one's neighbor, what language one spoke, to which organization one belonged, and even what products one bought and in what market one bought them, were all national political issues, explicitly recognized as such by all concerned. The labor market relations between Jewish and Arab labor and, even more accutely, between their organizations, was thus an intricate interplay of class and national interests.

The labor market itself is highly differentiated. Thus my argument calls for a placement of the labor market in a broader political and historical context and at the same time for "finer" distinctions within the specific labor market situations. The higher-priced and cheaper workers to which the SLM theory refers, meet, or potentially meet, in a wide range of settings. These settings differ in the nature of the threat posed by the cheaper workers, the strategies pursued by the more expensive workers, and the interests of the employers. The economy may be divided into different sectors according to the identity of the owners of the means of production. This might well effect their relation to the different groups of workers, because of shared noneconomic perspectives and interests. Furthermore, industries differ in the level of skill they require. This factor might be significant in determining the threat posed by cheap labor and the options available to the more expensive labor. Even within the same industry, enterprises might differ in terms of the way their labor is recruited and organized, and the way the labor process is set out and controlled. Thus an overall model of labor market relations should bear in mind the differentiation within the labor market, and its potential for bringing about various patterns of relations.

Bonacich's theoretical model focuses on two main actors—the cheaper and the more expensive groups of workers. The SLM theory implies that the cheaper labor accepts its role in the labor market passively, perhaps even happily, since the low cost enhances the workers' potential for employment. The more expensive labor, however, actively reacts to the threat of substitution, primarily through strategies aimed at excluding the cheap workers from the market. I argue that in both cases additional forms of response are viable, and are even to be expected. The cheaper and weaker labor force, in all probability, will not remain static. This has been recently demonstrated by Agnes Calliste, in relation to black workers on American and Canadian railroads, and to the conditions that affected their struggle to break out of the split labor market in which they were submerged.[26] The weaker group of workers is not an isolated labor force, but one affected by the class relations of the capitalist system. Furthermore, it is precisely the split labor market situation itself, and the visibility of the higher-priced labor, even if from behind barriers, that can be expected to catapult the "cheaper and weaker" out of their passivity. Their attempts at change might be made at an ad hoc level, or as part of a long, determined, well-planned struggle. They may be hesitant and tentative, their success might be partial and piecemeal or far-reaching. In any case, the analytical framework should take such potential developments into account.

The higher-priced labor might be less "exclusion minded" than Bonacich's discussion of her own model leads us to expect. Once again, the split labor market situation itself contains the potential for greater diversity. The availability of cheap labor poses limitations on the ability of the higher-priced workers to pursue their preferred strategy of closure. Under such conditions they might be expected to adopt an alternative course and attempt some form of equalization, instead of, or in an uneasy combination with, strategies of exclusion. In pursuing a strategy of equalization, higher-priced labor attempts to avoid being substituted or downgraded, by raising the value of cheap labor and thus eliminating, or mitigating, the competition between them.[27] This is a highly problematic course of action. It entails the loss of the relative advantage of the cheap labor and is difficult to conclude successfully. It is, not surprisingly, pursued less frequently than the strategies of closure. Nevertheless, I contend that equalization strategies are as integral an outcome of the split labor market situation as the more frequent, and more often studied, strategies of exclusion. Cliff Brown and Terry Boswell have recently pointed to the need for greater attention to be paid to cases of solidarity within split labor market analysis. They studied the conditions under which interracial solidarity developed during the great steel strike of 1919 as compared to the conditions under which strikebreaking took place.[28] Thus, by grounding both strategies of exclusion and solidarity in the concrete historical context in which they were pursued, we are able to identify the circumstances that led to each strategy and the contradictory tensions that developed between them.

The circumstances of the SLM in Palestine made equalization very difficult to achieve. Such attempts were, therefore, relatively rare and marginal both in terms of the resources allocated to them and the ideological commitment invested in them. And yet the marginality of an alternative should not marginalize it in the study of the society and the relations it embodied. While remaining marginal, the various attempts at equalization, each differing from the dominant Zionist labor orientation, continued to be made. They offered potential alternatives and signaled that the dominant labor orientation was not the only possible course of action, either because of its limitations or because of the opposition it aroused.

Thus the study of the relations of Arab and Jewish workers in Mandatory Haifa is related to two theoretical issues: (1) to the analysis of the Zionist settlement in Palestine and its interaction with the Arab population; (2) to the SLM theory and its historical grounding. Both issues set the framework for the case study of Haifa and underlie the discussion of its unique story.

The analysis of labor market relations in the following chapters moves from the most general level of Palestine as a whole to the most detailed level of a given work site. In part I, the study begins with an overall view of Palestine and its split labor market, a discussion of

Jewish and Arab workers in the three sectors of Palestine's economy, the Jewish, the Arab, and the government sectors. Then the discussion focuses on Haifa as a special case study, presenting the town, its development, its population, and the pull between cooperation and disengagement that characterized the relations between Jews and Arabs in Haifa, in all spheres. In Part II, the examination of labor market relations moves on to the labor market itself. Each of its four chapters is devoted to an industry that was important for the Haifa economy and society. The first two industries, construction and manufacturing, were owned by both Jews and Arabs and so formed part of the Jewish and the Arab sectors. The other industries, the Haifa port, the Palestine Railways, were owned and managed by the British colonial government. The relations between Jewish and Arab workers in each industry are explored in terms of the special characteristics of each economic sector (i.e., Jewish, Arab, and government), and of each particular industry within the sector. The specific interplay between economic and political-national considerations is examined in each case, as it played itself out in concrete issues and events, such as strikes, conflicts over wages, controversies over labor organizations, and the relations between the two nationally oriented labor organizations, the Jewish Labor Movement—the Histadrut—and the Palestine Arab Workers' Society. The overall trends and conclusions are presented in the concluding discussion.

Part I

The Split Develops

Chapter 1

The Split Labor Market of Mandatory Palestine: Actors, Sectors, and Strategies

The end of the First World War and the beginning of British rule in Palestine marked the start of a period of rapid demographic and economic growth. This was triggered, in large measure, by the influx of Jewish immigration and the consolidation of the new Jewish settlement. Jewish colonization led to a complex interaction with the resident Arab population. Palestine's economy developed into a split labor market, in which the Jewish labor force commanded the higher wages and the Arab labor force the lower wages. This chapter deals with the way this split labor market came about: how each group functioned within it, and within the three economic sectors—the Jewish, the Arab, and the Government—that made up the economy of Palestine.

DEMOGRAPHIC AND SOCIAL TRENDS

Palestine had been far from stagnant before the First World War, images to the contrary notwithstanding. By the mid-nineteenth century numerous changes had set the economy moving—the Ottoman land and tax reform of 1858, the growing involvement of European powers, the increased contact with the European market, the Jewish immigration, the import of capital in the last two decades of the nineteenth century, and the connection to the Hijaz railway in 1905.

With the beginning of British civil rule in Palestine, the economic and social damage wrought by the First World War was quickly overcome and the population of Palestine almost tripled between the years 1920 and 1945. The population was made up of the Arab inhabitants, a large, albeit shrinking majority, and the Jewish inhabitants, a continually increasing minority. Both communities were experiencing rapid growth. The Arab population in Palestine increased at a faster rate than in any other country in the Middle East, but the Jewish rate of increase far outdistanced it. The processes of growth were extremely different. The Arab population increased primarily through natural increase, while the Jewish population grew through immigration. The Jewish population was relatively indifferent to the growing number of Arab inhabitants. The Arabs, however, realizing the political and economic significance of the Jewish demographic growth, were deeply concerned by it.

Table 1.1 illustrates the high overall rate of growth and the distinct differences between the two communities. The Arab population doubled within two and a half decades; the Jewish community increased by almost tenfold in the same period. Arab growth was due to a high rate of natural increase, whereas a much higher rate of immigration accounted for the Jewish population growth. Natural growth from a high birth rate and a declining death rate accounted for 77 percent of the Arab population increase. Arab immigration into Palestine accounted for the remaining 23 percent.[1]

In 1882, when the Zionist immigration began, the Jewish community in Palestine numbered approximately 24,000.[2] The first waves of Zionist immigration, together with the continuing traditional, religious-oriented immigration, raised the Jewish population to about 85,000 on the eve of the First World War. The war dealt a heavy blow to the Jews in Palestine. Not only did immigration cease, but many of the Jewish inhabitants were removed. If they were citizens of the allied

Table 1.1. The Growth of Population of Palestine, 1920–1945

	Arabs	Jews	Total
1914	600,000	85,000	685,000
1920	600,000	66,500	673,000
1922	668,200	84,000	752,000
1931	1,033,000	176,600	856,700
1939	1,056,200	445,500	1,501,700
1945	1,255,700	554,300	1,810,000

Source: Gertz, *Statistical Handbook of Palestine—1947* (Jerusalem: Jewish Agency, 1947), pp. 46–47.

countries, they were deported. If they were Ottoman citizens, they were recruited into the army. The first assessment of the new British administration in 1920 set the Jewish population at about 66,600—a decrease of about 20,000 from the prewar population.[3] However, from 1920, when large-scale Zionist immigration, primarily from eastern and central Europe, began, the Jewish population increased rapidly. This was clearly a case of push-and-pull immigration, triggered by events in the country of origin that pushed large numbers of Jews to leave. They came to Palestine for ideological as well as economic, social, and political reasons. Immigration took a cyclical form. An upsurge of immigration combined with a large-scale import of capital created economic prosperity. This would last a few years and then both the immigration and the import of capital would come to a sudden halt, turning prosperity into depression. A few years later, circumstances in Palestine and outside it would change, and another cycle would begin.[4] The census of 1922 set the number of Jews in Palestine at 83,794.[5] By 1926, after the major wave of immigration known as the Fourth Aliya (1924–1925), the Jewish population had almost doubled, increasing to 149,500. By the end of the 1930s, with the coming of the Fifth Aliya (1932–1939), it almost tripled again so that in 1939 the Jewish population had reached 445,500. In 1947, the last year of British rule, the Jewish population was approximately 600,000.[6] This exceptional growth raised the proportion of Jews in relation to the total population from about 11.1 percent in 1922, to 30.6 percent at the end of this period.

During the same period, the Arab population in Palestine also grew rapidly. Starting with a population of about 400,000 in 1870, it increased to approximately 600,000 by the eve of the First World War, and doubled in the years of British rule. This was a faster rate of growth than that of many other Middle Eastern and Asian countries.[7] Nevertheless, the Jewish population growth shrank the Arab majority from 89 percent in 1922 to approximately 67 percent in 1947.[8]

The majority of the Jewish population was thus new to Palestine. They came from outside the country and its immediate surroundings, immigrating from Europe to a non-European, Middle Eastern country. Only about 10 percent of all Jewish immigrants came from Middle Eastern and North African countries, and they were on the periphery of the new Jewish community—the *Yishuv*. The Arab community, on the other hand, grew by natural increase and was complemented by immigration from the neighboring countries of Lebanon and Syria, Trans-Jordan and Egypt.

The Jews did not perceive themselves as strangers to the land. On the contrary, they saw themselves as returning, not to Palestine but to the Land of Israel—Eretz Yisrael. They saw themselves as reversing their long but "temporary" stay in the European diaspora and reestablishing a Hebrew entity in the land of their fathers. They saw themselves as settlers and colonizers, but of a very different type than that of the European settler movements. The Zionist settlers were themselves aware of the possible similarity between Zionist colonization and that of European settlers elsewhere and therefore they constantly emphasized what they considered to be vital differences: They were not foreigners but settlers returning to the land that had belonged to their forefathers. They did not intend or desire to exploit native labor; on the contrary, the essence of their return was that they themselves should do the work. They did not wish to dominate the local population but to establish their own, separate, national home, and they believed that their colonization would not harm the native population but would benefit it. The Arabs, however, perceived the Jewish immigrants to be foreigners and invaders, intent on dominating a land to which they had no claim, and dominating a people who, for centuries, had been the majority population.

JEWISH AND ARAB LABOR

The different processes of population growth affected the development of the labor force within each community. Where the population increased as a result of immigration, the labor force grew because there were more young and single adults among the immigrants and fewer young children and elderly people. Thus the Jewish workforce increased as immigration increased. However, where the population grew through natural increase, the weak and dependent elements increased and not the breadwinners. Thus, among the Arab community where the birth rate rose and the death rate dropped, the number of dependents in the population increased while the working sections of the population did not. The Jewish labor force grew in proportion to the overall Jewish population, whereas the reverse was true of the Arab labor force. Metzer and Kaplan calculated the annual average growth rate of Jewish labor for the years 1922 to 1935 at 14.6 percent per year,[9] while the average annual growth rate of the overall Jewish population during those years was 11.5 percent.[10] The Arab labor force, according to Metzer and Kaplan, grew at the rate of 1.9 percent per year, while the Arab population increased by 3.5 percent per year.[11] Thus immigration increased the potential labor force, while natural increase slightly lowered it.

Jewish Labor

Jewish immigrants, who were to become workers in Palestine, were an integral part of Zionist immigration. Both the Second Aliya (1904–1914) and Third Aliya (1919–1923) were identified as immigrations composed primarily of workers, or pioneers—*Halutzim*. Of the two later and larger immigrations, the Fourth Aliya (1924–1931) was perceived as comprising primarily lower middle-class immigrants from Poland, and the Fifth Aliya (1932–1939) was seen as including mainly middle-class immigrants from Germany. The facts are, however, that the majority of those immigrations were labor immigrants, with no capital of their own, who hoped to find employment in Palestine.[12] Most labor immigrants were affiliated in one way or another with the Zionist labor movement before immigrating to Palestine. About one-third had been members of the different Zionist workers' parties while still in Europe. Others had been members of the *Halutz* youth movement, or of other youth movements affiliated with the Zionist labor movement. In most cases, labor immigrants received their immigration permits through Zionist and labor institutions, thus reinforcing their links to these institutions. Many of the labor immigrants came to Palestine in groups that had been formed in the political and youth movements to which they belonged in their countries of origin.

The majority of Jewish workers were of European origin, hailing primarily from eastern and central Europe. They accounted for approximately 88 percent of all Jewish workers in 1926 and 83 percent in 1937.[13] In all these European countries there had been active workers' movements and in many cases revolutionary workers' movements who carried out either unsuccessful (e.g., Germany and Poland) or successful (Soviet Union) revolutions. Jewish youth were familiar with these activities and, at times, even actively involved in them. They frequently had previous experience of labor organization, usually, though not exclusively, within the Zionist movement.[14]

The majority of Jewish workers who immigrated to Palestine came from middle- and lower-middle-class families. The 1937 census conducted by the Histadrut[15] shows that the fathers of approximately 50 percent of all workers were traders and, given the Jewish occupational structure in Europe, they would have been mostly petty traders. Two and a half percent came from factory-owning families. Only a quarter of the workers reported that their fathers had themselves been laborers. The Jewish workers had a relatively high level of education and this is compatible with their class origin. Close to half had some secondary education and of these 4.5 percent had had higher education. One-third reported having had only elementary education, while the remaining 15 to 20 percent had some form of religious or home education.[16]

These relatively educated workers from lower-middle-class families included a disproportionately large number of men, young people, and single men and women. The Jewish labor force had many more male than female workers, which was typical of that period and later years as well. According to the 1926 Histadrut census of Jewish workers, women constituted about 13 percent of all the workers surveyed.[17] By 1930 they made up about 18 percent of the labor force[18] and in 1937 approximately 28 percent.[19] This small, but growing proportion reflected not only the lower level of participation of women in the labor force, but also the discriminatory immigration policy of the Jewish Agency by which women were granted immigration permits primarily as dependents of male wage earners rather than as future workers.[20]

A large proportion of the workers were young. In the mid 1920s, 60 percent of the Jewish workers were between the ages of twenty and thirty, and only 20 percent were above the age of thirty.[21] This high proportion of young people decreased somewhat in the 1930s, but even then they still composed almost half the Jewish labor force.[22] Similarly, the proportion of single men and women was high, though it too decreased slightly over the years.[23]

Thus the Jewish workers in Palestine were for the most part a newly proletarianized and newly arrived labor force. They immigrated under the auspices of the World Zionist Organization, with no private means of their own, from industrialized or industrializing countries and were familiar with political and labor organizations. Given their social, economic, institutional, and ideological background, it becomes clear that Jewish labor immigrants had to find employment and maintain themselves through their own labor. It is also clear that they came with attributes and experience that would enhance their level of organization and thus their ability to meet their basic needs. These attributes help explain much of the strength of Jewish labor and its ability to obtain higher compensation for its labor than would be expected in a country with an abundant supply of much cheaper, local labor and in an economy that was only beginning to industrialize.

The organization of Jewish labor was established in 1920. It brought under its auspices already existing organizations, established by the immigrants of the Second Aliya (1904–1914). These included political parties, mutual aid associations, and unions of workers of specific trades. The General Federation of Jewish Labor—*ha-Histadrut ha-Klalit shel ha-Ovdim ha-Ivrim be-Eretz Yisrael* (in short, the Histadrut)—contained a very high percentage of all Jewish wage earners, approximately

75 percent.[24] It fulfilled a wide range of functions: the protection of workers' rights and wages via their trade unions, the allocation of work via the Histadrut-controlled Labor Exchange, the creation of employment via the Histadrut-owned contracting company—Solel Boneh—and the provision of essential services, the most important being health services via Kupat Holim and cultural and recreational services. It was also active in Jewish colonization beyond the needs of wage labor, primarily in agricultural settlement and issues of defense. The Histadrut defined itself as "The State in the Making"—"*ha-Medina she-ba-Derekh*"—and was recognized as such by much of the Jewish community.[25]

The Histadrut contained only Jewish members. Nevertheless, it attempted, from time to time, to attract Arab workers. For this purpose, the Third Convention of the Histadrut (1927) decided to form the Palestine Labor League (PLL). Theoretically, this was to be a binational organization of Jewish and Arab workers, divided into two national units. In practice, the PLL came to refer only to the adjunct organization for Arab workers through which the Histadrut hoped to bring Arab workers under its auspices, to diminish their opposition to Zionist settlement, and yet to avoid incorporating them as full members in the Histadrut.[26]

Arab Labor

The Arab labor force was made up largely of peasants who were in the process of proletarianization. Arab society was predominantly an agrarian society in which the agrarian sector was undergoing crisis and deterioration under the impact of an increasingly capital-oriented economy. The peasantry, while still accounting for 55 to 65 percent of the population, was becoming less and less able to make its living from agriculture. Land was become scarcer than it had been due to the transfer of ownership of land to the Zionist settlement institutions. The amount of land purchased was not very large, in relation to the overall amount of cultivated land in Palestine, but it was the most productive land— large stretches of coastal and plain lands, and thus highly detrimental to the development of Arab agriculture. The customs of inheritance of the Arab villagers further exacerbated the shortage of land, as it forced repeated subdivisions of their plots. Heavy debts, which had been accumulating for a number of decades,[27] led the small peasants, the *falahin,* to forfeit land to debtors or seek additional sources of income. The small landowners were too hard-pressed to save and so lacked the resources for intensive agriculture, and the large landowners transferred

Figure 2. Arab workers in British army camps, 1935.

their money elsewhere, rather than reinvesting it and providing employment for the landless.[28]

Carmi and Rosenfeld, having documented the small amount of land owned by different levels of the peasantry and their inability to subsist off it, argue that all peasants were potential candidates for wage employment. Nevertheless, there were clear differences between villages and districts in their extent of proletarianization. These were due, according to Graham-Brown, to numerous factors, among them the ratio of population to land, the attitudes of the villagers to traveling away from home, and the existence of family members or other connections in a big town or in a work place where wage labor could be obtained. The crucial factor appears to have been the proximity to towns, to settlements with plantation agriculture or to army bases,[29] or more generally the opportunity for work outside of the village.[30] These opportunities evolved rapidly under the new British administration that initiated labor-intensive, infrastructural developments and services. The Jewish immigration triggered economic expansion that created different kinds of employment opportunities. There was thus a demand for casual and unskilled wage labor, and there was an almost unlimited potential supply of laborers from the agrarian sector. The combination of the supply of peasants-cum-workers and the casual nature of much of the work led to a high labor turnover. The villager who picked fruit in the nearby Jewish agricultural colony, the landless peasant who worked with scores of others laying the tracks of the Palestine Railways, the migrant laborer who excavated stone for construction in a quarry owned either by a Jew, an Arab, or the government, the poverty-stricken Hourani, who hoped for a day's work carrying heavy loads— each could easily be replaced by others like them. This exchangeability, Carmi and Rosenfeld argue, was the major factor that determined the low wages of Arab labor, the limited level of their proletarianization, and their tenuous relation to the towns.[31]

Throughout the twenties and thirties, Arab peasant-workers were, for the most part, temporary migrant workers. Some combined agricultural work with off-season wage labor, while others stayed in town as long as some kind of employment was available, shifting between jobs as the need and the opportunities arose. The migrant peasant-workers retained a wide range of rural connections. They kept close social contact with the family that remained in the village. They sent them money and returned to help during the height of the agricultural season. They also retreated to the village in times of unemployment or political upheaval in the towns. Within the urban centers they maintained close communal links through marriage, residential proximity, and communal associations. The rural-urban link was further reinforced by contractors who recruited rural labor for urban employment from their villages, in conjunction with the village leaders. This practice reestablished village connections, enforced dependence on village elders, and increased the insecurity of urban employment.

This intermittent, though relatively large-scale, proletarianization was accompanied by a process of urbanization. According to Gilbar, the proportion of Arab urban dwellers increased from 27 percent in 1922 to 36 percent in 1946.[32] The level of urbanization was strikingly different for Muslims and Christians. The Muslim Arab population was and remained largely rural. Nevertheless, Muslim urban dwellers increased from 23.2 percent in 1922 to 30.5 percent in 1946. Most of the proletarianizing peasants came from the Muslim rural population. Among the Christians, the process of urbanization had begun at the turn of the century and had steadily increased. In 1922, 63 percent of the Arab Christians were urban dwellers and by 1946, 80 percent of Arab Christians were living in the towns.[33]

The rate of urbanization was much slower than that of proletarianization. By the mid-1930s approximately half of all Arab workers were wage laborers, while only about 30 percent of the population were urban dwellers. During the 1940s, the process of proletarianization and urbanization stabilized. Army camps recruited peasants as workers on a large scale and for longer periods of time, and as a result the migratory nature of the Arab wage laborer changed. Whole families moved to the urban centers. Labor unions took on new life and a strata of urban workers began to form.

In addition to this rural-urban migration within Palestine, migrant workers came to Palestine from neighboring countries. Most came from the Houran and from Trans-Jordan. Others came from Syria, Lebanon, and Egypt. Estimates vary as to the number of Arab immigrants into Palestine.[34] It was a casual and seasonal migration, often undocumented, at times illegal. Vashitz sets the number of non-Palestinian Arabs in 1934 at 25,000 to 30,000,[35] which would account for about 25 percent of Arab wage labor.

There was differentiation and stratification within this new class of wage labor. The top stratum was made up of the veteran urban workers, most of whom were Christian. They had been independent artisans and were increasingly becoming skilled wage laborers. They earned four, five, and six times as much as casual day laborers, from whom they kept themselves aloof and distant.[36] Most of the wage workers were the Muslim migrant peasant-workers, who were casual day laborers. They concentrated in shantytowns on the margins of the towns, maintained communal links among themselves, and were spurned by the veteran urban population. And finally, ranked below them, were the non-Palestinian migrant workers, most of whom came from the Houran in southern Syria. Eliahu Agassi, a Histadrut activist well acquainted with the condition of Arab workers, described the Hourani migrants as arriving "in a spontaneous stream of thousands of simple peasant-workers, congregating around the ports, in the citrus orchards, in the army camps and the international companies."[37]

Because many of the workers migrated into town on a temporary or seasonal basis, labor organization was extremely difficult. R. Graves, formerly an official of the British administration in Egypt, surveyed the condition of Arab labor in Palestine in 1941 and reported:

> There is no lack of reasons why since the establishment of the Mandate the Arab workers have done little to organize themselves for their own protection. In the first place, they had no traditional associations which might have developed on the lines of modern Trade Unions. Secondly, the high wages obtained by Jewish labour caused, almost automatically, an important rise in the scale of Arab wages, which for unskilled labour leaped to the double of what was being

paid in Egypt, Iraq or Syria for similar work. The cost of living was doubtless higher for the worker than in the neighbouring countries, but the increase in wages combined with the low standards of comfort claimed by Arab workers represented a very important advantage which had been obtained without a struggle . . . Thirdly, the political energies of the Arabs after they had recovered from the relief of finding themselves freed from an oppressive war-time regime became concentrated on national objects and the idea of combining to achieve social reforms did not interest them. Possibly even the spectacle of the complicated and successful organization of labour by the Jews damped the enthusiasm of potential reformers, who would not be beholden to a rival even for an idea.

Finally, it must not be forgotten that the Arab *fellah*, who was and is attached to his village and to the leading families of his village, is much less likely to be moved by external influences than the urban industrial worker who has no territorial roots and loyalties. And it is to the former class that most of the Arab workers belong. The country notable, whose influence on his tenants and neighbours is very considerable, is not likely to encourage any tendency to working class consciousness among the villagers who often spend six months in their homes and six months working for contractors on roads or buildings.[38]

The factors that enhanced the relative value of Jewish labor and those that detracted from the value of Arab labor can be found in the origins of Jewish and Arab labor and in their different processes of proletarianization. Jewish labor was an educated and young labor force, not overburdened with family responsibility, experienced in organizing, and anchored in a relatively cohesive political movement with related institutions and a strong ideological commitment. Arab labor was unskilled and in unlimited supply with little organizational experience and little wider political backing. These differences explain the striking disparity in the value that each group was able to obtain for its work.

THE DIFFERENTIAL VALUE OF JEWISH AND ARAB LABOR

The wages of Arab and Jewish workers are well documented in both Jewish and government sources. Although the data are not identical, the overall pattern is clear and consistent. It shows a large disparity in the wages of unskilled Arab and Jewish workers and a much smaller disparity, if at all, between skilled workers.[39] A government commission appointed in 1928 to study the wages paid to unskilled workers, reported the following earnings for Jewish and Arab workers:

Arab rural 120–150 mils a day
Arab urban 140–170 mils a day

Jewish nonunion 150–200 mils a day
Jewish union 250–300 mils a day[40]

As for skilled labor, the report concluded that:

> This [disparity—D.B.] is absent in skilled labour, where there is no dif-
> ference between the levels of Arab and Jewish wage rates. . . . The dif-
> ference between Arab skilled and unskilled labour wage rates is much
> greater than between the similar Jewish rates.[41]

Other government sources reported lower wages, especially for unskilled Arab labor, than those stated by the Wage Commission of 1928.
The Report of the High Commissioner to the League of Nations for the
year 1929, for example, assessed unskilled Arab wages at 80 to 120 mils
a day in agriculture (rural labor) and 100 to 160 mils a day in industry
and building (primarily, though not exclusively, urban occupations).[42]
A few years later, in 1932, the Labor Legislation Committee appointed
by the government listed seven categories of unskilled labor according
to the minimum daily wage earned by adult males. European Jewish
immigrants living in the major towns earned a minimum of 250 mils
per day, Jewish labor in the new private enterprise agricultural villages
(the *moshavot*), earned a minimum of 200 mils, and Jews in other rural
areas and in minor small towns earned 150 mils per day. Arabs and
Oriental Jews living in the large towns earned a minimum of 120 mils
daily for their unskilled labor, while Arabs in small towns earned a
minimum of 100 mils per day. Rural Arabs and nomads earned a minimum of 80 and 60 mils per day, respectively. It is important to note that
the unskilled Oriental Jews earned the same wage as the unskilled
Arab workers. This points up the peripheral status of the Orientals in
the new European-oriented Jewish community and their peripheral
position in relation to organized Jewish labor.[43]

Other available sources compare the wages of Jewish and Arab labor
within specific industries. For most of the period, the wages of Arab
workers in agriculture were between one-third to one-half the value of
Jewish wages. Although the gap between Jewish and Arab wages did
decrease, the trend was not consistent and the wages never came close
to being equal. The disparity between the wages of female Jewish and
Arab agricultural workers was much larger than the disparity between
the wages of the males. The gap between the wages of Jewish and Arab
workers was smaller in construction than it was in agriculture. But,

Table 1.2. The Wages of Jewish and Arab Labor in Agriculture (mils p.d.)

	1934[a]	1938[a]	1942[b]	1945/6[b]
Jews	200–350	200–300	M 250–300 F 300	M 750 F 750
Arabs	80–100	80–150	M 140–180 F 90–110	M 300–600 F 200–400
Proportion of Arab wage to Jewish wage[c]	32.7	46	M 61.8 F 33	M 52.3 F 40

M = males; F = females.

Sources:

a. David Horowitz, *The Palestine Economy and Its Development* (Tel Aviv: Mossad Bialik, 1948), pp. 161, 168. The data does not include citriculture.

b. A. Gertz, *Statistical Handbook*, 300. Data concerning citriculture was omitted for the sake of comparison.

c. Proportion calculated in relation to the average wage within each category.

once the distinction is made between skilled and unskilled labor, the disparity is striking. In the 1940s, unskilled Arab labor earned only 40 percent of the wages paid to unskilled Jewish labor. Skilled workers also did not earn the same, although the difference in their wages was much smaller.

Wages in the manufacturing sector followed the pattern of the other industries. The disparity between the wages of Jewish and Arab labor is marked and consistent. It increased sharply in the 1940s, probably because of the large cost-of-living allowance obtained by the Jewish workers and the much smaller one won by the Arab workers. The distinction

Table 1.3. The Wages of Jewish and Arab Labor in Construction (mils p.d.)

	1934[a]	1938[a]	1942[b]	1945/6[b]
Jews	300–900	300–900	Unskilled 400 Skilled 750	Unskilled 1,250 Skilled 2,000
Arabs	100–500	Unskilled 117 Skilled 255–412	Unskilled 190 Skilled 500	Unskilled 500 Skilled 1,750
Proportion of Arab wage to Jewish wage[c]	30–50	30–50	Unskilled 47.5 Skilled 66.6	Unskilled 40 Skilled 87.5

Sources and comments:

a. David Horowitz, *The Palestine Economy and Its Development* (Tel Aviv: Mossad Bialik, 1948), pp. 161, 168. The data does not include citriculture.

b. A. Gertz, *Statistical Handbook*, 300. Data concerning citriculture was omitted for the sake of comparison.

c. Proportion calculated in relation to the average wage within each category.

Table 1.4. The Wages of Jewish and Arab Labor in Manufacturing

	1934[a]	1938[a]	1942[b]	1945/6[b]
Jews	200–700	150–750	756	1,440
Arabs	70–500	110–396	MS 459[c]	MS 617
			AS 262	AS 464
Proportion of Arab wage to	63	56	MS 61	MS 43
Jewish wage[d]			AS 35	AS 32

Sources and Comments:
a. David Horowitz, *The Palestine Economy and Its Development* (Tel Aviv: Mossad Bialik, 1948), p. 16.
b. Be'eri, *The Arab Worker in the State of Israel* (1948, unpublished mimeo), p. 27.
c. MS = Mixed settlement; AS = Arab settlement.
d. Proportion calculated in relation to the average wage within each category.

made by Be'eri between Arab wages in mixed settlements and those in homogeneous Arab settlements highlights the fact that Arab labor earned more in the mixed settlements. Thus, although the presence of Jewish labor did indeed raise the wages of Arab workers, the gap between the two nevertheless remained striking.

The breakdown of wages by occupation, rather than industry, given by Gertz for the years 1939 to 1944 indicates that the gap was as pronounced as ever in the different occupations that called for some degree of skill. For example, in 1943, a Jewish carpenter earned 764 mils per day while his Arab counterpart earned 425 mils. The Jewish machine printer earned 900 mils per day while the Arab machine printer earned 395 mils, and the Jewish fitter earned 836 mils while the Arab fitter earned 525.[44]

Jewish labor was thus earning between two to three times the wages earned by Arab workers in most industries for most of the period. The gap was smaller for skilled labor, but it certainly did not disappear. Thus a typical split labor market emerged in which two groups of workers, belonging to different national collectives, obtained markedly different value for their labor. Jewish labor was relatively high priced in relation to the much cheaper Arab labor.

So much for the workers and the two national groups to which they belonged. What of the labor market in which they competed? What impact did they have on each other? Where did they work? One of the particular features of the split labor market of Palestine was that in most cases Jewish and Arab workers, employed in the same occupation or industry, worked on different locations and for different employers and yet they competed with and influenced one another. To understand this relationship, we must outline the sectorial structure of Palestine's economy.

THE ECONOMIC SECTORS OF PALESTINE

The economy of Palestine was made up of two major economic sectors, the Jewish and the Arab sectors, that were supplemented by the government sector. The Jewish sector was primarily an urban, capitalist economy. The Arab sector was still largely agrarian, in transition from a semi-feudal, semi-subsistence economy to a market-oriented, capital-based economy. The economic structure of the Arab and Jewish sectors was very different. Agriculture dominated the Arab economy, while manufacture and construction played a much greater role in the Jewish economy. Services were of central importance in both cases, though there was probably proportionately far more trade in Arab services.[45]

From the early 1920s, the Jewish economy had a primarily modern, capitalist structure.[46] This was due to the very large one-directional import of capital by individual immigrants and by the Zionist institutions. The rate of capital inflow was extremely high such that Jewish capital imported into Palestine exceeded government revenue for many of the years between 1922 and 1947.[47] The previous experience of most immigrants in their countries of origin provided the resources essential for economic development. These included experience in wage labor; skills acquired prior to immigration by workers, entrepreneurs, and managers; international connections; as well as patterns of consumption that created a market for new local products. The political framework in which this immigration took place facilitated the efficient exploitation of these resources of manpower and capital. The rate of economic growth was exceptionally high, reaching an average annual growth rate of 21.7 percent between 1922 and 1935.[48]

The Arab sector was by comparison far more agrarian and less capitalized. It lacked many of the resources available to the Jewish sector of the economy. Nevertheless, it was undergoing rapid growth as well as significant transformation. The average annual growth rate of the Arab sector was 7 percent, with a lower growth rate in agriculture and a significantly higher growth rate in manufacture and construction.[49] These figures clearly belie the notion of a stagnant or nondeveloping economy. The Arab economy was to a large extent market oriented. A relatively large share of its agricultural produce was exchanged via the market—50.2 percent as early as 1921 and 64.4 percent in 1935.[50] The relatively large share of transport and trade—both market industries—in the net national product of the Arab economy also indicates a market orientation.

Abraham Cohen summarizes the changes that the Arab economy underwent in its transition from a traditional to a capitalist economy. In a traditional economy, claims Cohen, there are few external economic contacts, the main occupation is agriculture, most work as independent farmers, tenants, craftsmen, and traders, and there are relatively few wage earners. Public services fall way behind basic needs and no stratum can be identified as "intelligentsia." Cohen contends that the Arab society in Palestine no longer fit these criteria because import from outside the sector (including from the Jewish sector) amounted (by 1936) to 34 percent of the local gross product and its export amounted to 23 percent. In addition, by 1945, agriculture accounted for only about half of the workforce and 40 percent of the national product. Appproximately half of those employed were wage laborers. Education and health services were relatively advanced and a wide stratum had acquired experience in government administration, police services, education, and health.[51] Cohen nevertheless points out that these significant developments stopped short of a major structural and technological transformation. Nonmodernized agriculture retained a central role. Neither agriculture nor industry became highly mechanized. Investment was not due to capital saving but primarily to capital import from the Jewish sector, and the relatively large stratum of wage earners that emerged did not lead to a consolidated and organized proletariat.

The third sector of Palestine's economy was that of the Mandatory government. It included the government departments of agriculture, customs, education, justice, police, and finance as well as infrastructural services such as public works, railways, ports, and the postal service. The government sector also included regional commissioners and local government. Government financing came primarily from taxation of the local population, with revenue exceeding expenditure during most years.[52] The government sector was smaller and less varied than the two national sectors, yet it was the single largest employer in Palestine. In 1936, government departments alone employed over 15,000 regular workers and many more casual workers.[53]

INTERRELATIONS

The three economic sectors—the Arab, Jewish, and government sectors—functioned separately, with clear boundaries between them. Nevertheless, they were neither isolated nor insulated from one another. They were, in fact, interrelated in a complex combination of exchange, competition, and attempts at disengagement. The interrelations between the sectors included the mobility of labor between sectors, the movement of capital, the reciprocal impact on products, services, employment, and on the extent of industrialization.

The most important expression of this interrelatedness for the purposes of this study was the mobility of workers between the sectors. Arab workers were employed, to different extents, in all three sectors. In the Arab sector, only Arab labor was employed and the few Jewish workers who were employed in the Arab sector were the exception. In the government sector, Arab workers formed the majority and in the Jewish sector, they constituted about 10 percent of the labor force. Jewish workers were employed mainly in the Jewish sector, where they constituted 90 percent of the labor force, and in the government sector, where they accounted for between 12 and 20 percent.[54] Our main concern here is not with the specific levels of employment in each sector but with the extent to which both Jewish and Arab workers moved between the sectors. Arabs sought employment in the Jewish sector and thus competed with the Jewish workers. The Jewish workers, for their part, tried hard to increase their share of employment in the government sector, but did not seek employment in the Arab sector. Thus workers competed with one another in a wide range of settings. The difference in the levels of employment of each national group in the different sectors should be seen as a result of this competition, rather than as a given separation stemming from the structural difference between the sectors.

Capital also moved between the Jewish and Arab sectors both directly and indirectly. Jewish-owned capital entered the Arab sector directly through the purchase of land and goods and the payment of rent and wages, while Arab capital increasingly entered the Jewish sector through the purchase of goods and services. The indirect transfer of capital took place via the government budget. Metzer and Kaplan present a detailed breakdown of the Jewish-Arab transfer of capital for the years 1921 and 1935.[55]

In 1921, goods, services, and labor accounted for 66.5 percent of the payments made by Jews to Arabs and the purchase of land accounted for the remaining 33.5 percent. At that early stage of Jewish settlement, Arabs bought almost nothing from the Jewish sector and thus they transferred no capital to it. Fourteen years later (1935), the amount of capital transferred had not only increased greatly, but the pattern of this transfer had changed as well. The capital that moved from the Jewish to the Arab sectors had almost trebled, increasing from approximately 1.5 million £P (Palestine pounds) in 1921 to close to 4 million £P in 1935. Payment for land had increased from 33.5 to 43 percent of all Jewish capital transferred to Arab hands. Of the remainder, 60 percent was spent on goods, 24 percent on wages, and 15.6 percent on residential rent. By the mid-1930s capital was also moving from the Arab to the

Jewish sector, primarily via the purchase of manufactured products. In fact, Arabs spent about as much on Jewish manufactured goods as Jews spent on Arab agricultural and quarry products.[57] These reciprocal acquisitions demonstrate the links created between sectors as a result of the differences between them.

Aharon Cohen, writing in the mid-1940s, documented the transfer of Jewish capital to Arab hands between the years 1920 and 1941. He distinguished between the different classes of the Arab recipients and the basis of the transfer. He calculated that Jews imported approximately 115 million £P, of which 30 million £P were transferred directly to the Arab population: 11 million £P to the wealthy class, 11 million £P to the middle class, and 8 million to the poor.[58] Thus, if Cohen's calculations are approximately correct, they illustrate clearly the diverse distribution of Jewish capital within the Arab society and its impact on all its strata.[59]

The indirect transfer of capital from the Jewish to the Arab sector concerns the transfer of Jewish capital through government expenditure. Such transfer stemmed from the disparity between the contribution of each community to government revenue and the benefits it received from government expenditure. Specifically, it refers to government revenue collected from the Jewish sector that was spent on the needs of the Arab population. The assessment of such transfers was highly controversial. Although it was generally accepted that the Jewish community contributed more than its relative share of the population, opinions differed sharply as to its relative share in government expenditure. Jews constituted approximately 16 percent of the population and provided about 40 percent of all government tax revenue in the late 1920s and early 1930s. Metzer asserts that this figure was generally accepted by all the parties.[60] Jews and Arabs disagreed strongly, however, on the relative share of the Jewish sector in the benefits obtained from government expenditure. The contemporary Jewish assessment saw the Arab population as the major beneficiary of government moneys earmarked specifically for the two national communities. The Jewish interpretation saw only social services as explicitly divided between the two communities. They considered other items of expenditure to be beneficial to all. They argued that the government spent more on social welfare services for the Arab population than it received from them in revenue. Such expenditure was therefore made possible by the Jewish contribution to government revenue. In this way, Jewish capital was indirectly transferred to the Arab population.

The Arabs did not accept this claim. They reversed the argument and claimed that government expenditure on securing law and order and developing the economic and financial infrastructure answered the needs of the Jewish community and the Jewish National Home policy. These needs in fact created costs that would otherwise not have had to be met. Since they accounted for more than 40 percent of the government expenditure and the Jewish population contributed no more than 40 percent of the government revenue, it was the Arab sector, they argued, that was in fact subsidizing the Jewish settlement in Palestine. Thus the Jewish sector claimed that it subsidized Arab social services, while the Arab sector argued that it subsidized the Jewish National Home.

Another reciprocal effect of the Jewish and Arab sectors resulted from their catering to each other's needs. This was far more evident in the economic activity of the Arab sector, which responded to the needs of the expanding Jewish sector with its impressive purchasing power. Thus Arab construction expanded during the height of Jewish immigration.[61] Abramovitz and Gelfat emphasize the importance of the commercial links between the two sectors:

> The Arab market bought in 1935—during the period of economic prosperity and of good economic relations between the Arab settlement and the Jewish settlement in the country—goods to the value of 5 million £P from all the countries of the world and to the value of close to a million £P from the Jewish settlement. At the same time the Arab settlement sold of its produce to all countries of the world to the sum of close to 2 million £P, and—to the Jewish settlement to the sum of 800,000 to 1.000,000 £P, of which—600,000 £P were for agricultural produce, and the rest—building material and other industrial products. These figures indicate the close economic ties which existed between the neighboring settlements.[62]

The growing Jewish settlement also had an impact on the employment levels of the Arab population and thus on its economy. Again, the two opponents assessed the issue very differently. The Jews emphasized the benefits enjoyed by the Arab population through the increasing employment opportunities created by the Jewish settlement and denied that it had any harmful impact on Arab unemployment. They pointed to the increased economic activity that resulted from their settlement and the concomitant employment opportunities for Arabs in all three sectors. The expanding Jewish market, they argued, enabled the Arab sector to expand by catering to its needs. Jewish capital helped finance government works and so increased the jobs the government offered, and the expanding Jewish sector also created work. As Nemirovsky, a Zionist labor activist, wrote in 1935, "With few exceptions, it can almost be stated as a rule that, wherever Jewish immigration and Jewish construction have increased, the economic activity of the Arabs has developed."[63]

As for Arab unemployment, difficult to assess due to the migratory nature of Arab wage labor, the Jewish position consistently underrated the extent of unemployment and denied any responsibility for its existence. Jewish labor, it was argued, was not the cause of Arab unemployment, and did not displace Arab labor. Jews, in any case, were not employed in the Arab sector, and were only minimally employed in the government sector. They were therefore no threat to Arab employment. Organized Jewish labor claimed that the closure of the Jewish sector to Arab workers was not responsible for their unemployment. After all, the Jewish sector was established for the employment of Jewish labor and would not have been established otherwise.

The Arab position totally rejected the Jewish rationale. They saw Jewish immigration to Palestine, and the immigration of Jewish labor in particular, as a major cause of Arab unemployment. They saw Palestine as one undivided entity and one market. They rejected the Jewish perspective, which saw the Jewish *Yishuv* and the Jewish economic sector as a separate and autonomous entity. In the Arab view, Jewish workers served as substitutes for the local workers, the people of the homeland, the *watani'yun*. They contended that Jewish opposition to the employment of Arab workers in the Jewish sector increased Arab unemployment and was thus responsible for it.[64] They either ignored the creation of new employment opportunities, especially within the Jewish sector, or asserted that the labor opportunities existed only because the Jewish labor leadership was unable to block them. Thus Mansur stated with no little irony, "If some Jews still employ Arab labor in their orange orchards, either because they preserved an older tradition of friendly dealings or because Arab labor is cheaper and better for this purpose, then the fact can be used [by the Zionist—D.B.] as evidence of the employment provided by Zionism for Arabs. But if Arab labor can be pushed out by "picketing" and "pressure" that is much better."[65] Jewish spokesmen stressed "the fact that in practice our immigration and settlement, far from ousting other elements, has actually spelt more plentiful employment and a higher standard of life for the rest of the population,"[66] while the Arabs stressed the crisis of unemployment and the excessively high cost of living brought about by Jewish colonization.[67]

The high level of industrialization of the Jewish sector may indeed have restricted industrialization processes in the Arab sector. As noted, most Arab purchases from the Jewish sector were of industrial products. Jewish manufacture developed rapidly and industrialization was primarily a Jewish enterprise.[68] As early as 1930, Jewish industry was responsible for 55 percent of the industrial products. By the eve of the Second World War, this had increased to 70 percent.[69] Although Jewish industry faced various difficulties because of the small market and the absence of a protective policy, it had the advantages of a large inflow of capital, know-how, and experience, as well as the ability to utilize previous connections. It also had some government support. These advantages, it has been forcefully argued by Palestinian writers, jeopardized the development of Arab industrialization by creating insurmountable competition.[70] The development of a modern proletariat, an essential element of class struggle and liberation movements, was thus also inhibited.[71] The restricting impact of Jewish industry on Arab industrialization has also been acknowledged by Zionist-oriented scholars, though they claim that it is only one of many factors that inhibited such development and not necessarily the most important one.[72]

The different economic sectors thus affected one another in multiple ways. The main impact of the Arab economic sector on the Jewish sector stemmed from its cheap resources that were also a source of competition. Its cheap labor competed on the labor market and its cheap products competed on the commodity market. The Jewish economic sector affected the Arab sector by enhancing the processes of capitalization, providing capital and employment, and needs to which to cater. It also set a rate and pace of growth that far exceeded both the forces of production and the class formations evolving from within the Arab economic sector and society. The government sector also had a profound impact on the two national sectors, as a channel for the transfer of capital, as the developer of infrastructural services essential for economic growth, and as a source of large-scale employment.

FROM SECTORS BACK TO ACTORS

Arab and Jewish labor competed with one another within and between the different sectors of Palestine's economy. Newly proletarianized workers, both Jewish and Arab, competed for work on the new economic projects—new roads, new railway lines, new public buildings. Jewish immigration created new needs, and the new capital resources triggered economic development—construction of residential buildings, quarrying for stone, transportation for growing numbers of people, cultivation of food for their consumption. All these created new employment opportunities—for whom? The newly semi-proletarianized workers from among the rural *fellahin* of Palestine saw the work as naturally coming to them, the native sons—*Ibn'a al-balad*, the people of the land, the *watani'yun*. The Zionist settler workers, recent immigrants, also saw the work as naturally coming to them, the pioneers, the *halut-zim*, so that they could establish the Jewish National Home. Thus economic expansion, growth of labor, and competition within the split labor market were multiple interacting strands of the same ongoing processes.

The fact that in most cases Jewish and Arab workers were competing over new sources of employment, rather than directly displacing each other, did not lessen the reciprocal threat that both perceived from the other. The Zionist leadership asserted that Jews had the right to immigrate to Palestine, and to be employed in the Jewish sector, which was developed by Jewish capital, with no regard for unemployment among Arab workers. Furthermore, they contended, Jewish labor had the legitimate right to expect a "fair" share of the employment opportunities within the government sector as part of the British commitment to a Jewish National Home. These legitimate rights were threatened by the low cost of Arab workers and their unlimited number. Again and again Jewish labor spokesmen expressed the existential problem faced by Jewish workers as a result of the competition from cheap Arab labor, and asserted the legitimacy of their demand for employment with "adequate," "civilized," European wage levels. One quote will suffice to illustrate their position. It is taken from the 1934 annual report of the Haifa Labor Council (HLC), and was written by its powerful secretary, Aba Houshi. He draws attention to the multiple facets of the threat posed by Arab labor. It threatened the employment of Jewish workers, the work opportunities available for new immigrants, the employment potential for future immigrants, and the standard of living of present and future Jewish settlers; in short, it threatened the Zionist enterprise itself:

> It is not for nothing that Ben Gurion has said that if we are to express our whole ideology concerning Eretz Yisrael in one sentence, it would be "Hebrew Labor!" Our struggle for Hebrew labor is not only a Zionist struggle for a place of work for the worker and the immigrant who are already registered in the Labor Exchange. After all, this last year we were not short of work, on the contrary we were short of workers. It is a struggle for our existence in this country. It is a struggle for the possibility of massive immigration of workers to the country and of ensuring our ability to provide them with work. It is no less a struggle to protect the labor conditions and standard of living of the Hebrew workers, already working in the country. . . .
>
> The Arab economy is totally closed to the Jewish worker and im-

migrant. In the government and municipal sectors the proportion of Hebrew labor is almost nil. We have not even begun to enter the sector of international capital, and in the basic Jewish economy, in wage labor agriculture, the proportion of Jewish workers has gone down . . . to 30–33 percent percent. Furthermore, the affliction of cheap labor has begun to spread and infest other branches of the economy in both the *moshava* and in the town. Thousands of cheap workers—Houranis, Syrians, Egyptians and Sudanese—work in construction, porterage and other services, taking the place of thousands of Jewish immigrants who are suffering from starvation and unemployment in the diaspora. They are reducing the conditions of labor and the standard of living of thousands of Hebrew workers in the country, endangering their very existence.[73]

Arab labor felt threatened as well. Despite the attraction of its low cost, it feared the political and organizational power of Jewish labor. Arab spokesmen articulated their fears of the detrimental impact of Jewish immigration and development. They felt excluded from the benefits of such development, and feared that Jewish workers would encroach on the government sector, the major employer of Arab wage labor. As early as 1924, after four years of British civil administration, the Arab Executive stated in its report to the League of Nations:

Immigration to Palestine, or to any other country, should take place in consideration with the absorption capacity of that country, otherwise immigration can cause disaster not only to the country of entrance but to the immigrants themselves . . .

Many immigrants who hoped to find the "land of milk and honey" did not find any work. Others who came with a small amount of capital, lost most of their money shortly after arrival. Highly skilled and professional people could not find an outlet for their energy. . . . As a result the issue of unemployment, which was aroused in this quiet country for the first time in its history, poisoned the atmosphere and caused demonstrations and outbursts of quarrels in the streets. . . .

From now on the role of the government on the one hand, and of the Zionist Executive on the other was to provide work for the Jews who were the victims of its hasty policy. The government employed many of them in road repairs . . . instead of the Arab workers who had been engaged in such work till then. The Zionist Executive put pressure on Jews to employ Jewish workers at higher rates instead of the cheap workers from among the Arabs . . . .This created bitter resentment among the Arabs, as the result of this policy was soon to be felt in the form of the crisis of Arab unemployment.[74]

Ten years later, at the height of the economic boom that created prosperity for both Jews and Arabs, R. J. Davies, M.P., wrote of the Jewish
workers after his visit to Palestine:

> One thing is obvious: if the Mandate is carried out even on the present
> restrictive lines, the Jew, with his modern conceptions of life in Eu-
> rope, and his genius, higher intelligence, and culture, is bound to win
> in the struggle against the poor, uneducated Arab. The Arab becomes
> more jealous, in the very nature of things, just as the Jew succeeds. If
> the Jew came down to his level and lived as he does, the Arab would
> probably be more satisfied than is the case at present. He feels he is
> being pushed aside at every turn: and the fact that the Jew is more
> competent avails nothing with him. Whatever the reasons may be, the
> fact remains that he is losing ground in his native country.[75]

ALTERNATIVE STRATEGIES

The fear of substitution and displacement led Jewish labor to organize itself. This response is not unique to the Jewish settlement in Palestine. Bonacich deals at length with the different strategies pursued
by higher-priced labor when threatened by displacement. She em-
phasizes particularly the efforts made by higher-priced labor to
avoid competition by blocking cheap labor's access to employment.
This is usually done by attempting to close the labor market completely to the cheap labor, and failing that, by "caste formation."[76] In
the case of Jewish labor in Palestine, the dominant strategy was closure , known as "the Conquest of Labor" or "Hebrew Labor." This
strategy was compatible with, and complementary to, the overall
strategy of Zionist settlement—the formation of a distinct and separate socio-political entity, the Jewish National Home. The central ten-
ets of Zionist settlement led directly to separatism, as we noted in the
Introduction. The threat to Jewish labor was one of the crucial factors
that reinforced the separatist perspective and fostered its institution-
alization. In turn, this separatist orientation facilitated economic and
labor market separatism and the political, financial, and social steps
toward its implementation.[77]

Jewish labor's achievement of ensuring employment for Jewish
workers is noteworthy, given the unlimited supply of cheap Arab labor
and the disparity in wage levels. The ability of Jewish labor to devise
complex and far-reaching strategies to block Arab labor stemmed from
the basic characteristics of Zionist colonization. These included the development of the Jewish settlement as a separate and distinct social,
political, and economic entity, under the auspices of the World Zionist

Organization (WZO). The WZO provided the political and financial support as well as the infrastructure necessary for Jewish colonization. Specifically, the WZO aided wage labor through a combination of financial subsidies and political pressure. The subsidies helped meet the added cost of the higher-priced Jewish labor, and enabled employers to hire Jewish labor without suffering significant losses. This support was complemented by social pressure on Jewish employers and by class action, both of which were initiated by the Jewish labor movement and the Histadrut. These means of organization and action were most successful in the Jewish sector of the economy, and were indeed effective in consolidating a high level of closure of that sector to Arab labor.

Within the Jewish sector, employers and higher-priced Jewish labor shared the goal of establishing the Jewish settlement in Palestine and, more specifically, the Jewish National Home. They also had the support system of the political and economic institutions that had been set up to advance that goal—the World Zionist Organization, the Jewish Agency, and their various national funds. This context alone explains how and why Jewish labor was able to achieve a high level of closure, and why Jewish employers were willing to forgo, in large measure, the readily available cheap Arab labor. This context also explains how higher-priced Jewish labor was able to obtain most of the employment in the Jewish sector, for at least minimally adequate wages, without creating too inhibiting a cost to their employers.

Jewish employers were willing to forgo the option of maximizing profits by employing cheap labor. They recognized that Jewish labor's demand for employment and a decent wage was a necessary condition for increasing the Jewish population. At the same time, they were not willing to forgo profits, and indeed as a class they could not do so. Hence it was essential to find ways to mitigate the added cost of employing higher-priced Jewish labor by making use, directly and indirectly, of the institutional and political apparatus of the Jewish settlement. When the product was aimed mainly at the local Jewish market, the added cost was frequently passed on to the consumer, raising the relative price of commodities produced within the Jewish sector. This was complemented by a major drive, carried out jointly by organized Jewish labor and employers, to persuade the Jewish population to use commodities produced by Jewish labor, under the slogan "Buy *Tozeret Ha-Aretz*," "Buy the Produce of the Land." In addition, the Zionist leadership applied political pressure on the British administration to enlist the aid of the state in building the necessary infrastructure and levying protective taxation. Although this state support was not related directly to the employment of Jewish labor, it did enable profitable economic growth, and thus made it possible for Jewish employers to curtail their need for cheap labor. Zionist institutions also provided some measure of financial support for the development of Jewish industry. Eight and a half percent of the Jewish funds were directed to urban trade and industry.[78]

Jewish labor, in turn, organized in ways that would increase its chances of employment. It created a highly comprehensive labor organization, the General Federation of Jewish Labor—the Histadrut—that served a dual function for Jewish labor. It provided a wide range of services that improved the living standard of Jewish workers. It also provided employment by serving as a contractor for government projects and for projects funded by Jewish public institutions. In its role of contractor it was aided by financial support from the Jewish national funds.[79]

The higher-priced Jewish labor was thus employed by both private and public Jewish employers, including its own labor organization. The shared interest in the demographic growth of the Jewish settlers' society, and the support given by the institutions of that evolving society, enabled Jewish labor to gain a quasi-monopoly over the labor market of the Jewish sector, and a substantial measure of closure of that market to cheap Arab labor.

In the government sector, where the interplay of class interest and political goals was very different, the strategy of closure could not be effective. The colonial Mandatory government in Palestine had no prior commitment to employ higher-priced Jewish labor. It did not set aside a given share of public sector employment for Jewish labor, disregarding its higher price, as did the South African government, for example, in the case of higher-priced white labor.[80] On the contrary, the stated policy in Palestine, as in the rest of the British empire, was to minimize the costs of government expenditure. At the same time, it could be argued that the government did have an obligation to provide employment for Jewish labor because of its commitment, under the Mandate granted by the League of Nations, to aid in the establishment of the Jewish National Home: "The Mandatory shall be responsible for placing the country under such political, administrative and economic conditions as will secure the establishment of the Jewish national home."[81] It is to this commitment that the Zionist leadership appealed, and not to economic considerations, when it urged the British political leadership, in London and in Jerusalem, to ensure the employment of Jewish labor. The Zionist leadership attempted to establish criteria by which a given share of government jobs, unskilled as well as skilled, would be secured for Jewish labor, at wages suited to its higher standard of living. They argued that Jewish labor should be employed in proportion to the share of the Jewish population in government revenue.[82] Alternatively, they argued that Jewish labor should receive half of all government work as it composed half of Palestine's wage labor.[83] The Executive Committee of the Histadrut asserted that the government had a responsibility to its citizens (i.e., to its Jewish citizens):

> We have the feeling that government is but little concerned with as-
> suring the existence of the Jewish worker, the citizen of the country,
> with the standard and requirements of a cultured man. Government
> would appear to be indifferent to his fate and is ever ready to surren-
> der him in the interests of a disgraceful exploitation of cheap labour,
> both from Palestine and from outside.[84]

The government weighed various considerations, searching for a delicate balance between economic and political criteria. "Indeed if economic forces were allowed free play," wrote a senior official, "it is probable that no Jewish unskilled labour would obtain employment on such works [referring to Public Works Department, the Haifa Harbour etc.—D.B]."[85] The government responded to Zionist political pressure and accepted that some employment had to be secured for Jewish labor. The High Commissioner stated:

> The problem is how to secure the employment on public works of a
> fixed proportion of Jews with as little interference as possible with
> the general principle that in the interests of the taxpayer, public
> works should be constructed at the lowest possible cost and that
> when works are put out to public tender the lowest tender should be
> accepted.[86]

The government response to Jewish political pressure was balanced against the complementary and conflicting commitment stated in the Mandate for Palestine—"The Mandatory shall be responsible . . . for safeguarding the civil and religious rights of all the inhabitants of Palestine, irrespective of race and religion."[87] The Palestine administration tried to placate the opposition of the Arab majority, which objected to any form of government aid to the Jewish Zionist settlement. Allocation of government work to Jewish immigrant labor, especially under preferential wages, was bound to become a focus of Arab opposition and ensuing unrest.[88]

The pattern of employment of Jewish labor in the government sector was the outcome of these complex and conflicting dilemmas. It consisted of a set of shifting compromises that allowed for the employment of Jewish labor, albeit to a lesser extent than demanded by the Zionist leadership, but to a greater extent than justified economically or than accepted by the Arab leadership. It allowed for the employment of Jewish labor primarily in the skilled and nonmanual categories, while the unskilled manual work was allocated by tender, to Jewish contractors, who then employed both Jewish and Arab labor, at differing wage levels.

Because the government sector could not be closed to cheap labor, higher-priced Jewish labor was compelled in that sector, and in it alone, to combat the competition of cheap labor by strategies of equalization. This refers to attempts at eliminating competition by raising the standard of cheap labor, rather than by blocking its access. Bonacich sets out three types of equalization strategies, each of which can be found in the case of Palestine:[89]

1. Pressure on the government to establish and enforce minimum standards for all workers. The Jewish leadership advocated the enforcement of a minimum wage for unskilled labor, especially in the case of works and contracts allotted by the government.[90] These proposals were consistently rejected by government agencies and committees.

2. Organization of the cheap workers to "bring them into the unions and political parties of the high-priced group."[91] The Histadrut attempted to organize Arab workers under its auspices, though usually in a cooptative manner, and not as full and equal members. The results were meager.

3. Support for "the liberation movements of oppressed peoples who are being used as cheap labor."[92] This was probably the most difficult since it usually entailed direct confrontation with the national movement of the higher-priced group of workers. The Palestine Communist Party, organized by Jewish workers and predominantly Jewish till the mid-1930s, was probably the closest equivalent to that form of action.[93] The Palestine Communist Party, which was illegal for most of the time, vehemently opposed not only the government but the Histadrut and all institutions of the Jewish settlement. It, however, had little impact on the Palestine labor market and remained marginal in terms of the actual policies upheld by the vast majority of Jewish organized workers.

Strategies of equalization faced massive economic and political obstacles. Closure and equalization, although attempted in different contexts, contradicted each other. Although closure could not be enforced in all cases, it made equalization difficult to implement. The overall emphasis—political, economic, organizational, and ideological—on separatism, made equalization strategies, and especially cooperation and joint action, extremely difficult. Thus, while equalization strategies, piecemeal, halting, halfhearted, cooptative as they were, never disappeared, they were unable to overcome the deep political, ideological, and organizational divide between Jewish and Arab labor. While closure was not always possible, cooperation was seldom a viable alternative.

From the split labor market of Palestine as a whole, we shall now shift our focus to one locality—the town of Haifa. How did the SLM operate in this mixed town? What kinds of relationships developed between the two communities? What were the reciprocal affects?

Chapter 2

Haifa—Growing and Growing Apart

EARLY TREMORS OF GROWTH

1920
A town of the East slumbers by the Mediterranean shore
Narrow alleys snake through the polluted oriental market
A smattering of Jews in a lonely Hebrew neighborhood by the foot of
   the Carmel
Cemeteries lie between the town and its daughters—separating
The railway lies between the town and the blue sea—separating
On the slopes of the mount midst the vast emptiness, a giant building
   not yet completed.

1921
Pioneers of the nation come in their tens from all over
The town opens its eyes from its lazy slumber
The alleys widen and break loose their fetters
Jews pass over the boundaries—leave their neighborhood
Houses spring up among the cemeteries—a new life in the kingdom of
   the dead
The giant building, now completed—new homes rise up around it

1922
Onwards! Onwards! Up the ancient mount. Here they come in their
   hundreds
Young, enthusiastic, vibrant . . .
The town wakes to a new life . . .
Exuberantly the wheel of life turns in a new town, eager to create
Hadar Hacarmel takes its first steps—to build, to renew

1923
The pioneers in their thousands conquer, as in a whirlwind, the city of
 the future
The songs of building and creation are heard on high, by day, by night
Gigantic buildings rise up on all sides
And tower over the alleyways of the ancient city
The city will receive its new look, the Hebrew look
Hadar Hacarmel will blossom in the garden of the new settlement
The Carmel will wake to a new life above the future city—abuilding.[1]

To the young Jewish laborers, arriving in Haifa in the early 1920s, the
town seemed heavy with sleep. It was they who shook it awake, they
thought. This was not quite so. The slumbering small Arab settlement
had begun to awaken in 1831 when Ibrahim Pasha, the son of the Egyptian ruler Muhammad Ali, conquered it from the Turks. Consular representatives of European powers, foreign traders, and churches of different denominations then established themselves in Haifa. In the
1860s, the German Templars chose Haifa as the place for their central
settlement in Palestine.[2] Arab landowning families, both Christian and
Muslim, in search of urban land and an urban link, moved into the
town, as did increasing numbers of Jews from the holy cities of Safad
and Tiberias and from overseas. Large numbers of rural Muslim day laborers gravitated to the town as its population grew.

Acre, at the northern tip of Haifa Bay, with its harbor and strong
fortifications, was the major town of the northern coast of Palestine at
the beginning of the nineteenth century. It was the seat of the Ottoman
administration, the abode of European representatives, and the main
importing and exporting port of northern Palestine and its agricultural
hinterland. The change in the relative positions of Acre and Haifa
began with the easy conquest of Haifa from the Turks by Ibrahim
Pasha, who then made it his headquarters. He conquered Acre only
after months of fighting that devastated much of the town. This gave
the first push to both local rich merchant families and foreign consuls,
to move out of Acre and into what promised to become the new center.[3]
Ibrahim Pasha's lenient policy toward non-Muslims encouraged European representatives, churches, and Arab Christian families to locate in
Haifa. Others followed, especially after the improvements carried out
by the Russians in the Haifa port, the building of a new pier, and the
introduction of new sailing techniques, better suited to the deeper waters of the Haifa harbor. Ibrahim Pasha's rule in Palestine ended in
1840, before it had had much impact on the country as a whole. In
Haifa, however, the trends he had set in motion continued to develop.
In 1868, the Christian Templars from Germany settled in Haifa,

bringing with them additional links to Europe.[4] Their most important contribution to the development of Haifa was the example they set by their economic enterprise. They planted vineyards, founded a dairy, and imported agricultural machinery and European methods of fertilizing. They built a foundry, founded the first modern soap factory in Palestine (1872–3), and set up a workshop that used machinery to assemble wagons. They invested their acquired wealth in land that they sold when prices spiraled.

The Ottoman land reform of 1858 had a decisive impact on the social development of Haifa. It enabled the inhabitants to acquire official and permanent property rights for the first time in the history of their town. The rich Muslim and Christian Arab families who moved to Haifa in the last decades of the nineteenth century invested their wealth in urban and rural land and urban property. Their economic status also gave them access to political, municipal, and religious positions. These newcomers, from Palestinian towns such as Acre, Nazareth, and Nablus, from Palestinian villages and from outside of Palestine, from Beirut, Damascus, and Anatolia constituted the strata of notables and dignitaries of the Arab community in Haifa of the later Ottoman period, some of whom retained their status during the British Mandatory period as well.[6]

Prominent among these newcomers to Haifa were Salim Khouri, Muhamad Taha, and Mustafa Pasha al-Khalil. Khouri, a well-to-do Beirut Christian Maronite merchant, moved to Haifa in the early 1870s. He sold his property in Lebanon, purchased large tracts of land in Haifa and in the surrounding rural areas, and became one of the largest merchants and exporters in Haifa. He sold Jewish investors the land on which the Nesher cement factory and limestone quarries were established in the mid-1920s.[7] Muhammad Taha moved to Haifa from Nablus, during the rule of Ibrahim Pasha, and worked as a guard of the French vice-consul. He took advantage of his consular connections and the opportunities created by the 1858 land reform and bought large tracts of land. He became one of the largest property owners in Haifa. He married into a veteran family of notables, and used his position to help family members obtain work in the Haifa Ottoman municipal administration and in the religious establishment.[8] His son, Khalil Taha, rose to a position of propertied opulence by becoming a tax farmer and trading in agricultural produce.[9] Mustafa Pasha al-Khalil also acquired large tracts of land in Haifa and nearby villages. He probably came from Kafr Lam, a village on the Carmel coast. The important offices that he held included the post of mayor, member of the Administrative Council, and member of the Education Committee.[10] Both the Taha and al-Khalil families enjoyed good connections with the Jews and sold land to Zionist institutions.[11]

This large-scale accumulation of land was facilitated by the 1858 land reform, which required that the ownership of land be registered. At the time, many small landowners refrained from registering their land under their own name for fear of heavy land taxation. They preferred to register their property under the name of a large landowner and dignitary, without intending to formally hand over the ownership of the land. Many of these small landowners did eventually forfeit their property and thus further increased the holdings of the large landowners. These holdings created one of the reservoirs of property from which the Zionist institutions were able to purchase land at the beginning of the twentieth century.[12]

Possibly the most important boost to the development of Haifa came when it was connected to the Damascus-Hijaz railway. This major railway line, constructed by the last Ottoman ruler, Sultan Abd al-Hamid the Second, for the use of the thousands of Muslim pilgrims, linked Damascus with the holy town of Medina in the Arabian Peninsula.[13] In 1903, the construction of the Haifa link to the main line, at Dar'a, in Trans-Jordan, was begun.[14] The construction work and the railway's operation after its inauguration in 1908 triggered unparalleled demographic and economic growth.[15] The Hijaz railway link established Haifa as the main port of entry for Palestine. Imports and exports of the provinces east of the Jordan passed through it. Muslim pilgrims arrived en route to the holy cities of Medina and Mecca. The large amounts of material necessary for the construction of the line were imported through the port and agricultural produce from east of the Jordan was exported. The head offices of the Hijaz railway and its main railway workshops were located in Haifa. This, in turn, spawned other economic activity. Workshops and commercial enterprises sprang up and foreign businessmen invested in Haifa.

Work was thus plentiful in Haifa—so much so, that during the construction of the Hijaz railway, it won the title of *"Um al-Amal,"* "the mother of labor."[16] The large-scale government projects also provided employment. Haifa had already become the focus of labor migration and attracted unskilled Muslim rural migrants, many of whom stayed on in town, reinforcing its Arab character. It also attracted Italian, Greek, Armenian, Turkish, and German artisans and skilled workers, who strengthened its heterogeneous and cosmopolitan character.[17] Thus, at the beginning of the twentieth century Haifa was a small, somewhat rundown town, yet alive with the promise of its geographic-strategic potential. The port linked it to Europe and the west, and the

railway linked it eastward to its agricultural, social, and political hinterland. Haifa began to assume the profile that was to shape later perceptions of it.

The Jewish settlement in Haifa expanded as well. In the early nineteenth century, Jews made up only 3 percent of the population and
numbered approximately one hundred souls.[18] They were mostly poor
peddlers who sold their merchandise in nearby villages. By the turn of
the century the Jewish community had grown to 1,500 to 2,000 persons—about 12 percent of the of the population.[19] They came from
Safad and Tiberias and from overseas. They were mainly Sephardi Jews
who had originally come from North Africa and the Levant. They were
joined by a smaller number of European Ashkenazi Jews, who established the first hotels and hostels for Jewish pilgrims and immigrants
arriving at the Haifa port.[20]

The major change in the Jewish community came with the Zionist
settlement. The Zionist activists, like the European powers, recognized the importance of Haifa. Theodore Herzl, the charismatic Zionist leader, envisaged Haifa as a grand metropolis of the Mediterranean.[21] On a more practical level, Arthur Ruppin, the head of the
Palestine Office of the World Zionist Organization (WZO) and the
senior official determining settlement policy and land purchases,
wrote on the eve of the First World War: "Haifa is the future port of
Eretz Israel. Our influence in the north of Palestine will depend primarily on our standing in Haifa."[22] Zionist immigrants, primarily
from eastern Europe, aided by Zionist institutions and funds, cata-
pulted the Jewish community into a period of rapid development. Private entrepreneurs established industrial enterprises, most important
of which was the Atid factory. It produced soap and machinery and
employed close to one hundred people from the local Jewish community. Jewish enterprises expanded and entered the export and import
market. Much of the money that Baron Rothschild invested in the agricultural colonies found its way to the Jewish suppliers and workers
of Haifa. Zionist institutions established their headquarters for the
north of Palestine in Haifa. It was also chosen as the best location for
the Technikum (later the Technion), the first Jewish institute of higher
education in science and technology in Palestine.

The rapid development and consolidation of the Jewish community, with its new Ashkenazi majority, aroused the admiration of
some. In their survey of the district of Beirut, at the beginning of the
First World War, the two Ottoman officials, al-Tamimi and al-Halabi,
concluded:

There is nothing in Haifa which those, coming largely from Russia, won't achieve with their brain and their obstinance. Their institutions function with energy and efficiency and do wonders in serving their interests. They have established large factories. They live in new houses, and their traders compete successfully with the Christians and the Muslims. The Jewish schools are of the best in town. Their teachers earn good salaries, free medical care and comfortable living accommodations. Their community and organizations function in an exemplary manner, and every official carries out his obligations faithfully.[23]

They did, however, note the underlying tensions among the different groups within Haifa, as each group contended for dominance in the society.

Not all the Arabs were as enthusiastic as the Ottoman officials. There were those who viewed these achievements with trepidation, fearing that the Jews were out to displace the Arabs from their trade and their land, despite the generally friendly relations between them.[24] The most consistently outspoken proponent of this view was the Christian journalist and editor Najib Nassar, whose newspaper, *al-Karmil*, from its first appearance in 1909, warned against the scheming intentions of the Zionists.[25] His strong anti-Zionist position was shared by most Muslim and Christian intellectuals. As early as 1910, Abdullah Mukhlis, one of Nassar's close associates, wrote, "We see that the [Jewish] soap factory in Haifa, and the other enterprises run by Jews employ only from among their people. . . . The Jew does not buy from the shops of his Christian or Muslim fellow countrymen. He runs only to the warehouses of his co-religionists."[26] He went on to express his respect for the unity of the Jewish community, but appealed to the Jews to remain part of the Ottoman society and to forsake their steps toward segregation, for otherwise "Palestine will be in danger. Within a few decades the struggle for survival will have begun."[27]

EXPANDING COMMUNITIES AND NEW NEIGHBORHOODS

Haifa suffered hardship, hunger, and disease during the First World War. Its fortunes changed in 1918 when the war ended and the British assumed the Mandate granted it by the League of Nations. For Britain and her empire, Haifa was strategically located to provide protection for the Suez Canal, and a link over land to Iraq and further on to India. It was a crossroad of the Empire.[28]

Demographic Growth—Absolute and Relative Change

The small town that had begun to rise and stretch, to crack its shell and look beyond its boundaries, was now about to become the center of growth. Under British rule, the earlier demographic growth accelerated, creating rapid expansion. In 1880, there were 6,000 people living in Haifa. By the end of the First World War the population had almost quadrupled to 22,000–23,000 residents. The population doubled between the two major censuses of 1922 and 1931, and had tripled by the end of the mandatory period so that there were 150,000 people living in Haifa in 1946.[29]

As in all of Palestine, the demographic growth of Haifa resulted from different, parallel, and interrelated processes within the Jewish and the Arab communities. Both communities grew at astounding rates. Both communities grew mainly through immigration. The growth of the Jewish population in Haifa followed the pattern of growth of the Jewish settlement in general. On the other hand, the rapid growth of the Arab population in Haifa was not due primarily to natural growth, as it was in most of Palestine, but to the internal migration of people attracted by Haifa's rapid economic growth.

The Arab population of Haifa grew faster than anywhere else in Palestine, surpassing the increase of the Arab population as a whole. According to Gilbar, the rate of growth of the Muslim population from the year 1922 to 1946 was 337.2 percent, and of the Christians, 238.5 percent. The Jewish population growth, however, exceeded both of these groups, reaching a growth rate of 1,091.5 percent over the same twenty-four-year period. By the early 1920s, the Jewish community had already recovered from the years of the war when it declined from an approximate 2,000 to 1,500, due to the deportation of citizens of allied countries. With the British conquest, and the prospects of British rule, Jewish immigration and settlement quickly picked up again. The census of 1922 indicated that the Jewish community in Haifa had already reached 6,230 people. During the 1920s, the community reached close to 16,000 persons, to be followed by the far greater growth of the 1930s. By 1938, according to the census of the Jewish community, its members had reached approximately 54,000 and by 1946, 74,000.[30] This growth radically changed the relative proportion of the religious and national groups in Haifa. The most striking change was the increase of the Jewish population from a small minority of 10.0 percent prior to the War, to a quarter, a third, and by the mid-1930s, to one half of the total population of Haifa. This was not merely a demographic shift. Writing in 1936, Vilnai commented

Figure 3. Jaffa Street, downtown Haifa, circa mid-1930s.

Some years ago the Muslims constituted the majority in Haifa, their religion, their Arabic language, their customs and holidays stamped their mark on the experience of the city. But in recent years, due to the large Jewish immigration, their percentage has been declining, and with it their influence. The Muslim character of the city is disappearing.[31]

Spatial Growth—the Formation of New Neighborhoods

The demographic growth of Haifa was accompanied by geographic expansion. The influx of so many newcomers, from all groups, led to the formation of new neighborhoods. The spatial distribution and the internal differentiation of these neighborhoods determined the sociogeographic layout of the city. This, like most else in Palestine, had political significance and political repercussions. The basic pattern of spatial distribution, which emerged at an early stage, was the establishment of Christian neighborhoods in the western part of Haifa, Muslim neighborhoods in the eastern part, and Jewish neighborhoods on the lower and upper slopes of Mount Carmel.

New neighborhoods necessitated the acquisition of land on which to construct new dwellings. By the second half of the nineteenth century,

Christians had purchased land to the west and Muslims to the east. When further building within the old town of Haifa became all but impossible, new Arab neighborhoods were developed on this land. The Palestine Office of the World Zionist Organization and Zionist settlement institutions also bought large tracts of land during the last years of Ottoman rule. The importance attributed to Haifa led to the purchase of land, even before large-scale Jewish immigration took place. The purchase was facilitated by the establishment of special societies that raised funds, bought a large tract of land, and then subdivided it and sold it in small plots to individuals. They used the proceeds of the sales to acquire more land and repeat the procedure. In this way, they were able to continue with further purchases.[32] Most of the land in Haifa was bought from individual landowners, but important purchases were also made from churches, and from the German Templars.[33]

The demand for land, created by the Jewish immigration, made it more profitable for the landowning families of Haifa to sell their recently acquired holdings than to let them out for cultivation. They invested their returns in urban property, construction, and commerce.[34] It would appear that all, or almost all, landowning families sold land to Jewish individuals or societies. David Hacohen, one of the leaders of the Jewish community who was well acquainted with the Arab elite, wrote in 1936:

> Arab leaders and notables of well-known and distinguished families, who frequently appeared as the leaders and spokesmen of the Arab national movement, were the first to negotiate with the Jewish settlement over the selling of land . . . in the most open manner. Among these were notables who for years have been leaders of the Muslim community in Haifa like Tawfik Bek al-Halil and his brother Ibrahim Bek al-Halil, (the late) Hajj Halil Taha, and Hajj Tahr Qaraman, or the leader of the Catholic community Ibrahim Sahyoun and the chairman of the Christian Orthodox community Mikhail Touma. Many others too, who were affiliated with the Arab national movement as members of the national-religious councils, would sell their lands to Jews, or would speculate in the purchase of land, to be sold later to Jewish buyers.[35]

These land acquisitions by Jews, for the new Jewish neighborhoods, were crucial points of contact between the two communities. They served as one of the main channels for the transfer of capital to the Arab community. This capital became a major resource for the Arab elite and a major factor in triggering economic activity in the Arab sector. The large profits available from the sale of land help explain the sharp contradiction between the economic behavior of many of the Arab elite, and their political stance that strongly condemned such land sales.[36] Indeed, land sales to Jews became one of the focal issues of the radical nationalist opposition before and during the Arab Rebellion of 1936–1939. Many members of notable families who had sold land were murdered. Among the most prominent victims were Ibrahim Bek al-Khalil, Khalil Taha, and his son.[37]

Let us now return to the spatial distribution and location of the neighborhoods of Haifa. The old town became more and more crowded as the Hijaz railway and its related projects attracted large numbers of workers. New housing therefore sprang up on the outskirts of the old town and beyond its boundaries. At first, the segregationist pattern of the old town, with Christians on the west and Muslims on the east, was reproduced in the new neighborhoods. Jews had also lived within the boundaries of the old town. They lived close to the Muslims, unlike the Christians, who were clearly segregated from them. They were concentrated in three streets, a number of alleys, and a square, which were known as Harat al-Yahud (the Jewish Quarter). This quarter was incorporated physically and socially within the Muslim sections of the old town.[38] Even when Jews began moving to the eastern outskirts of the old town, to establish a new Jewish section, Ard-al-Yahud, they settled within the larger Muslim neighborhood of Ard-al-Balan. For example, a group of Jews, mainly from Damascus and Beirut, bought 60 dunams in this area from Muhammad Taha. Each built a home on a one-dunam plot and planted vegetables and fruit trees around it.[39]

The new Arab neighborhoods were located on the narrow coastal strip at the foot of the Carmel. They were clearly segregated by religious affiliation and socio-economic status. The Muslim neighborhoods spread eastward, from the old town with its conglomeration of crowded alleys and dilapidated houses, on to Ard al-Balan where better built stone houses mingled with factories, warehouses, and shops, to Wadi Salib, where houses were built, at random, along its gentle slopes, to Halissa, where the middle- and upper-class Muslims built their more modern homes. Further to the northeast, along the strip of sand on the outskirts of the town, at Ard al-Ramal, the poor Muslim migrant workers lived in shacks of beaten tin and other cheap materials. These shacks were known as *Buyut al-Tanak* (the tin shacks) or "*al-Mantanah*," the place that stinks, because of the absence of sanitary facilities and its stagnant swamps.[40] Time and again the municipality or other government authorities tore down the shacks, for reasons of health or political unrest,[41] only to have them crop up again.

The Christian neighborhoods spreading to the west of the old town were similarly differentiated, though their standard of housing and living was generally higher. The housing spread to the west along Wadi Nisnas and along Allenby Road where the homes mingled with educational institutions, churches, business enterprises, and shops. The Christian elite lived further up the slope of Mount Carmel in grand houses on Abbas Street and its surrounding. The one small, poor Christian neighborhood was located closer to the coast. The railway ran through this neighborhood which included small workshops and the rural migrant workers' low quality housing.[42] The new Jewish neighborhoods represented a radical break with the past developmental pattern of Haifa. They were situated at a distance from the Arab neighborhoods and clearly segregated from them. The first neighborhood, Herzlia, was established in 1909 by a group of middle-class Jews, who were determined to remove themselves from the Muslim neighborhoods and to stop paying rent to the Arabs—"who then build houses with our money."[43] They set about constructing a separate neighborhood, following the example of the Jews of Jaffa who were building the new neighborhood of Tel Aviv. They declared, "As the people of Tel Aviv build on the sands, so we will build on the rocks. The slopes of the Carmel will be our fortress."[44] After the war, Hadar Hacarmel began to develop, starting with the plots of land surrounding the Technion, and spreading south and east.[45] It was a well-built, well-planned—albeit crowded—highly organized neighborhood and it became the nucleus of the new Jewish community of Haifa. The land on which the Hadar developed had been bought by Ruppin before the First World War, but because of the war the first houses were built only in 1920.[46] Once again, the founders stated their intentions clearly:

> Here, in the town of Haifa, where the Jewish settlement is but a small minority compared to the Muslims and Christians, we feel the great need to establish a central Hebrew neighborhood, which will bring together all those who are dispersed in the Arab neighborhoods, and will thus create the stronghold which will secure our position and our existence in the town of Haifa with its grand promise for the future.[47]

Hadar Hacarmel developed rapidly covering 1,730 dunams by 1940 and numbering 32,820 persons by 1938 when it housed over half of the Jewish community in Haifa.[48] It thus became the geographic, municipal, and social heart of the new Jewish settlement.

Other new Jewish neighborhoods developed in the 1920s. Those that were contiguous with Hadar Hacarmel were eventually incorporated

Figure 4. Herzl Street, central street of Hadar Hacarmel.

into it. Neve Sha'anan (1922) was located on one of the eastern plateaus of the Carmel, and Bat Galim (1923) was the only Jewish neighborhood along the western coastal strip.[49] Many of the German Jewish immigrants of the 1930s settled on the Carmel.[50] The Valley of Acre was settled in the 1930s and residential quarters for members of the General Federation of Jewish Workers—the Histadrut—were built there.[51]

The socio-economic differences among the Jewish neighborhoods were far less marked than in the Christian and Muslim neighborhoods. This reflected the absence of the very rich and the very poor. Hadar Hacarmel, for example, was established by the new Jewish middle class (engineers, lawyers, doctors, educators, etc.) but many skilled workers also lived there.[52] Neve Sha'anan, which had been established by lower-middle-class families, was also a mixed neighborhood where clerical and skilled manual workers lived. The special workers' quarters helped to prevent the formation of slums, as did the modern planning of the new neighborhoods. Nevertheless, the large influx of people did create the Jewish equivalent of the migrant Muslim workers' shanties. Tents and wooden huts were an integral and constant feature of most of the Jewish neighborhoods. The first large tent camps were built by the Haifa Labor Council (HLC), while many of the wooden huts were constructed by individual families.[53] Although conditions were better here than in the Muslim workers' slums, there were nevertheless health hazards and sanitation problems. The municipality exerted much pressure to dismantle these temporary dwellings but to little avail since they were often the only housing to be had. When the plague hit in the summer of 1941, the remaining wooden huts were torn down, together with the petrol-tin shacks of Ard al-Raml.[54]

By 1940, a new Haifa had emerged. It was not only larger geographically with its many new neighborhoods, but it also had a distinct pattern of religious-national dispersion. The Arabs lived along the coastal strip and the lower slopes of the Carmel, while the Jews lived in dispersed neighborhoods, on the middle and higher slopes. Both national groups found this spatial distribution problematic, each for its own reasons. The Jewish leadership defined its problem in terms of its basic goal, the creation of a separate, autonomous, segregated municipal entity. For that purpose, contiguity and easy accessibility from one neighborhood to another were of vital importance. They therefore devoted much effort to building connecting roads between the neighborhoods. The costs were covered by the residents themselves, by Zionist institutions, or by loans from the Haifa municipality.[55] The Arabs resented this, as Seikally reports, "These measures were criticized very bitterly by the Arabs who felt that needed improvements in their quarters were deliberately ignored, and that loans were made available only to carry out construction in Jewish quarters."[56] In addition, the Jewish community regarded Arab neighborhoods located between the Jewish ones, and Arab homes and property on strategic thoroughfares, as a "physical interruption" and a security hazard, especially during the recurring clashes of 1929, 1933, 1936–39 between Jews and Arabs in Haifa.[57]

The Arab leadership, on their part, perceived the new Jewish neighborhoods to be encircling them.[58] The rapidly expanding Jewish population, in searching for territories in which to establish separate neighborhoods, spread in all directions. In the case of Haifa that meant north, and northeast along the Haifa Bay, southeast and south on the lower and higher slopes of Mount Carmel, west, once again along the coast. There were large gaps between these neighborhoods; nevertheless, the predominant perception of the spacial dispersion of the Jewish community by the Arab population was one of encircling. This was further exacerbated by the geographic layout of Haifa, with the slope of Mount Carmel coming down close to the coast and to the old, predominantly Arab, town. Most of the new Jewish neighborhoods were thus located above the old Arab neighborhoods, and above the new ones that emerged as an expansion and a continuation of the latter. The Arab population, responding to the rapid changes taking place in its midst and around it, saw itself as being both encircled and towered over. This phenomenon was evident as early as 1924 when E. Mills, assistant to the Chief Secretary of the Palestine Administration, reported: "There is in Haifa claustrophobia. The town is ringed round by Jewish enterprises and Jewish-owned lands."[59] Thus, for the Arabs, the spatial dispersion served to reflect and reinforce their perception of the Jewish goals and the threat they posed. Fahmi Abbushi, of Jenin, warned: "The Jews have encircled the town from the mountain to the plain and the coast; the Arabs should be aware of this encirclement out of fear for their fate.[60]

HAIFA — THE POLITICAL CONTEXT

The complex of intra and intercommunal processes in Haifa grew out of, and reflected, the national conflict that shaped life in Palestine. It is therefore pertinent to look at the relations between Jews and Arabs in Haifa within this political context.

The 1920s were a period of relative calm in relations between Jews and Arabs in Haifa, as it was in all of Palestine. Despite the Arab leadership's obvious displeasure, there seemed to be a de facto acceptance of the new situation. Even the deep recession of 1926–27, which created large-scale unemployment among the Jewish workers, seems to have had less of an impact on the Arab economy and on unemployment among Arab workers. The violent outburst of hostility that occurred in Jerusalem in August 1929 took the Jewish settlement by surprise. Despite the absence of religious conflict in Haifa, of the kind that had triggered the outbursts in Jerusalem, other foci of conflict had developed during the decade. The social, economic, and demographic factors that Hope-Simpson argued were at the source of the outbursts, were certainly evident in Haifa too.[61] Social tension within the Arab community had increased, as did the internal differentiation between those who benefited from the new order and those who did not. The poverty and marginality of the thousands of Arab peasant-workers, on the one hand, and the prosperity of the burgeoning Arab middle class on the other, created the potential for violence. Once the clashes began in Jerusalem, they easily spread to Haifa.[62]

The 1930s were a decade of political shifts and upheavals. The opening of the newly developed Haifa port in 1933, and the large-scale Jewish immigration from central Europe during 1932 to 1935, ushered in several years of growth and prosperity.[63] This, in turn, increased the migration of Arabs in search of work that was far beyond the absorption capacity of the town. As a result, the number of poor migrants increased, the internal differentiation sharpened, and intercommunal relations became fraught with tension. The invasion of Ethiopia by Italy in October of 1935, and the international crisis that ensued, brought economic activity to a sudden halt. Unemployment spread among both Jewish and Arab workers.

Haifa, the center of economic growth and the target of migrant workers, became a breeding ground for social and political unrest. After the short years of the economic boom, the many Arab villagers who moved into town keenly felt the hardship of unemployment. Sheik Izz al-Din al-Kassam, who held important religious positions in Haifa, had worked among the new urban poor from the early 1930s and won their confidence. He was the first to realize the political and social potential of the uprooted urban-*falahin* and, together with them, began his armed activity against both the British and the Jewish settlers, in November 1935.[64] The activity of al-Kassam was short-lived. In November 1935, he and several followers were surrounded during one of their attacks and killed.[65] The militant activity of Izz al-Din al-Kassam can be seen as a forerunner of the general strike and the Arab Rebellion that broke out in April 1936 and lasted, off and on, till 1939.[66] The Arab Rebellion transformed Arab-Jewish-British relations in Palestine. It polarized the relations between Jews and Arabs, deepened the separation between the two communities, and increased Jewish autonomy and self-sufficiency. It temporarily created close cooperation between the Jewish settlement and the British, but ultimately led to the White Paper of 1939 that severely restricted Jewish immigration and therefore aroused vehement Jewish opposition. The Arab population of Haifa did not fully join the general strike, despite very strong pressure by the national leadership in Jerusalem.[67] Nevertheless, the general strike created havoc within the Arab Palestinian society of Haifa, weakened its elite and its leadership, and deeply affected its economy. Economic activity dropped drastically and many workers left Haifa to return to their villages of origin. The Palestine Arab Workers' Society (PAWS), the main Arab labor organization, which had gained momentum during the years of prosperity, totally disintegrated.[68] Most Arab councilors of the Haifa municipality resigned and the Town Council was replaced by one appointed by the District Commissioner of Haifa. Internal terrorism was directed against those who opposed the national leadership of Hajj Amin al-Husseini. It struck at many of Haifa's most distinguished families, as a belated "punishment" for selling their lands to Zionist organizations and individuals.

By the early 1940s, after four to five years of depression, Haifa's economy and society slowly regained some of its momentum, to prosper during the years of the Second World War. The British war machine and its needs were in large measure responsible for this boom. Tens of thousands of workers, Jews and Arabs, worked in the military camps, in construction and maintenance, and in the many industrial enterprises that were established to meet the need for products that could not be brought from elsewhere. The political mood was far more apprehensive. The bombardment of Haifa during the first year of the war created grave anxiety. The anti-British feeling among the Arab community, which focused mainly on the British support for the Jewish National Home, led them to hope for the defeat of the British. Tension between Jew and Arab heightened.[69] When the balance of the war shifted in 1943 and the possibility of a German invasion disappeared, relations between Jews and Arabs began to improve. The economic boom, the rapid rise in the cost of living, and the relative breakdown of barriers between the Jewish and Arab economic sectors, facilitated cooperation between the Arabs and the Jews.[70]

The end of the war brought uncertainty about the future. Unemployment spread as the British army closed down its projects. Among Arab workers, unemployment was a major problem.[71] It was less evident among Jewish workers. The Jewish economy had managed to develop a sound base during the war and was thus able to absorb the thousands of workers who had been employed by the military, as well as the returning soldiers. The Arab economy, which had also prospered during the war, was not able to fill the same role.

The political future was unclear. Arab and Jewish opposition to the continuation of British rule increased, and so did the hostility between them. The United Nations and the United States became involved in the search for solutions. The political conflict became even more pervasive. While neither side yet realized it, the countdown had begun.

SPHERES OF COOPERATION AND THE PULL OF SEGREGATION

In a town like Haifa, with a mixed population, we can expect to find various forms of interaction and cooperation between members of its different communities. Haifa began as a mixed town, and remained so throughout the period of British rule. And yet, the dominant trend was toward the increase in the autonomy of the Jewish community. This process was initiated primarily by the Jewish community and its Zionist leadership, and was in line with their goal of establishing the Jewish

National Home. This was evident in each of the three spheres to be discussed, the social, municipal, and economic spheres, where the systematic increase in the autonomy of the Jewish community was accompanied by an increase in its separation from the Arab community. The pull between autonomy and cooperation existed in all spheres. It took different forms and followed different courses.

Social Relations

The sphere of personal, social relationships between Jews and Arabs in Haifa was characterized by decreasing contact. Informal social relations existed during the late Ottoman period at the neighborhood level. Both research and personal memoirs emphasize the close day-to-day social relations between Jews and Muslims, who, as noted, lived in the same neighborhoods.[72] This was primarily true of the Sephardi Jews, who constituted the majority of the Jewish community into the beginning of the twentieth century.[73] In his memoirs Khalfon recalls:

> On the whole relations between neighbors were compatible and frequently they were relations of friendship. I recall reciprocal visits on occasions of festivities and of mourning. On the Passover eve my parents would send me to our Arab neighbors carrying a tray full of dried fruit and "matsot." In turn, at the end of the holiday our Arab neighbors would bring us trays piled with "pitot" and "labaneh," cheese, eggs, olives and the likes.
>
> I further remember that opposite us lived a highly respected Muslim family; the head of the family was Mustaffa 'Aamr, a very rich man who was a member of the city council, appointed by the Ottoman government. He was a frequent guest in our home, and would visit us mainly on our holidays. Another Muslim neighbor was Za'ablawi, whose son was well known in Haifa and outside it for his pranks. A scoundrel he was, with his hand on the sword and dagger. Everyone feared him, but whenever he saw my father, who was . . . a Rabbi, the young Arab paid him great respect, kissed the hem of his gown and asked him for his blessing. My father would lay his hand on the youngster's head and bless him.[74]

The creation of the new Jewish neighborhoods that were geographically separated from the Arab neighborhoods signaled the beginning of the end of informal social relationships. Over the years, more and more of the Jewish community, spurred by demographic growth and the aspiration for autonomy, lived within these new neighborhoods. The recurring outbreaks of hostility also pushed Jews out of the mixed neighborhoods. During the riots of 1929 and in 1936, Jews living in the mixed downtown neighborhoods fled their homes. Most remained in the new neighborhoods when the hostilities subsided. By the late 1930s, only a small proportion of the Jewish community remained within the mixed neighborhoods. They were mostly Sephardi families and they had become a minority in the predominantly Ashkenazi Jewish community. Haifa had become a largely ethnically / nationally segregated town.[75] For those who remained in the mixed neighborhoods, close social relations with their Arab neighbors continued. For the rest, informal day-to-day contacts were rare.

Municipal Relations

At the level of local government, Jews and Arabs continued to cooperate fully in the Haifa municipality.[76] At the same time the Jewish community consolidated its separate communal institutions, in order to increase its autonomy and self-sufficiency. The municipal authority was composed of an elected mayor and town council. The mayor was chosen from among the Muslim Arabs, the largest community, and the town council was composed of a given number of representatives from each religious community in conformity with the Ottoman millet system. In the first municipal elections, held in 1927, a council made up of four Muslims, four Christians, and two Jews was elected. The council was headed by Hasan Shukri, a member of the front opposing the Arab nationalist leadership, and one of the few members of the Arab elite who was positively inclined toward the Zionist enterprise.[77] In the second municipal elections, held in 1934, Hasan Shukri was reelected as mayor and the composition of the council was changed to match the demographic changes, noted in the 1931 census. A council of twelve was elected, composed of four Muslims, four Christians, and four Jews. During the Arab rebellion, most of the Arab councilors resigned, and the elected town council was replaced by an appointed commission, nominated by the District Commissioner of the Haifa district, and headed by the elected mayor. Hasan Shukri escaped to Lebanon in 1937, after several attempts on his life, and the Jewish councilor, Shabtai Levi, substituted for him as mayor.[78] When Hasan Shukri died in 1940, Shabtai Levi, an Arabic-speaking Jew of Turkish origin and the longest serving Jewish councilor, was appointed mayor.

Relations on the town council appear to have been good. Discussions focused almost exclusively on matters of the town, with relatively little national polarization, except for the period of the Arab Rebellion, 1936–1939. Vashitz claims that both communities preferred candidates who were known to be moderate, inclined to cooperate with each other, and who would best advance the interests of the town.[79] Seikaly, however, contends that most of the Arab councilors came from wealthy elite families who benefited from the British colonial rule and were thus willing to cooperate with the Jewish representatives, even to the detriment of Arab interests.[80]

The role of the Jewish representatives was seen, within the Jewish community, mainly as a "defensive" one, to secure the share of the Jewish community in the resources of the municipality and to protect its interests when they appeared to be at odds with those of the Arab population. Concomitantly, an additional, separate and autonomous institutional system was developed within the Jewish community, which took on itself most of the responsibility for its local urban needs. It was a two-tiered system functioning both at the neighborhood and at the community level. The neighborhood committees were the first level to be set up. Of these the most important was the neighborhood committee of Hadar Hacarmel. It took on a wide range of functions, among them the acquisition of land, construction and maintenance of the neighborhood's infrastructure, financial aid, as well as negotiations with the government and local authorities. It also set regulations for the moral and social life of the neighborhood.[81]

The Community Council (*Va'ad ha-Kehila*) was established in 1932 as a roof body. It included the older, pre-Zionist institutions of the Sephardi and the Ashkenazi communities, the new representatives of all the Jewish neighborhoods, and the Jewish representatives on the Town Council.[82] The declared purpose of the Community Council was to protect and advance the needs and rights of the Jewish community, but it appears to have considered itself to be a supplementary or surrogate municipality.[83]

The creation of semi-municipal institutions, at both the neighborhood and the community level, was seen within the Jewish community as an inevitable step. It was intended to compensate for the inherent weakness of the Jewish community as a minority in an essentially hostile environment. Within the Arab community, local municipal relations were viewed quite differently. In the early 1930s, they already saw the municipality itself as "a Jewish stronghold"[84] and the Arab press portrayed Hasan Shukri, the mayor, as an "Arab who was being used as a stooge by the Jewish councilors."[85] They perceived the consolidation of autonomous Jewish institutions as contributing to the widening differential between the two communities in the standard of living and the level of services. The Arab community depended only on the government and its local authority—the municipality—which did very little to advance the welfare of the town, while the Jewish community had an additional system that compensated for the indifference of the local government.

The mixed municipal authority in Haifa did serve as an arena of cooperation. It was, however, supplemented by a system of separate institutions whose autonomy and authority increased over the years and contributed to the growing separation between the two communities.

Economic Relations

In the economic sphere, as in the others, the dominant trend was toward the increased segregation of the Jewish and Arab sectors. Segregation, even to the extent of reciprocal boycotting, was an economic goal and a political rallying cry among different elements of both national communities. And yet, despite its undoubted predominance, the pull toward segregation varied in intensity and consistency in different strata of each community, and in different periods.

What little economic cooperation there was appears to have been among the bourgeoisie, the new middle classes, rather than among the working class. As the following chapters deal at length with attempts at cooperation between Jewish and Arab workers, it will suffice at this point to sketch the central argument. Jewish and Arab workers were in direct competition with each other, for each group feared the other would displace it. Thus, despite some attempts of the Histadrut to organize Arab workers, and despite joint work sites, little effective cooperation developed between the two collectives.[86] The segregation policy of the Histadrut and the Haifa Labor Council, which called for the employment of only "Hebrew Labor" in the Jewish economic sector, created a deep chasm between Jewish and Arab labor, and made cooperation extremely difficult. It was from among the bourgeoisie, and almost only from among them, that reservations were voiced about full segregation. The Jewish commercial and construction circles in Haifa did not reject the policy of employing only Jewish labor and purchasing Jewish manufactured products. Indeed, they supported these courses of action, as part of their strong Zionist commitment. But they did reject the totality with which these demands were propounded and enforced, and the vehement rhetoric in which they were expressed. The Arab economic elite in Haifa, in turn, did not reject the strong nationalist opposition to the Zionist colonization. On the contrary, most of them identified with it, and some even led the political struggle. But they did express strong reservations about boycotting all economic transactions with members of the Jewish community.[87]

The Jewish members of the Chamber of Commerce in Haifa adopted a policy of segregation. In 1921, they left the Haifa Chamber of Commerce to form their own separate, Jewish only, organization. This step was economically and symbolically linked to their goal of a separate autonomous Jewish community in Haifa.[88] They did, however, make an effort, especially at the informal level, to retain decent relations with the Arab Chamber of Commerce and with its leading merchants. There were commercial interactions between Jews and Arabs that no one wanted to damage. The kinds of personal informal relations that occur between people who interact over long periods of time, even in a hostile environment, did exist. One of the few to state this explicitly was A. Rosenfeld, one of the largest Jewish importers in Haifa, who said in 1936, "I have been working with an Arab contractor for 16 years, I cannot bring myself to behave ungratefully. There is an emotional involvement, besides the question of prices."[89]

Similarly, Arab merchants had reservations about the Arab boycott that had been declared during the Arab Rebellion of 1936–1939 banning all economic relations with Jews. Numerous reports told of the limited participation of most Arab merchants in Haifa in the boycott, and of the many ways developed to bypass it.[90]

Large merchants and contractors supported economic cooperation, which was beneficial to both sides. The Jewish businessmen could provide financing, European connections, and know-how; their Arab counterparts could provide cheap labor, land, as well as connections with local and Middle Eastern markets. Thus cooperation developed in those economic activities in which cheap labor was of prime importance (construction, excavation, agriculture in rural areas), or in which market connections could be shared beneficially (import, export, wholesale, retail). Catran provides us with an example of such cooperation. He was a Sephardi Jew who imported Manchester textiles. Working with Arab agents and traders, he sold about 70 percent of his merchandise to Arab customers in Haifa, as well as in other towns and villages of Palestine, and in Trans-Jordan.[91] Grain merchants, mainly Sephardi Jews and Christian Arabs, also cooperated among themselves, establishing ad hoc partnerships from time to time.[92] Such cooperation also existed in contracting. Emil Sahyoun was an Arab contractor for gravel, who went into partnership with the contracting office of the Haifa Labor Council. Yehiel Weitzman, a Jewish contractor and leading figure in the Hadar Hacarmel community, set up numerous partnerships with Arab contractors. The contractor T. Dunia and the engineer Katinka established one of the biggest partnerships in Palestine with Joseph Albina, the Arab financier from Jerusalem.[93]

These close interactions and economic relations fluctuated. During periods of depression and periods of overt hostility, each community conducted its economic activity primarily within its own boundaries. However, during years of prosperity, interactions increased, breaking down some barriers. In the early 1930s, during the big economic boom in Palestine from which Haifa benefited greatly, both communities prospered and had much to offer each other. David Hacohen, a leader of the Jewish community, a member of the city council and one of the executives of the Histadrut-owned construction company Solel Boneh, remembers this time:

> Those were years of great economic prosperity brought about by the immigration of Jewish capital. All strata of the Arab population bene- fited greatly. The land owners, some of whom were almost bankrupt, recovered and began to accumulate a fortune. . . . The large merchants and smaller traders increased the scope of their business. They prof- ited from their new Jewish customers, and from the thousands of Arab workers who came into town to supply the labor needed by the expanding and developing market. This development created an or- ganic necessity for ties between Jews and Arabs, and no national am- bitions could stand in their way.[94]

The economic crisis of late 1935 and the Arab Rebellion of 1936 brought all this to a virtual standstill. The rebellion and general strike widened the separation between the two communities and consolidated it. The trend toward separation seemed irreversible. However, the years of the Second World War proved that in the economic sphere, at least, this trend could change. The prosperity of the war years created close rela- tions once again. The breakdown of trade with Europe enhanced the economic importance of the local and foreign Arab market. More voices within the Jewish community called for the mitigation of the segregationist policies and a committee was appointed in 1940 by the World Zionist Congress to study and recommend possible ways of cooperation between Jews and Arabs.[95] In Haifa, the two communities resumed their commercial connections.

The war came to an end. By 1946, both the economic and the politi- cal scene had shifted once again. The end of the war economy led to widespread unemployment, primarily among the Arab workers. The national struggle was renewed and the Arab national leadership in Palestine and surrounding neighboring countries declared an eco- nomic boycott of the Jewish economy, which came into effect on the 1st of January, 1946.[96] Its implementation, in Haifa, was again partial and piecemeal. Vashitz concludes: "We see how closely interrelated the two economic sectors were and how similar the reactions of the Chambers of Commerce were. Both were doubtful about boycott and counter-boycott."[97] This time there was no opportunity for renewed prosperity. The final countdown was about to begin.

It is within this complex context of growth and internal differentiation, of sharp economic fluctuations and of the ever-present interplay between the economic and the political, that Jewish and Arab labor faced each other in the Haifa labor market.

ARAB AND JEWISH LABOR

Both Jews and Arabs gravitated to Haifa in search of work. Both created new strata in their respective national communities. Both grew as a result of the expanding economy, enjoyed years of prosperity, suffered unemployment in years of depression, and experienced hardship during much of the period. In the following chapters we will focus on their mutual impact, the competition between them, the threat each posed to the other, and the rare cases of cooperation between them.

Arab Labor

Arab wage labor in an urban, capitalist economy was a new phenomenon in Palestine. Haifa led the way in 1903, with the jobs provided by the construction of the Hijaz railway. Later, under British rule, unskilled workers found employment in the extension and maintenance of the Palestine Railway, the development and running of the Haifa port, the Haifa municipality, stone quarries, oil refining, and a number of Arab industrial enterprises.

Some of the workers had particular skills. They were the sons of veteran Haifa families, of small merchants and artisans, who did not continue their fathers' businesses or crafts but became skilled wage laborers. However, the vast majority of the Arab workers were unskilled, migrating in the thousands to Haifa from rural areas. It is difficult to estimate the numbers of these workers, or their exact distribution. There were no government censuses or surveys, and the Arab institutions, unlike the Jewish ones, did not conduct surveys of their labor force. The temporary nature of Arab labor migration, which fluctuated according to season, supply of employment, and level of political stability, makes such estimates even more difficult. The one detailed census of Arab workers in Haifa was conducted at a rather late stage, in 1943, by the Haifa Labor Council (HLC).[98] Despite the problems of possible inaccuracies and underaccounting due to the probable lack of cooperation on the part of the Arab workers, it appears to be relatively comprehensive, and the information it collected is similar to that obtained from more piecemeal sources. This census counted 15,672 Arab workers. Of these, approximately 20 percent originally came from Haifa, 60 percent migrated to Haifa from within Palestine—40 percent from rural settlements and 20 percent from urban ones—and 20 percent migrated from neighboring countries.[99] It is likely that the number of migrants from outside of Palestine is underestimated in this census. Thus seasonal migrant workers from the Hauran, in southern Syria, probably played a larger and more important role in the unskilled labor force of Haifa, than the 1943 survey indicates.[100]

The rural migrant laborers, studied in detail by both Vashitz and Yazbeck, usually remained on the periphery of Haifa's social fabric.[101] They lived in makeshift dwellings, and sometimes in shantytowns. Hundreds of workers could be seen, night after night, asleep in sacks in the town streets. Hundreds of families lived in the caves of Wadi Rushmiya with no sanitary facilities.[102] George Mansur, a labor activist from Jaffa, noted that in 1935, "There were in Haifa alone, 11,160 Arab workers living in 2,473 huts."[103]

The migrant peasant-workers kept in close contact with their villages of origin, lived near others of the same village, helped each other find work, established associations according to their community of origin, and married among themselves. Vashitz notes that the transition from village life to urban dwelling followed several stages. The first time in town, the villager looked for a place of work. Anything would do. The villager was not choosy and would accept low wages. When the work ended, or when the agricultural season arrived, he would return to his home village. By the second and third time the villager came to town, he was more selective about the work he accepted. He would stay in town for longer periods, returning on the weekends to his village, where his family was likely to have remained. Many workers worked for years as temporary-seasonal migrants. Others moved on to the third stage, which was characterized by the worker no longer returning to his village for the seasonal agricultural work. He now had a more or less permanent place of work in Haifa, and was acquiring new skills, becoming "experienced" or "semi-skilled." His earnings improved. At this stage the villager became an "owner of two homes" and he might continue in this manner for as long as ten or twenty years. Finally, the migrant laborer became a city dweller. He became a skilled worker. His family settled permanently in Haifa and his children grew up in town. They were part of the new urban working class.[104]

An illustrative account of this process, as it had evolved by 1943, was presented by one of the workers' organizations—The Federation of Arab Trade Unions and Labour Societies (FATULS).[105] In an address to the Wage Committee, appointed by the government in 1942, the Federation stated:

> The majority of our unskilled workers are villagers drifting to town searching for their livelihood through manual labor, fleeing from the specter of starvation which hovers over the Arab village due to shortage in arable land and the increase of the population. They came to town and were prepared to work in any job and at any wage in order solely to earn their daily living and that of their families. The demands and needs of these unskilled villager workers were simple at the beginning, but their contact with skilled workers in the town and their comparative instinctive understanding of the social elevation, forces them to drift with the stream of the new life before them. A great number have lived in towns for five or fifteen years and a greater part severed their bonds with the village retaining only family relationships. They have therefore, these being the circumstances, become dependent for their livelihood on their work in towns.[106]

The temporary migrant peasant workers were not generally considered the ideal manpower for the establishment and consolidation of a labor movement. Yet Eliyahu Agassi, a Histadrut activist who was in close contact with the Arab workers in Haifa, maintained that they were more amenable to labor organization than the urban workers.[107] He argued that the urban workers came from better-off urban families and in many cases retained their petty-bourgeois perspective and conservative outlook. The rural migrant workers, on the other hand, came from rural communities with a tradition of cooperation and solidarity. The prosperity years of 1932–35 transformed the rural workers from part *falahin*–part laborers into wage workers, yet they retained many of their old ways, as Agassi observed in 1935:

> Their social orientation and personal characteristics did not change markedly. And as in the village their social life was organized in a particular way—they belonged to "*hamulot*" and to clans, and the individual felt the living link which connected him to a particular social association—thus in the town they remain amenable to associations and organizations, and replace their missing communal ties with an affiliation to labor associations. . . . This would explain why the rural workers in the IPC strike, and in almost any other strike, were far more consolidated and patient than the urban workers.[108]

The PAWS—the Palestine Arab Workers' Society—was established by skilled and semi-skilled workers of the Palestine Railway who came from Syria and Egypt.[109] By the 1930s, the peasant workers had begun to join unions. Some, like Sami Taha, became very active and influential. He moved to Haifa from his native village of Arabah, near Jenin in the early 1930s. He soon joined the PAWS where he was employed as a low level clerk. He worked his way up within the organization, so that by 1937, when he was still in his twenties, he was appointed its secretary-general. He had only completed the fifth grade of elementary school, but he studied on his own and became highly knowledgeable in issues of labor and labor legislation, as well as proficient in the English language. He became a powerful and influential labor leader, and was appointed the representative of labor on the Arab High Executive.[110] Sami Taha's career was certainly outstanding. Other workers of peasant origin also became lower level activists in the PAWS and, despite the fact that the urban workers who had founded the PAWS retained their central position, by the mid-1940s, almost all of the Society's activists were of peasant stock.[111]

Haifa was the birthplace of the PAWS and was its stronghold. It was established in 1925 and held its first conference in Haifa in January 1930. Haifa was also the venue for its two other conferences in August of 1946 and August of 1947. Strikes were more frequent among Arab workers in Haifa than elsewhere in Palestine. These included recurring strikes at the quarry of the Nesher cement works, at the Mabruk cigarette factory, at the Palestine Railways, and, most important, the large strike at the Iraq Petroleum Company (IPC) in March 1935. The PAWS played a significant role in most of these strikes.[112] Despite splits in 1942–43, and later in 1945, which led first to the formation of the Federation of Arab Trade Union and Labor Societies, and later to the establishment of the Congress of Arab Workers, the PAWS remained the largest and most influential Arab labor organization, and Haifa retained its position as the PAWS' stronghold and center.[113]

The primacy of Haifa in labor organization was due to its large concentration of wage workers and the large size of many of the workplaces. The PAWS may have been spurred to act because it feared the impact of the Zionist-affiliated Histadrut on the Arab workers. These workers were surely aware of the benefits—provision of employment, rate of pay, labor conditions, and social services—obtained by Jewish workers through the Histadrut, and specifically through the Haifa Labor Council (HLC).

Jewish Labor

While Arab labor was on the periphery of the Arab community in Haifa, Jewish labor was at the very center of the highly organized Jewish community. The HLC was one of the most powerful of the local labor councils, whose impact on Haifa in general, and Jewish Haifa in particular, is illustrated by the epithet—"Red Haifa"—"Haifa *ha-Aduma.*" It succeeded in organizing Jewish labor, so that 90 percent of all Jewish construction workers and an even higher percentage of manufacturing workers were members of the Histadrut and directly affiliated with the HLC.[114] The membership was significantly lower in a number of other sectors, such as government works and small workshops.

The number of Jewish workers in Haifa increased sharply during the Mandatory period. According to the Jewish Agency census, there were 3,001 Jewish workers in Haifa in 1930,[115] and as many as 17,927 in 1937.[116] This phenomenal increase (590 percent) exceeded both the growth of the Jewish community as a whole and the growth of Jewish workers in other major urban settlements.[117]

In the 1920s and the 1930s, Jewish workers gravitated to Haifa. It was the port of entry for many of the immigrants, some of whom chose to settle in Haifa, rather than move elsewhere. Others belonged to the hinterland of Haifa. They were members of agricultural collectives or employed in government public works, laborers working in road construction. They moved to Haifa when their previous jobs were no longer suitable or available. Finally, there were those who were attracted to Haifa by its natural beauty and economic promise.

In the 1930s, this sense of promise had a sound base. Haifa flourished. The deep water port had opened and the Jewish immigrants from Germany invested much of their private capital and industrial know-how in Haifa, where a large industrial area was developing. Yet, the promised economic boom never came. The short years of prosperity (1924–25; 1932–35) were followed by years of economic depression (1927–30; 1936–41), when the labor market of Haifa could not provide employment for all the workers who had come to the town.

Jewish labor in Haifa faced frequent unemployment. "Every Jewish immigrant who settled in Haifa, or any worker coming to Haifa from elsewhere," writes De Vries of the 1920s, "could expect an extended period of total unemployment or a more or less constant state of partial unemployment."[118] As a result, relations between workers were replete with tension. Jewish workers competed among themselves for work, primarily in the Jewish sector. "Veteran" workers, those who had immigrated several years before, were wary of more immigrants. Members of cooperative groups guarded against the unemployed, who were allocated work by the HLC Labor Exchange. The organized workers, members of the Histadrut, feared the competition from the nonorganized workers who undercut them, and Haifa'ites preferred to close ranks against Jewish workers coming from out of town, even when they were also members of the Histadrut. Concomitantly, Jewish workers competed with Arab workers, primarily, though not only, over employment opportunities in the government sector. When the economy prospered, there was work for all and wages and labor conditions could be improved. As soon as the economy slowed down and unemployment spread, tensions increased and wages fell.

The Haifa Labor Council, established in 1921, was led by two strong secretaries, David Cohen in the 1920s and Aba Houshi in the 1930s and 1940s. Under their respective leadership, the HLC consolidated into a powerful institution, probably the most powerful of the labor councils in all of Palestine. It was highly centralized so that all functions related to it were brought under the direct control of the Council's secretary and the inner circle of functionaries. The functions of the Council encompassed all aspects of the lives of its members and their families, from their immigration to Palestine, to their initial absorption, their work, housing, nutrition, health, education, and recreation. Thus the council and its leadership exercised immense influence on its members who became dependent on them. How was this control achieved? The ideological commitment of the vast majority of Histadrut members provided the basic solidarity necessary for the HLC to achieve its control, and exercise its authority. In addition, the Council applied sanctions, such as withholding vital services that the HLC provided for its members.[119]

Thus, from a position of weakness, or at least of vulnerability, Jewish labor was able to build an organization that became the dominant force in the Jewish community of Haifa. De Vries concludes:

> The concept "Red Haifa" described both a condition and a process: a condition in which the social and cultural power was in the hands of the workers and of the Histadrut, and a process in which this power continually increased. "Red Haifa" was characterized by a consistent growth of its working class and of members of the Histadrut within the Jewish community. Its political climate focused on the power of the Histadrut, taking its centrality as a given. To the members of the labor movement, the concept expressed a way of life, a form of identification with the movement and a source of pride. To its opponents, the concept expressed their fears for the future of the town. Common

to all the different uses of the term "Red Haifa" was the recognition of
the unique nature of Haifa in the 1930s and the 1940s as a workers'
town, and of the dominance of the Histadrut in the life of the Jewish
community.[120]

While the HLC dealt primarily with Jewish workers, it also extended
its attention to Arab workers, to a greater extent than any other local
labor council. It began by establishing a club for Arab workers, in 1925,
as a result of rank-and-file pressure by those Jewish workers who
worked in close proximity with Arab workers. Later the HLC supported the activity of the Palestine Labor League (PLL) in Haifa. The
PLL was established in 1927, by the third Histadrut Convention, as an
adjunct organization for those Arab workers who wished to affiliate
themselves with the Histadrut. It was run by Jewish labor functionaries, the most important of whom was Eliahu Agassi, an Arabic-
speaking Jew from Iraq. Agassi managed the affairs of the PLL in Haifa
between the years 1932 and 1937, in close conjunction with the HLC
secretary Aba Houshi, and became very knowledgeable in all matters
of the Arab workers in Haifa. The PLL was thus the vehicle through
which the HLC appealed to Arab workers and tried to influence them
in ways which were seen as compatible with the interests of Jewish
labor.

The strength of the Histadrut in Haifa did not necessarily ensure a
high standard of living for its members. The rank and file of the Jewish
working class was affected not only by the strength of its organization,
but also by economic and political vicissitudes. Long spells of unemployment led to hardship and poverty which the organization could
cushion only minimally.[121]

Wages and Differentials

The far-reaching differences in the history, characteristics, and organization of Jewish and Arab labor in Haifa were manifested in their
earnings, which reflected the wage pattern of the whole country (see
Chap. 1). Unskilled Arab workers were paid between 120–200 mils per
day; 120–150 mils per day in the lower paying jobs, and 150–200 mils in
the better-paying jobs. The Hourani laborers were the lowest paid casual workers and they received around 70–100 mils per day, while the
more experienced or skilled workers earned between 250–350 mils.
Most unskilled Jewish workers earned as much as the experienced or
skilled Arab workers, approximately 250–350 mils. In the government
sector, however, the Jewish unskilled worker seldom earned more than

220 mils per day. The more experienced and skilled Jewish workers could command as much as 1,000 mils, but they usually earned between 350–750 mils per day.

The documentation indicates that the main factor affecting the wage of Arab workers was the large supply of peasant-workers from the rural areas of Palestine and from the Houran. In times of prosperity the rural migration into Haifa increased. This abundance of labor neutralized the opportunity of using the increased demand for labor, which came with prosperity, to demand higher wages. The wages of Jewish workers were affected primarily by economic fluctuations. During times of prosperity the demand for labor exceeded the supply and wages would rise, but they would fall during the depression that followed.

With these differences in mind I have chosen one point in time, 1934–35, the years of prosperity, to look more closely at the Haifa labor market. We have fairly detailed figures for the earnings of Jewish and Arab workers at this time through which to obtain a more detailed and concrete picture of Arab and Jewish workers in the Haifa labor market.[122] Let us "tour" Haifa and meet the workers at their places of work. It is 1934–35. We approach Haifa from the North and visit the Haifa Bay area. The coastal area is being developed as an industrial zone on land leased by the Jewish National Fund (JNF). The international oil companies are located here. Many new factories like the Phoenicia glass factory are just now going into production. It opened in 1934 and employs both unskilled and skilled Jewish workers. The unskilled earn a beginning wage of 300 mils and the skilled 400 mils.[123] Just beyond the land owned by the JNF is the Ata textile factory, which opened in 1935. Its Jewish male workers, primarily skilled workers from Czechoslovakia, earn approximately 350 mils while the young female Jewish workers, who learn the skills on the job, earn a beginning wage of 200 mils.[124] Close by, the Iraq Petroleum Company (IPC) is in the final stages of construction.[125] About 110 Arab workers are employed at the site at the minimum wage of 120 mils per day and a small number of highly skilled workers receive 500 mils.[126] No Jewish workers are employed here.

Approaching Haifa from the east, we pass the Nesher cement factory where approximately 500 Jewish workers are employed. The prosperity has benefited the workers who have just received significant wage increases. The minimum wage of the unskilled worker is 448 mils, while the wage of the skilled workers varies from 480 mils to 740 depending on level of skill and seniority.[127] The Nesher quarry is close by. About 300 Muslim Arab workers, mainly from villages in the Jenin area, are excavating the raw materials. They work under an Arab contractor and earn from 100 to 125 mils per day.[128] More stone and lime quarries are located at the eastern approach to Haifa. Among them are Arab-owned quarries that employ mainly Hourani workers at the rate of 100 mils a day. They work twelve hours a day for six or seven days a week. The quarries of Even Va-Sid, owned jointly by the Histadrut contracting company Solel Boneh and the Arab entrepreneur Hajj Taher Qaraman, are located nearby. Both Jews and Arabs are employed in different sections of these quarries. The Arab workers earn a higher wage than other Arab quarry workers—150 mils per day,[129] with a maximum of 200–220 mils.[130] The Jewish workers receive the wage agreed upon by their trade union—320 mils to begin with, and 385 mils after six years of work. Skilled excavation workers earn 420 mils per day.[131]

Moving into downtown Haifa, we come to an area of residential housing, small workshops, and a few factories. Among them we see the large tobacco and cigarette factory, Mabruk, owned by Qaraman, Dick, and Salti, which employs between 600 to 800 workers. The men earn between 70–200 mils, the women between 70–130, and the children between 40–100 mils.[132] Moving on in the same direction, we come to the Haifa port where few Jews work. Hundreds of Arab workers, Houranis and Palestinian villagers, work as porters. The Houranis earn 80–120 mils a day and the Palestinian villagers 150 mils. They tell that they work an unlimited number of days a week and hours a day.[133]

During these years of prosperity there is much construction. Going through Wadi Nisnas, a Christian residential area, we come across workers employed by the large Arab contractors Jeda and Shublak. There are Hourani workers digging foundations for 100 mils a day.[134] Unskilled to semi-skilled workers, mainly migrant villagers, do most of the actual construction work for approximately 200 mils, and the skilled workers, usually urban Christians, earn 250–350 mils for their day's work. At adjacent sites and in the Jewish neighborhoods, Jewish workers are doing most of the construction work. Their wages range from 330–380 mils a day for the "regular" construction worker, to 450 for the medium range "experienced" worker, and to as much as 750 mils for the skilled worker.[135]

We continue with the tour and meet municipality cleaning workers working under the supervision of foremen. They are villagers who earn 120 mils a day while the foremen earn 200–400 mils.[136] We enter small Arab workshops, such as a metal workshop (150–200 mils a day for unskilled, 250–300 for skilled work),[137] or a carpentry shop (200–250 mils).[138] It is harder for us to find small Jewish workshops but those we do come across, likely as not, employ Arab workers or the owner himself does his own work. Skilled Jewish workers, hard to come by in times of prosperity, are well paid and command between 500 to 750 mils.

And so we end our tour. The wage picture is clear. The majority of Arab workers earn between 100 and 200 mils; the majority of Jewish workers, between 300 to 350 mils. While skills and experience raise the daily wage of Jewish labor, in many cases, to 500 mils and over, they only increase the wage of most skilled Arab workers to around 350 mils per day.

The significantly higher wages paid to Jewish labor did not necessarily indicate that they lived at a high standard of living. Unemployment was frequent and thus the actual money earned per month could fall well below the basic costs of a Jewish family. Even in the short periods of prosperity the high cost of living, especially the high cost of food and accommodation, meant that many families had to live very carefully. According to a survey conducted by the HLC among Jewish working families, the cost of living for a family of four, in the mid-1930s, was 11.700 £P—5.500 £P for food, 2.800 £P for accommodation, 1.650 £P for clothing and culture, 1.000 £P for taxes, and 0.750 £P for education. Even during full employment, a worker earning the basic 300–400 mils per day would be earning between 6.900 to 9.200 £P per month.[139] This was barely enough to cover the costs of board and keep according to the survey.[140] Thus the publication of the HLC concludes:

> In most cases the worker's family reduces its food, cuts down on its clothing and does without culture and recreation. If we add to this the fact that thousands of workers have to help other members of their families, some by sending money abroad, and others by bringing their families here and supporting them, the picture becomes clear.[141]

We do not have equivalent cost of living information for the Arab workers. Comparisons of this kind are extremely complicated. No doubt the expenses of the Arab worker were much lower, but from the outset his earnings limited his standard of living. Accommodation did not cost the Arab workers 2.800 £P, but for precisely that reason they often lived in tin shacks or even in caves. Food was cheaper for the Arab workers. Some were able to get food from their villages but certainly not all. Food was cheaper in the Arab market, but then Jews bought some of their supplies there as well. When the issue of the comparative standards of living arose, mainly in the 1940s, Jewish spokesmen tended to emphasize that the Arab worker had the advantage of being able to return to his village in case of need. Arab spokesmen, in turn, pointed out that Jewish families were small, and wives were often employed, while they were the sole providers for their large families.

My intention is not to make a direct comparison. How can one compare levels of expectation about standards of living? Do such expectations determine costs, or do they themselves result from of the means at one's disposal? In terms of the dynamics of a split labor market, the issue does not matter. Jewish workers earned significantly more per work day, and were therefore under the constant threat of substitution by cheaper Arab labor. In their daily experience, however, both Jewish and Arab workers were familiar with hardship and deprivation.

TO CONCLUDE

In many respects the major trends within the Haifa labor scene were similar to those observable in Palestine as a whole—the predominance of separatism in the orientation of the Jewish community, the formation of a split labor market, and the intricate interplay between economic and national-political factors. At the same time, Haifa was unique in that its population included both Jews and Arabs, who shared issues and interests to a greater extent than was the case in most other places. Despite the trend toward separation, there still remained a number of points of contact that could, at least potentially, create the conditions for greater interaction and closer cooperation between Jews and Arabs. The following chapters will examine this potential, by focusing on the relations that developed within the labor market of Haifa, in four different industries: construction, manufacturing, the port, and the railways. In the construction and manufacturing industries, workers were employed by either Jewish or Arab employers and entrepreneurs. The railway and port workers were employed by the Palestine government.

Part II

In the Labor Market

Figure 5. Haifa port and adjoining storage and business area circa 1935.

Chapter 3

Construction—Competing at the Work Site

Construction demonstrates better than any other urban industry the dual process of interpenetration and separation between the Jewish and Arab sectors. The abundant availability of cheap and experienced Arab labor, in a labor-intensive industry, threatened the position of Jewish workers. This threat led the Jewish labor movement to invest much effort in erecting barriers and blocking the access of Arab workers.

Building and Aliya, Building and creation, Building and cultivation. . . . In the Jewish, Zionist imagery of the period the act of building and the act of national redemption went hand in hand. Construction was central to the Zionist colonization project. To colonize the land meant to settle it, to acquire land and till it, to acquire land and establish new settlements on it. Taking hold of the land meant transforming it, cultivating it, and building on it. *"Nekhasekh Salmat Beton va-Melet"*—"We shall cover thee with a gown of concrete and cement," sang the pioneers to the motherland. The construction workers, the builders, were the elite of the urban workers, the urban pioneers. Construction was not merely a process of putting brick upon brick and erecting a building, it was part of a process of creation—'*Binyan ve-Yetsira,*' part of the process of colonization—'*Binyan ve-Aliya.*'

Construction became a central element in the economy of the Jewish settlement, not only in its imagery and pathos. It was closely linked to the large-scale Jewish immigration in multiple ways. Immigrants created the demand for increased building and supplied both the necessary labor power and the capital. Thus the sharp fluctuations in immigration and in capital import brought about extreme fluctuations in the construction industry, the ramifications of which contributed to the overall fluctuations of the Palestine economy. Economists were well aware of the unique role of construction in Palestine. In 1938, Horowitz and Hinden wrote:

> In Palestine, building has acted as the medium through which new purchasing power is pumped into the economic life. But this effect . . . has been accomplished not by organized planning, but by an extraneous factor, the influx of capital and immigration. The new immigrants exert a continuous demand for housing, which is supplied by the capital influx. The import of capital by a small number of capitalists—who have never exceeded 12% of the total annual immigration—could not itself stimulate economic life. It had to be diffused among all strata of the population, and in this work of distribution, the building trades have played a leading role. An exceptionally high proportion of investment in building is paid away in wages, and these wages create a market for agricultural and industrial products. In this way, the demand for consumers' goods in Palestine has been in advance of supply, and the new capital invested in building has had an immediate impact on all branches of the country's economic life. The building trades are a temporary station through which immigration passes before it is absorbed in the more permanent branches of current production.[1]

Not surprisingly, construction became the urban industry in which the competition between Jewish and Arab labor was most blatant and direct, and in which the threat of substitution of Jewish labor by much cheaper Arab labor was most salient. During periods of prosperity, in which there was a large inflow of Jewish immigrants and private capital, construction expanded. New contractors appeared. They increased the competition and hence the need to cut expenses. The unlimited supply of Arab workers and their low wages seriously threatened the Jewish workers. This threat led to intense organizational efforts, aimed at closing the Jewish construction market to much cheaper Arab workers. The competition between Arab and Jewish workers, the organizational steps taken in support of the Jewish workers, the resulting confrontation and its ramifications in both communities, will be the major theme of this chapter.

Construction was the industry in which there was the most interchange between the Arab and Jewish sectors. Capital was transferred from the Jewish to the Arab sector through the purchase of land for construction, through rent paid by Jewish immigrants to Arab homeowners and through the wages paid to Arab workers by both Arab and Jewish contractors who were building for the Jewish market. As noted in the previous chapter, construction was among the small number of industries in which Jewish and Arab contractors and engineers cooperated at the entrepreneurial level. Indeed the Jewish construction industry had a strong impact on the Arab economy and society.

CONSTRUCTION — FLUCTUATION AND SCOPE

Let us review the construction industry in some detail, as it evolved in Palestine in general and in Haifa in particular, during the 1920s and the 1930s. We shall follow the fortunes of the Jewish and Arab sectors and note the indications of interdependence between them. In the late 1930s, private building activity dropped dramatically, and remained at a very low level throughout the Second World War. Our discussion focuses on the period prior to this when private construction was a central component of Palestine's economy and ends with the outbreak of the Second World War.

Construction accounted for an unusually high proportion of economic activity in the Jewish sector in Palestine. It was proportionately higher than that in the Arab sector and indeed in the economies of most other countries.[2] According to Metzer and Kaplan, the value of the output of construction in the Jewish sector, in relation to the combined value of agriculture, industry, and construction, varied from 6.7 percent at its lowest level, to 16–20 percent during much of the period, and reached 32–34 percent during peak years. In the Arab sector, the proportion of construction was 3 percent at its lowest, 4–5 percent during much of the period, and 10–12 percent at its highest.[3]

There were extreme fluctuations of construction, as measured by the value of the output. Short periods of intensive construction activity, measured by sharp leaps of output, alternate with longer periods of low levels of activity. These fluctuations occur in both the total output of construction in Palestine and in the Jewish sector. Since the Jewish sector accounted for between 60–80 percent of the industry, during most of the period, congruence in the pattern of fluctuation is to be expected. The boom of the 1930s was far more dynamic than that of the 1920s. During the 1920s, the fiscal value of construction increased four-fold in two years. This was largely due to the Jewish immigration from Poland, known as the Fourth Aliya, which brought with it substantial private capital. In the 1930s, the leap was even more impressive. Construction increased twentyfold. This reflected the impact of German-Jewish immigration (the Fifth Aliya) between 1932 and 1935. This was the largest wave of immigration and it brought with it an extremely large amount of private capital.[4] Toward the end of 1935, construction dropped sharply because of the Italian invasion of Ethiopia and the economic crisis that followed, the drop in Jewish immigration, and the outbreak of the Arab Rebellion in 1936.

Construction in the Arab sector fluctuated as well, though far more moderately. During the period 1926–27, when declining Jewish immigration brought about a sharp drop in Jewish building activity, the Arab sector continued to flourish. This may have been due to the earthquake of 1927, which severely damaged Arab towns in the inland hill area of Samaria, and as a consequence created an urgent demand for construction work. On the other hand, Arab building activity did follow the Jewish pattern in the 1930s, though at a much slower rate.

Building activity in Haifa reflected the pattern of Jewish immigration to the town. In the 1920s, the immigrants of the Fourth Aliya congregated mainly in Tel Aviv and the rate of building activity in Haifa fell below that of Palestine as a whole. In the 1930s, many of the Fifth Aliya immigrants settled in Haifa heralding a period of prosperity and intense building activity. During the decade of the 1930s, the increase in construction in Haifa far surpassed that of Palestine. The available comparison between Jewish and Arab building activity in Haifa is limited but illuminating. During the 1920s, there was more construction by Arab entrepreneurs than by Jewish. This changed in the 1930s, when Jewish building activity exceeded Arab activity in both commercial and residential construction. Nevertheless, although it had lost the lead in the industry, Arab construction followed the Jewish trend of a rapid increase in building during the early and mid 1930s, and a sharp drop during the second half of the decade.

An additional point of comparison between the Arab and Jewish construction industry is the nature of the employers. In the Arab sector private contractors—big and small—were the sole employers. The financial resources for buying urban land and funding construction came primarily from three sources: savings from the late Ottoman period and the years of the First World War, income from the sale of land, the price of which was increasing sharply, and rental income. In some cases, profits from other economic enterprises were invested in urban construction.[5] In the Jewish sector there were both public and private contractors. Because of the importance of building as a source of employment and the paucity of private investment during periods of depression, the Histadrut itself became, early on, a contractor and provided its members with work. It initiated building projects, largely with national funding, and took on contracts for government works. Solel Boneh, the Histadrut contracting company, became the major factor in the Jewish construction industry, particularly in Haifa.[6] It was augmented by large and small private contractors, who were prominent during the periods of prosperity. The funding for construction in the Jewish sector came mainly from imported private capital and from the Zionist national funds. The shift within the Jewish sector from private construction during periods of prosperity to public construction during the years of depression was significant for the competition between Jewish and Arab labor. Private Jewish contractors gave priority to economic considerations and therefore preferred cheaper Arab workers. Public contractors, on the other hand, assigned a higher priority to social and political considerations and thus gave unconditional preference to Jewish workers. As a result, competition between Arab and Jewish workers increased in times of prosperity, and declined in times of depression, a point to which we shall return in detail later on in this chapter.

And what of the workers who actually carried out the building activity? They were plagued by extreme shifts in the level of employment because of the sharp fluctuations that characterized the construction industry. Their number rose and fell as did their proportion of the labor force. In Haifa, in the 1920s, there were a few hundred Jewish construction workers. They accounted for 10–14 percent of the local Jewish labor force. By the mid 1930s, the number of Jewish construction workers had increased tenfold to three and four thousand and, at the height of the boom, to as many as five thousand. Their relative share of the Jewish labor force increased from 14 to 28 percent.[7] A publication of the Haifa Labor Council (HLC) recorded the rapid growth:

> The year 1933 brought immigrants to our shores, refugees from the German hell. The capital that entered the country and the urgent need to provide dwellings for the immigrants, sharply increased the building activity in the town. . . . Many workers moved permanently from the countryside to town while others took advantage of the new work opportunities in town in order to improve the economic condition of their settlement. Hundreds of villagers, the young and the veteran turned to construction and joined the Union of Building Workers. Within a short time there was a shortage of construction, especially skilled workers. More than 5,000 workers were employed.[8]

By 1936, with the end of the Fifth Aliya and the outbreak of the Arab Rebellion, employment levels had fallen drastically:

> The scope of work was cut dramatically. Construction was down by 90 percent in comparison to the previous years. Contractors disappeared from the market. Thousands of workers dropped out of their places of work. The number of construction workers which had

Figure 6. Jewish construction workers, new immigrants from Germany, 1934.

reached more than 4,000 dropped to 400–500 and they worked only part-time. In the years of prosperity the Union of Building Workers had 4,000 members and as many as 5,000 were employed in construction work. Now approximately 2,500 members are registered and only 800–900 are actually employed. Recently, at the beginning of 1939 the number was down to 500.[9]

DILEMMAS OF ORGANIZATION

Organizing labor within the construction industry was extremely difficult. It was a highly competitive industry. Workers could enter construction either as experienced workers or they could learn the basic skills at the work site. Both Arab and Jewish newcomers to Haifa were therefore drawn to construction work. They then competed with those already on the job. It was also quite easy to become a contractor, a course sometimes taken by workers—individually or as a collective. They then employed other workers and thus introduced further competition into the market. The fluctuations in building activity were a major factor in the competitiveness of the industry. Prosperity brought more and more workers to construction, who were then forced to compete against each other when the depression set in. Since construction was a labor-intensive industry, this competition inevitably lowered wages.

In 1930, the HLC reached a collective agreement with most of the building groups that acknowledged the authority of the Histadrut in allocating workers and in determining their conditions of work. In 1931, the annual report of the HLC noted the improvements in labor conditions that the Histadrut had won, the most important of which was the setting of an agreed minimum wage and an eight–hour workday.[10]

The HLC attempted to consolidate its members, who were all Jewish workers, in trade unions. Its goal was to create a strong, cohesive, and comprehensive organizational structure, which could be mobilized to ensure the control of the HLC over Jewish construction. It encountered serious difficulties that stemmed both from the threat of the reservoir of cheap Arab labor and from the objection of the contractors to the intervention of the Histadrut. Among these contractors were both individual, private entrepreneurs and collective groups of workers who formed a building collective, hired other workers, and took on construction tenders. Through intensive and persistent activity, the Council succeeded in setting up a diverse, yet highly centralized, organization. It was made up of trade unions in the different occupations related to construction, the Union of Building Workers, the Union of Wood Workers, the Union of Metal Workers, the Union of Paint Workers, and the Union of Cart Drivers.[11] The unions were then subdivided into "sections" according to specific skills. After 1932–33, when the labor force grew dramatically, this organizational structure no longer seemed adequate to maintain Council control over the individual workers. It was therefore reinforced first by an elected workers' committee for every contractor or employer and, soon after, by a shop steward who was responsible for all work matters at each and every work site. These various organizational levels—from work site, to employer, to "section" to Union—were all coordinated so as to remain under the direct supervision of the trade union and of the HLC leadership. The task of coordinating all of these levels, beginning with the activists at the work site, was no easy matter, as Aba Houshi, the authoritarian Secretary of the Council, testified in his report of 1934:

> The problem we faced was how to bring all these loyal workers together and how to link them to the "section" committees and the union committees. In short, how to make out of this army of loyal

workers a consolidated responsible block with a burning will for action and with a joint commitment. We attempted to solve this problem
by organizing periodic meetings of the loyal workers in each trade
with the committee of their union. Furthermore, we organized periodic meetings with the representatives of the unions, the sections,
committees at worksites in which we tried to clarify all the questions
which troubled the workers in all work sites, in all trades and in the
Histadrut as a whole. This appears to be the only way by which the
Histadrut can gain control over all the places of work, and over all
the workers and create a closely knit organization binding together
the mass of members and the Histadrut.[12]

By 1934, the HLC had set up the Union of Building Workers to which
about 90–95 percent of all Jewish construction workers in Haifa belonged.[13] According to Biletzki, this was a higher membership rate than
in other areas where only 80 percent of construction workers joined the
union.[14]

In contrast to the complex organization of the Jewish construction
workers, there was little organization among Arab construction workers. The organization of urban Arab workers had just begun. During
the prosperity of 1932–35, the Palestine Arab Workers' Society (PAWS)
began to organize workers, concentrating on the manufacturing industry rather than on construction. The explanation for this may well be
that factory work created a more cohesive link among the workers
themselves, and between them and their employers, than did the short-
term and shifting relations of construction workers who moved from
one building site to another, and from one contractor to another. Factory workers, employed in international and Arab-owned firms, went
out on strike several times between 1932 and 1935.[15] The one strike of
construction workers, which took place in Haifa in 1932, can be seen as
the exception that confirms the rule.

One hundred and fifty Arab workers, skilled and unskilled, were
employed by the big contractor Aziz Khayat in the construction of a
large office building for the Iraq Petroleum Company and for the Customs Department. Work went on daily from 6.00 A.M. to 6.30 P.M. On
the 12th of July, 1932, the stone cutters, all forty of them, having consulted with the PAWS, left work at 4.00 P.M. and announced that from
that day on they would be working eight hours a day.[16]

Khayat informed them that he had no need of workers who would
not work twelve and a half hours a day, and replaced them with stone
cutters from Nazareth and Jerusalem. The striking workers found
other places of work and nothing was done to stop the strikebreakers.

Within a few days, other skilled workers, employed on the same site, put forward similar demands. The rough carpenters and the metal workers announced to Aziz Khayat that they too would not work more than eight hours a day. Aziz Khayat was able to scare them back to work. He then fired their spokesman, Gorgi, an Armenian worker who was one of the two chief rough carpenters. The second chief carpenter was a Jewish worker and a member of the Histadrut. He suggested to his mate that he ask the HLC for its help. Aba Houshi, the Secretary of the HLC, realizing that most of the workers were affiliated with the PAWS, proposed joint action in order to help enforce an eight-hour day for all construction workers in Haifa. His letters to the PAWS were never answered. The PAWS suspected that the HLC wanted to take advantage of the strike in order to replace the striking Arab workers with Jewish workers. It was not ready to embark on any joint struggle with the Zionist-affiliated Histadrut, but at the same time it showed little initiative of its own. The skilled Arab construction workers then asked the British District Commissioner to intervene and institute an eight-hour workday. The Commissioner met with the big contractors of Haifa, among them Aziz Khayat, and concluded that Palestine was not yet ready for such regulation. However, the contractors acceded to his request that they shorten the workday from twelve and a half to ten and a half hours. The workers, angry and confused, were split among themselves as to how to respond and the struggle petered out.

The case of Aziz Khayat and his workers demonstrates the difficulties that the Arab construction workers faced. The stonecutters, rough carpenters, and metal workers did confront their employer, did put forward their demands, did go out on strike, and they even approached both the PAWS and the HLC for help, but they were not a typical group of Arab workers. Unlike most construction workers, they were skilled workers and they were employed in a very large and long-term project. Even these advantages were not sufficient for them to win their demands because they had no labor organization able to lead their struggle. The PAWS expressed support, but did little. The HLC also supported the workers' demands. An eight-hour day as a general practice would have decreased the pressure on Jewish workers and would have alleviated the competition. But the PAWS would not embark on a joint campaign, and the HLC did not have the organizational capacity to lead the struggle on its own. The District Commissioner could hardly be expected to be the one to win an eight-hour day for the workers. The colonial perspective that he represented opposed any change in class relations.[17] The Arab construction workers thus had little prospect of effective labor action.

WAGES AND COMPETITION

The wage for construction work ranged from a low of 80–100 to a high of 600–700 mils per day. The skilled worker earned more than the unskilled and the Jewish worker earned more than the Arab worker. The gap between Jewish and Arab workers was the greatest among the unskilled, with the Jewish workers earning close to three times as much as the Arab workers. The gap was smaller among the skilled workers, ranging from almost identical wages to a 20–25 percent addition for Jewish workers. Systematic data is available for Jewish labor, and to a lesser extent for Arab labor, for the years 1930, 1933–35, and 1939. The data for these years can serve to demonstrate the disparity between the wage of Jewish and Arab workers, and its fluctuation in years of prosperity (1933–35) and of depression (1939). In 1930, after several years of deep depression, construction work began to expand.[18] Jewish unskilled workers were earning 300 mils per day and the skilled workers 300–400 mils per day. Arab skilled workers, most of whom were employed by the government and by international firms, were paid at similar rates.[19] There is no data for the unskilled Arab workers for that year.

Significant changes took place during the years of prosperity (1933–35). In 1933, the HLC was able to enforce an agreed wage scale for its members on almost all Jewish contractors for the first time. Wages ranged from 330 mils per day for unskilled and beginning construction workers to as high as 750 mils.[20] By 1935, only new immigrants were earning 330 mils per day. Experienced unskilled construction workers earned about 400 mils per day, while skilled workers earned between 450–750 mils per day, depending on their grade of skill.[21] Thus the unskilled Jewish workers had won a small wage increase (from 300 to 400 mils) since 1930, while the skilled workers had substantially improved their earnings (from 300–400 to 450–750 mils).

There is no equivalent data on the wages of the Arab workers. This discussion is based on questionnaires filled out by Arab workers in 1935.[22] The Hourani unskilled workers, who earned between 80 to 100 mils per day, were by far the cheapest laborers. They probably composed between 20 to 40 percent of all Arab construction workers. Those unskilled workers who were not specifically identified as Houranis earned about 150 mils per day. They were probably unskilled rural migrant workers. The skilled workers who hailed from the towns earned between 250–350 mils, and on occasion, 400.[23] Skilled and unskilled Arab workers reported in their questionnaires that they were working twelve hours a day.

Thus the wage disparity between the Arab and Jewish worker grew during the years of prosperity. The unskilled Jewish worker earned two to three times as much as the Arab worker. The skilled Jewish worker, who had previously earned the same as his Arab counterpart, now earned significantly more.

By 1939, after three years of depression, the picture had changed once again. Though no new contract was signed, the three years of depression and unemployment (1936–39) led to a significant drop in the wages of all workers. The unskilled Jewish workers received 315 mils per day, down from 380–400, while the skilled workers received 450–470 mils, down from 600–750.[24] According to Gertz, the unskilled Arab worker now earned 109 mils per day, while the Arab skilled worker maintained his wage level, earning between 250 and 400 mils per day. The gap between the wages of the Arab and Jewish skilled workers narrowed but did not disappear.[25] In his statistical handbook Gertz noted:

> Generally, the year 1939 experienced an economic depression and wages fell (a decrease of 30%) as compared with the boom of 1933–35. Wages in the building trade are, as a rule, influenced by the extent of construction, for the laborers are limited in number. As a result, there is a shortage of specialized workers in times of intense building activity and wages rise considerably.[26]

The substantial disparity between the wages of Jewish and Arab construction workers, all through the 1920s and 1930s, led many Jewish contractors to prefer Arab workers. Since construction was a labor-intensive competitive industry, the wage level was significant. Indeed construction was the urban industry in which the threat of substitution was felt most keenly by Jewish workers. This threat was acknowledged at the national level, in the early 1920s, by the secretary of the Histadrut, David Ben Gurion, who stated: "Cheap labor governs the market in construction, no less than in agriculture."[27] At the local level, there was constant concern about the prevalence of Arab workers in construction work in Jewish neighborhoods. Yet the issue of competition between Arab and Jewish labor was not continuously on the agenda. During periods of prosperity the issue was exacerbated, while it was absent during periods of depression.

This phenomenon can be explained both by the extent of building activity during prosperity and depression, and by the identity of the building contractors. As construction expanded, the work opportunities for cheap labor increased. As it contracted, these opportunities decreased. During periods of prosperity, the contractors were mainly private entrepreneurs whose priority was to cut expenses and increase profits. They were therefore likely to prefer cheap Arab labor. However, during periods of depression, the private contractors disappeared and construction was carried out, in large measure, by Jewish public institutions that gave priority to social and political considerations rather than to economic ones. They therefore preferred Jewish workers, their higher wages notwithstanding.

This relationship between prosperity and competition between Jewish and Arab workers can be chronologically demonstrated. In the early 1920s, especially in the years 1922–23 when new Jewish neighborhoods were being established, the employment of Arab workers became an issue. It continued to arouse strong feelings during 1924–25, when the large Fourth Aliya led to an increase in private, residential construction. However, with the onset of the depression at the end of 1925, construction work decreased and the issue of Arab employment all but disappeared. The beginning of the Fifth Aliya (1932) and the renewed prosperity to which it gave rise, led to a sharp increase in construction and simultaneously a sharp increase in references to the employment of Arab workers. Again, with the onset of the depression of 1936, the issue of Arab employment all but disappeared as construction work decreased. Thus Arab labor seems to have threatened organized Jewish labor precisely when construction expanded, when work was plentiful, and there was a shortage of Jewish workers. The threat, therefore, was not so much one of direct displacement but rather a threat to organized Jewish labor's control over Jewish-owned construction. It threatened organized Jewish labor's ability to ensure employment for potential new Jewish immigrants, and to maintain the relatively high wages and improved conditions of work that it had managed to win. It is therefore not surprising that at such times the HLC reinforced its organizational apparatus and mobilized it against the employment of Arab workers.

Let us now demonstrate this close relationship between prosperity and competition in greater detail.

In the first half of the 1920s, the HLC officials frequently complained about Jewish contractors who employed Arab workers. In December 1921, the newly established HLC complained to the Zionist Executive, whose representatives managed the construction company "Haboneh," that "Haboneh used Jewish contractors who employed Arabs in order to exploit them and to make quick profits."[28] The new neighborhoods built in 1922–23, Neve Sha'anan and Bat Galim, were frequently condemned for employing Arab labor.[29] During the last months of 1924 and throughout 1925, the employment of Arab workers was continuously on the agenda of the HLC. In November 1924, Yoseph Erdstein, one of the leading activists of the HLC, reported to the Council:

> Two weeks ago I was informed that there were Arabs working in Hadar Hacarmel. . . . In the meeting of the neighborhood council it became clear that that indeed was the case, and that the secretary of the Council was aware of the fact. . . . The Arabs had been brought in, for one week, as expert workers. As they had done an excellent job, they were kept on and continued their work.[30]

In 1925, the HLC alerted the Histadrut Executive to another form of substitution. Work was allocated to a foreign contractor, German, Italian, or other, who, as a matter of course, employed the cheapest available labor:

> We are calling your attention to the fact that some of the buildings now being built on Mount Carmel have been given to a German contractor who employs only Arab workers. There are grounds to fear that other buildings will be handed over to the same contractor. . . . The fact that foreign labor has been used from the beginning, on Mount Carmel, might serve as a precedent for the large Hebrew neighborhood to be built there, and the Hebrew worker will find himself totally excluded.[31]

By June 1925, the HLC officials were even more worried. The employment of Arab workers "was becoming a usual and accepted matter," complained Berl Repetor, in one of the many debates devoted to the subject. Milson, of the Labor Exchange, added that, while Arab labor in Haifa was nothing new, matters were more serious and more dangerous than they had ever been.[32]

Little had changed by December of that year. The Hadar Hacarmel neighborhood council had indeed begun to enforce the employment of Jewish workers, but other neighborhoods were still being built by Arab labor. The HLC kept discussing the matter:

> Arab labor was being used on Mount Carmel which was some distance away and thus difficult to control. . . . In Bat Galim, as well, three houses were being built by Arabs. . . . There was no difference in the wages for skilled work, since skilled Arab workers received the same payments [as skilled Jewish workers—D.B.]. The problem was with the unskilled work. It might be possible to organize the skilled [Arab—D.B.] workers, but we will never be able to organize the unskilled

workers because they don't live in Haifa. . . . They come from the Hauran and from other places, and do not work on a regular basis.[33]

This concerted effort on the part of the HLC to ensure jobs for Jewish workers met with little success. Neither their letters to the institutions of the Yishuv nor the public pressure that they applied in Haifa had much effect. And yet, after December 1925, the issue disappeared and the employment of Arab workers was no longer mentioned. The first signs of depression were evident, construction dropped, and the Histadrut's concern shifted to the problem of Jewish unemployment.

During the following seven years the issue of Arab labor was dormant. It was raised again at the end of 1932 when the Fifth Aliya began and with it the expansion of construction. The Labor Exchange of the HLC writes to the Hadar Hacarmel Neighborhood Council: "We have recently noted frequent cases of Arab labor in the neighborhood. . . . It is needless to explain the danger in this negative development."[34]

By 1934, the cause of Jewish labor in construction had become the cause celebre of the HLC. Aba Houshi, who had finally managed to organize the labor market of the building industry, was up in arms and the HLC adopted several measures to end the employment of what they referred to as "alien labor" or "cheap labor." They monitored building activity in Jewish neighborhoods closely and warned Jewish contractors and owners who employed Arab workers against doing so. The contractors were summoned by the HLC and threatened implicitly or explicitly with public pressure if they did not employ Jewish workers. The HLC sent the following letter to Mr. Brunstein, the pharmacist, who had hired a Sephardi contractor known to employ cheap (i.e., Arab) labor:

> We are sure that his honor will not want to exclude himself from the Jewish collective and will do all in his power to terminate the work of the cheap workers immediately and to compel the contractors to hire Jewish workers.
> We await his reply by 10.00 a.m. tomorrow and we will be grateful if he will meet with us by then.[35]

When such pressure did not help, the HLC recruited neighbors, colleagues, the neighborhood councils, even the rabbinate, as well as other members of the community to persuade the offender. The HLC thus attempted to mobilize all strata of the Jewish community, emphasizing that the struggle for Jewish labor was not the issue of the Jewish worker alone. After all, stated a leaflet distributed by the Council, the wages paid to the Jewish construction workers were then passed on to all classes of the Jewish community via the tradesmen and the craftsmen, "the restauranteur and the tailor, the shoemaker and the shopkeeper."[36]

There were confrontations at specific building sites. Of these, the best known was the confrontation at the Borowski building, in Hadar Hacarmel. Other building sites which were picketed included the houses of Judge Harkavi, Mr. Zukerman and Mr. Hefetz in Bat Galim, and the homes of the wealthy Sephardi families, Abutbul, Negri, and M. Levy.[37]

It is difficult to know how many Arab workers were employed in the construction of buildings financed by Jewish owners. Even Aba Houshi acknowledged that there was no shortage of work for Jewish workers at the time. On the contrary, the demand for workers far exceeded the supply. Thus Aba Houshi's battle was not only, and probably not even primarily, against the employment of Arab labor. He was struggling, at least as strongly, to maintain the HLC's recently consolidated monopoly of the market and its level of organization. That monopoly was threatened by the Arab workers who were already employed and by the large numbers available for employment in the future. Jewish workers who were not members of the Histadrut also threatened the Histadrut monopoly. Most of these workers belonged to the Revisionist Movement and its National Association of Workers, and to other small workers' organizations affiliated with political parties that opposed Mapai, the dominant workers' party. There were also nonorganized Jewish workers, many of whom were of Middle Eastern and North African origin. Workers who were not affiliated with the Histadrut and the HLC were not allocated work via its Labor Exchange. They therefore had to seek employment directly from the contractors, who exploited their situation to undercut the wage demanded by the HLC and to weaken its monopoly. The workers were thus caught between the HLC, who would not provide them with employment, and the contractor who cut their wages. For the militant Revisionist workers, who strongly opposed the employment of Arab workers by Jewish contractors, the situation was painfully ironic since they themselves were employed by those contractors who employed Arab workers. Aba Houshi was well aware that the HLC monopoly was challenged as much by the nonorganized Jewish workers as by Arab workers, and he attempted, at least rhetorically, to tie the two issues together. He repeatedly argued that only the employment of "organized Jewish labor" could remove the threat of the Arab workers invading the Jewish labor market.[38]

Figure 7. Aba Houshi, sectretary of Haifa Labor Council,
in downtown Haifa, 1946.

The HLC continued to struggle against the employment of Arab workers until the end of 1935 when the depression forced it to divert its energies to finding jobs for the unemployed Jewish worker. Once again, the depression heralded the disappearance of the issue of Arab workers displacing Jewish workers. Jewish unemployment had been caused not by the cheap Arab labor which the Histadrut feared but by the stagnation of the building industry.

* * *

The overall pattern manifested a complex interplay of economic, organizational, and political factors. During periods of prosperity and boom in the construction market, the issue of competition from cheap Arab labor was conspicuous; during periods of depression it disappeared. Thus when Jewish building expanded, with private entrepreneurs playing a major role, Arab workers were attracted to the Jewish sector, and their low wages made them an appealing substitute for Jewish labor. At such times Jewish labor made every effort to block the entrance of Arab labor to the Jewish construction market. The HLC did not attempt to organize Arab construction workers and to equalize their working conditions with those of Jewish workers, as the unlimited supply of unskilled Arab workers from rural Palestine, from the Hauran, and from neighboring countries precluded any likelihood of success.

During periods of depression when private Jewish construction came to a standstill, and the arena in which Jewish and Arab labor competed shrank, there was little demand for either Jewish or Arab labor. Then the issue of Arab labor displacing Jewish labor virtually disappeared. Construction carried out during those periods, especially in the second half of the 1930s, was largely initiated and built by Jewish public institutions for whom considerations of profitability were secondary to political and social considerations. They initiated the construction of large public buildings such as a new major commercial center in Hadar Hacarmel, schools and buildings for Histadrut enterprises, as well as infrastructure development.[39] These projects were initiated primarily to provide work for Jewish workers, and were funded by monies allocated to alleviate unemployment. The threat to Jewish labor was thus circumvented and the lower wages of the Arab workers had little impact. No concerted effort had to be made to prevent their employment.

This complex reality in which macro and micro reflected each other, in which economic, organizational and political factors were intimately intertwined, can be further illustrated by moving closer to the work site, the scaffolds, and the picket lines. And so we move to the Borowski Building where construction was in progress during 1934.

THE BOROWSKI BUILDING

In August 1934, Mr. Borowski, of Warsaw, decided to invest in the construction of a large apartment building in the new Jewish neighborhood of Hadar Hacarmel in Haifa. He intended to rent the apartments and stores to the Jewish inhabitants of the expanding neighborhood.

He engaged two Jewish engineers, Mssrs. Shecter and Rutenberg, to oversee the construction. They hired Mr. Sam'an Tarsha, an Arab contractor, who recruited Hourani laborers and set them to work digging ditches for the building's foundations. Within three days, the HLC had learned of the project. It was not a new phenomenon for Jews to use Arab workers in this way, since even Jews prominent in the community were exploiting cheap Arab labor to build their homes. However, the HLC was particularly outraged by Mr. Borowski. He was investing in the construction of a large building in a Jewish neighborhood, to profit from the high rents that would be paid by the Jewish tenants. The HLC felt that the least he could do was to give Jewish labor the benefit of employment. The HLC was determined to make an example of him. At 5:00 A.M. on the 27th of August, a picket line of Jewish workers, all members of the Histadrut, appeared at the site. The Hourani workers were still asleep in the ditches.[40] They woke up and continued their work while the Jewish workers remained seated in the ditches. An hour later, the contractor summoned the police. Quiet picketing was permitted, but the obstruction of work was not. Seventeen members of the picket line were detained. "They went through the streets of Hadar Hacarmel singing, and the passers-by greeted them with applause."[41]

The struggle had begun. The HLC mobilized its full organizational strength. The same day, immediately after the arrest of the first group, another picket line was sent to the site and a call went out to all members of the Histadrut to register for picketing. The following day (August 28) the HLC met with the representatives of the General Association of Engineers and Architects, the Organization of Builders, the Organization of Building Contractors and the Association of Craftsmen. The HLC expected them to pressure their members not to employ Arab workers and not to supervise the construction of buildings where the contractors employed Arab labor. The HLC also expected them to persuade those members who were already employing Arab labor to desist forthwith. The meeting ended with a declaration, addressed to the Community Council, emphasizing the support of all the participants for Jewish labor, and calling on the Council to convene a meeting to "find ways and means to protect the Hebrew economy in Haifa from being swamped by cheap labor."[42] That evening the HLC also met with representatives of the Union of Metal Workers and the Union of Electric Workers, to organize the recruiting of their members for picket lines.

During the next three days, work at the site of the Borowski Building continued under police protection. The picketing continued as well. Eighty British and Arab policemen armed with shields, steel helmets, and truncheons were sent to the site. There were daily clashes between the picketing workers and the police. The Jewish workers refused to vacate the site, even when explosives were used for excavation. Police removed them by force, only to have them return to be removed once again.[43] Scores of Histadrut members took part in the picketing: male and female workers from the HLC trade unions; youngsters from the Histadrut youth movements; members of kibbutzim temporarily stationed in town, and members of Hapoel Hamizrahi, the religious party allied with the Histadrut. Over seventy pickets were arrested in the four days of picketing, often after violent clashes with the police in which many of the workers were injured. They were quickly brought to trial. Ironically, they appeared before the Jewish judge, whose own house was being built by Arab workers in the Bat Galim neighborhood. His sentences were severe—three weeks imprisonment in the Acre prison for most offenders, and five weeks with hard labor for those who had physically clashed with the police.[44]

By the 30th of August, the HLC had called a wide network of meetings in order to involve as many sectors of the community as possible in its mass campaign. The Council of the Association of Engineers and Architects persuaded the engineers Shecter and Rutenberg to resign. They sent the following telegram to Warsaw: "Under pressure from the Association of Engineers and of public opinion, and after the arrest and injury of workers, we feel constrained to resign."[45] On August 30, representatives of the HLC met with the British District Commissioner to explain their objections to the employment of Arab workers in the Jewish sector. They also warned that the large number of Hourani workers in town competed unfairly with both Jewish and Arab local workers.[46] On the same day, the Jewish Community Council invited representatives of all Jewish neighborhoods along with representatives of various commercial organizations to a meeting that issued a statement fully supporting the principle of "Hebrew Labor" and the struggle of the HLC.

> The organized Jewish community in Haifa warns all those who employ foreign workers that by doing so they are causing severe damage to the life of the community and are endangering its normal economic development. These transgressions might cause dangerous political complications. We extend a serious warning particularly to the neighborhood institutions of Bat Galim and Kiryat Eliahu and call upon them to prevent the spread of Arab labor in their neighborhoods and to bring such employment to an immediate halt wherever it is happening. The residents of these neighborhoods are called upon to use all means at their disposal to prevent foreign labor.[47]

They thus took the issue way beyond Mr. Borowski and his building. The day ended with a youth rally that declared its support for the workers imprisoned in the Acre prison. The youth then went singing through the streets. Two days later, on the 1st of September, four thousand people participated in a rally at a Haifa theater. They listened to the speakers "with bated breath."[48]

After several days of clashes between the police and the picketers, Mr. Tarsha, the contractor, agreed to suspend work for a few days. Pickets were no longer needed at the Borowski site, but the workers had been mobilized and the HLC did not want to lose the momentum. They therefore sent the pickets to the Jewish neighborhoods of Haifa to monitor the extent to which Arab workers were employed in construction. They went from house to house in what was called "the wandering picket line."[49] Day after day *Davar*, the Histadrut daily, reported on their findings:

> One group in the Tel Amal neighborhood found ten Houranis at work in the home of Mizrahi, the wagon driver. At the request of the pickets, the mistress of the house dismissed the Houranis while some of the pickets remained on guard. At the home of Mr. Epstein, a member of the Tel Amal Neighborhood Council, they found two Houranis. After a brief exchange, the landlord sent them away. This also happened at the home of Kaplan on Yalag street and at Herzl #2, the home of Moshe Bechar.[50]

> The wandering picket line is continuing its circumnavigation in Hadar Hacarmel. At the home of Lulu, the owner of a commercial enterprise—six Houranis! The landlord agreed to dismiss them. Contractor Knopf had Arab plasterers working at his home. Five Houranis were working at the home of Benjamin, the shoemaker and his son. They were all dismissed at the demand of the pickets.[51]

The Arab press also reported these events. Although their facts were similar to those in the Jewish press, their emphasis and conclusions were different. While the Jewish reports focused on the employment of Jewish labor, the Arab reports focused on the dismissal of Arab labor. The Jewish press reported on the Histadrut's attitude to the Jewish home-owners, the Jewish engineers, the Arab contractor, the police, the judge, while the Arab press reported on the Histadrut's attitude to the Arab workers—"The Histadrut and the Arab Workers," read the headline of August 28th in *Filastin*. "They Oppose the Employment of Arab Workers,"[52] declared *Filastin* the following day, and continued with

"The Struggle of the Histadrut against the Arab Workers,"[53] and "The Persecution of the Arab Workers by the Jews."[54] They reported other cases in which the Jewish labor leadership had called for a boycott of Arab labor and continued:

> They (the HLC) also distributed leaflets calling on people not to buy drinks from shops which employed Arabs. Only after the owner dismisses the Arabs are they willing to have anything to do with him.[55]

They also reported:

> We have learnt that the Histadrut required all the craftsmen in Haifa to dismiss their Arab workers and employ Jews in their place.[56]

The Arab press soon drew its own conclusions: "They persecute the Arab workers and we go on buying from their shops."[57] "We must learn from the past, the Arabs should unite and learn a lesson from the event. We are not advising Arabs to keep away from (the Jews), but we are asking them to be wise and to know what is good and what is bad."[58] A week later, the PAWS distributed leaflets calling on those Arab workers who had joined the Histadrut-affiliated Palestine Labor League to resign immediately because the Histadrut was inciting against Arab workers.[59]

The HLC was aware of the repercussions within the Arab community. It portrayed the reports quoted above as incitement and as exploitation of the events by Arab national leaders to turn Arab workers against the Jews. Having mobilized all the elements of the Jewish community to promote Jewish labor and dismiss Arab workers, the HLC proceeded to present its case to the Arab workers in a leaflet dated 3–9–34 and written in Arabic. The HLC addressed the workers as "brothers" and continued:

> The Jewish workers in Palestine and those immigrating to it neither want nor intend to remove the Arab workers from their jobs with Arab residents. But they consider it their right to be the *only* workers to work for Jewish residents with no partners or competition.
>
> The Jewish workers are employed under good conditions and earn a wage which enables them and their families to live a simple life. If others—non-Jews—were to work at the work sites of the Jewish residents they would be working under poor conditions and earning a low wage. At the same time they would be taking work away from the Jewish worker and would be preventing him from working at those sites. Thus they would be eliminating the one source of employment

available to the Jewish worker after Arab residents and the government and international companies shut the door of employment in his face. Therefore for the past fifteen years, the Jewish worker has had to protect his right of employment with the Jewish residents and has had to do all he could to obtain good conditions of work and a higher wage. His struggle has benefited the Arab worker as well, for his wage and standard of living have also increased. The immigration of Jews to Palestine has also brought about an increase in jobs for Arab workers with Arab employers, thus further benefiting the Arab worker in Palestine. Furthermore, thousands of cheap workers from the Houran have begun to come to Palestine and they have brought about a reduction in the wages of both Jewish and Arab workers, and have compelled both to work under inferior conditions.

The Jewish worker considers it his right and his duty to protect his work and to ensure a better wage and good labor conditions for himself. Therefore, the picket lines of the Jewish workers are not turned against any man or group. Their aim is solely to protect the Jewish worker's just demand for work so that he can make a living.

Arab brothers, people are spreading rumors. Don't let them influence you. Stand on the side of justice![60]

Did the HLC really expect the Arab worker to appreciate the "justice" of the Jewish worker's desire to maintain the benefits he had won? Did the HLC genuinely expect them to understand the threat they posed to the Jewish worker and graciously bow out?

The arguments in this leaflet are typical of those used by Jewish labor to explain its position to Arab workers, according to which the Jewish workers intended no harm to the Arab workers. They did not wish to incite against them or to persecute them. The Jewish workers were merely protecting their elementary rights and interests, and they could not be expected to do any less. Hence, the HLC contended that there was no contradiction between their rejecting Arab workers as wage earners in the Jewish sector, on the one hand, and their attempt to organize them in the Palestine Labor League, on the other.

The "wandering picket line" continued its activities for the following two weeks and then the picketing slowly ceased. The battle cry was heard again when the first prisoners were released. They were welcomed as returning heroes,[61] but the campaign was not resumed. It was difficult for even the HLC to sustain so high a level of mobilization at a time of full employment.

Despite the massive mobilization by the HLC, and the many declarations of support, its campaign, with its clashes, "wandering picket lines," and vehement rhetoric, did not win the approval of all the members of the Jewish community. Reservations were expressed even from within the labor movement. *Mapai*, the leading labor party, debated the issue in its Central Committee, on the 6th of September, 1934, following the first week of physical and verbal clashes. David Hacohen of Haifa, a member of the Central Committee of *Mapai* and the Labor representative in Haifa's municipal council, had close ties to the Arab community. He reported having been asked by an Arab friend: "How can you be so petty as to grudge a Hourani a day's work. He hardly earns a 'grush' [piaster—D.B.]. He is starving. How can you remove him when you are short of workers yourselves?"[62] Hacohen continued, "As far as I am concerned I have to admit that there is little I have to say to such an argument. My conscience as a human being tells me that this is wrong."[63] Yoseph Shprintzak, another member of the Central Committee,[64] told of the reaction of Jewish Yemenite workers, who also opposed the militancy of the HLC. They felt that there was work enough for all, so why not let the Arabs make some money as well?[65] Moshe Shertok, the chairman of the Political Department of the Jewish Agency, feared that the picketing would get out of hand and lead to violence between Jews and Arabs. He called for a change of tone, for fewer picket lines and less publicity.[66] It should be noted that none of these remarks and reservations was reported in *Davar*, which gave ample coverage and full support to the HLC's "valiant" campaign.

To the left and the right of *Mapai*, opposition to the HLC campaign was stronger and more incisive. On the left were *Poalei Tzion Smoll* (the left wing *Poaeli Tzion*) who supported joint Arab and Jewish class struggle and mixed unions. They, therefore, strongly opposed the picketing against Arab labor at the Borowski site, and the massive mobilization of public opinion that had accompanied it. At the height of the campaign they distributed a leaflet, addressed to the Jewish workers of Haifa, calling on them not to be "dragged into the anti-Arab net of *Mapai*." This was reported in *Davar*[67] with little comment. On the right was the Revisionist movement, which opposed the HLC campaign on other grounds. They objected to the employment of Arab labor but they also strongly opposed the powerful position of the Histadrut and *Mapai*, its leading party. They saw the picketing against the employment of Arab workers primarily as a means of reinforcing the Histadrut monopoly and not as a defense of the rights of Jewish workers. *Hayarden*, the daily newspaper of the Revisionist movement, repeatedly claimed that the Histadrut turned a blind eye to the employment of Arab workers by its own members and affiliated institutions, and confronted only those employers with whom it had political scores to settle.[68] After the first week of the campaign, *Hayarden* came out with headlines such as "The Red Guards," "A Struggle for Hebrew Labor or the Desire for Dictatorship in the Labor Market,"[69] and "The Picketline Theater Continues."[70] It argued that

> We hold that it clearly is not the issue of Arab labor which brings the leftists to the picket lines but issues of a completely different kind. The people of *Mapai* need to "keep things moving" so that their "comrades" will not be open to other matters. The people of *Mapai* must be kept busy with some "militant" class issue (for even Hebrew Labor is a class issue for them) so that they will not weigh the issues of the world . . . lest they fall, Heaven forbid, under the influence of the "courageous" "warriors" of *Hashomer Hatzair* or worse yet of *Poalei Tzion Smoll.* And to this end the people of *Mapai* invent all kinds of perils which require "pickets" and "actions." After the picket line in K'far Saba [against the employment of Arab workers in the citrus harvest—D.B.] they move the "Purim Shpiel" to another venue and begin their performance there. And after Haifa comes the turn of Tel Aviv. The failure of the pickets in K'far Saba can be expected in Haifa too. Because as long as we can say to the workers in the picket lines of Haifa or elsewhere, "Hypocrites! First, look to yourselves! Put your own houses in order regarding the issue of Hebrew labor and put the houses of your associates in Magdiel, Haifa and Tel Aviv in order (in transportation and other building work), only then can you come to us with your demands"—till then picket lines will be of no avail.[71]

Davar responded to the Revisionist critique with far more vehemence than it had expressed toward the major target of the campaign, the Jewish home-owners and the Jewish employers who hired Arab labor.[72] The Revisionists formed the main opposition to *Mapai* and to the *Mapai*-controlled Labor movement. *Mapai* and the HLC perceived them to be the main enemy of the Jewish worker and portrayed them as such. The two movements frequently exchanged vicious insults that sometimes led to violent clashes.[73] In Haifa, where Aba Houshi strove for a total monopoly and concentration of power, the Revisionists were so viciously attacked that even the labor and *Mapai* leadership voiced objections.[74] The political clash between the Histadrut and the Revisionists had direct implications for the Haifa labor market. As the workers who identified with the Revisionist movement were excluded from the Histadrut and its Labor Exchange, they were forced to accept work under conditions imposed on them by contractors who bypassed the HLC, undercut its wage demands, and employed Arabs. There was thus much bitterness between the Histadrut and these workers. These complex and tense relations between the Histadrut and the Revisionists were expressed in the ridicule of *Hayarden* and in the vehement rhetoric of *Davar*.

The Borowski Building was eventually completed by a Jewish contractor who employed Jewish workers.

In presenting the struggle for Jewish labor in the Borowski Building, the Histadrut publications and manifestos stressed the active role of the Jewish worker and the passive role of the Arab worker. They presented the Arab workers as non-actors. They "were found" on the premises, they "were removed" from the building site, or they "were dismissed" by the master or mistress of the house, while the Jewish workers "formed" picket lines, "moved" from place to place," checked," "demanded," and "insisted." They presented the Arab workers as having no presence of their own, and no interests to defend. The Histadrut publications did not mention or record any of the actions or responses of Arab labor and its spokesmen. This presentation highlights the extent to which the Jewish community was absorbed in its own self-perception, insulated from the Arabs surrounding them. It highlights the facility with which the Jewish leadership did not see and did not hear what was experienced within the Arab community. This was the case for the majority of labor activists and for *Davar*, the daily paper. The reservations of people like David Hacohen, Yoseph Shprintzak, and Moshe Shertok remained in closed forums.

The case of the Borowski Building demonstrates the relationship between the organization of Jewish labor and the extent to which it felt threatened by the possibility of substitution by Arab workers. It demonstrates the power that the HLC was able to consolidate through its complex and centralized organization, and through its diverse links with the Jewish community, and its effective use of these links to counter the threat of cheap labor. At the same time, this very threat served to mobilize and reinforce the HLC, and promote its position within the Jewish community.

TO CONCLUDE

Construction, better than any other urban industry, demonstrates the dual process of interpenetration and separation between the Jewish and Arab sectors, the fluidity and disjunction between them. It is precisely the many possible and feasible exchanges between the Jewish and Arab sectors that drove Jewish labor to invest so much effort in erecting barriers. Thus the story of construction is that of creating separations in a context vulnerable to (or hospitable to, depending on one's perspective) movement through tentative boundaries. It is the story of the limitations of these boundaries, but also of their relative success. Even more, it is the story of the high level of control won by organized Jewish labor over the Jewish labor market, and its successful mobilization of other strata of the Jewish community to its cause. The threat of cheap Arab labor was a stimulus for organization, and a rallying cry for further internal consolidation. It was a process in which Jewish labor played an assertive, at times, aggressive role, and in which Arab labor was largely passive though not indifferent.

The Jewish and Arab construction workers did share common interests, but these were not strong enough to withstand national priorities and to form a basis for cooperation. Both groups of workers were employed in hard physical labor by contractors intent on ensuring their profits. Both could have benefited from joint action to secure decent conditions of work. However, the unlimited supply of Arab workers and the threat of substitution that haunted the Jewish worker foreclosed any chance of joint action.

Chapter 4

Manufacturing Industry—Almost Separate

As we move from construction to manufacturing, from the building site to the factory, the reciprocal impact that Jewish and Arab labor had on each other takes on a very different form. In contrast to the direct competition between Jewish and Arab construction workers and their fear of possible substitution, Jewish manufacturing workers were hardly affected by the availability of much cheaper Arab labor. In construction, Jewish and Arab contractors and their Jewish and Arab laborers undertook the same tasks and therefore competed directly with each other. In manufacturing, the Jewish-owned industry and industrial work was very different from Arab industry. The experience, know-how, financial resources, and organizational infrastructure of the Jewish sector enabled it to develop a varied, skilled, and mechanized industry. The past experience of the Arab sector, on the other hand, was more restricting, as far as the development of manufacturing was concerned. The Arab urban notables and entrepreneurs invested their capital mainly in commerce, construction, and urban property. They also invested in labor-intensive, agriculturally based industry, but here their investment was more limited. Both Jewish and Arab manufacturing workers came up against specific difficulties, but these did not stem, primarily, from the challenge each posed to the other.

The Jewish manufacturing industry faced competition from cheap imported goods, and Jewish workers were dependent on their employer's ability to remain in business. Here, the main rallying cry of organized labor was "Buy *Totzeret Ha'aretz*" "Buy Products of the Land"—products of Jewish industry, and not the call for "*Avoda Ivrit*"—employment of "Hebrew Labor." Arab workers who were employed in

Arab-owned, labor-intensive industries also faced competition, but this was primarily competition from the large reserve of rural labor, ever ready to replace them. Arab labor was also affected by the low level of development of Arab-owned industry. This absence of industrial development and of medium or large factories, restricted the development of a modern working class. At the same time, the relatively advanced level of Jewish-owned industry impeded the growth of Arab industry. It thus limited, at least indirectly, the options available to Arab labor.

Manufacturing was the one economic sphere in which the Jewish aspiration for separation from the Arab economy and labor market was, in large measure, realized. This was due primarily to the fact that there were few Arab industrial products to compete with the Jewish products, and few Arab workers with the necessary skills to compete with the Jewish factory workers.

Precisely because Arab workers did not threaten Jewish industrial workers with substitution, despite their lower wages, and because Jewish workers did not threaten Arab workers, despite their higher level of organization, the potential for a noncompetitive, nonconflictual relationship existed. Arab workers, no longer in direct confrontation with Jewish workers, could turn to them for help in what they seemed able to do so well—improve their labor conditions. Jewish labor, in turn, had nothing to lose by extending such help. On the contrary, having received help, the Arab workers might be more sympathetic toward the Jewish workers, or so at least the HLC hoped. Nevertheless good relations with the Arab workers was not a high priority for them, and they allocated few resources to this end. The HLC and the PLL (Palestine Labor League) did extend help to groups of Arab industrial workers on several occasions, but this help was usually short term and sporadic and not the beginning of an ongoing relationship. Given the ambivalence of the Histadrut and the HLC toward cooperation with Arab workers, it is not surprising that their attempts to help met with little success. Both groups were, as a result, wary of further joint ventures. Furthermore, the Zionist goal of separation, and the Arab national opposition to Zionist settlement, made any form of joint action extremely difficult to pursue and pursue successfully.

This chapter examines the development of the Jewish and Arab manufacturing industry in Haifa: their different courses, major enterprises, the men who owned and managed them, as well as the workers who worked the plants. It notes points of contact between the Arab and Jewish sectors and devotes special attention to those cases in which Jewish labor extended help to Arab workers, or in which the two groups reached some level of cooperation.

TRENDS IN MANUFACTURING IN PALESTINE

Jewish Industry

During the First World War, Palestine was cut off from Europe and suffered gravely from a lack of basic commodities. However, during the Second World War, when it was again cut off from Europe, Palestine prospered. Its manufacturing industry had developed so significantly during the interim years that it was able to supply the needs of the much larger local population as well as those of the British army in Palestine and Egypt.[1] This growth was brought about, to a major extent, by Jewish entrepreneurship, capital, and labor. The economic and social dynamics of manufacturing differed markedly from that of construction for it did not have the ideological aura of construction and agriculture.[2] It was not explicitly included in the act of "the redemption of the people" or "the building of the land." And yet, in manufacturing the Jews reached a predominance and a level of separation from the Arab sector unequaled in any other economic sphere. The development of manufacturing was closely linked to Jewish colonization and immigration, to the inflow of capital and experienced manpower, but it was not as directly dependent on immigration as was construction. Manufacturing was able to sustain a steady growth, despite the cyclical nature of Jewish immigration. Indeed, at different times it did advance at different rates, but it did not experience the sharp and recurring fluctuations so typical of construction. Capital, especially large-scale capital, once invested in manufacturing could continue to sustain economic growth, even when the inflow of additional capital and manpower had temporarily ceased. Rather than contributing to unemployment, as was the case with construction during the years of depression, the manufacturing industry was able to absorb many of the unemployed and to increase the percentage of industrial workers in the Jewish labor force. Finally, manufacturing, with its dependence on relatively skilled labor and entrepreneurial expertise, was far less vulnerable to competition from Arab labor or from Arab industrial products. The major problem for Jewish industry was the import of cheap products from abroad that were often preferred by the Jewish consumer. Thus the major campaign of the Jewish industrialists and Jewish labor was to persuade the Jewish consumer to buy goods produced by Jewish-owned industry. Just as social pressure was brought to bear on contractors who employed Arab workers, so pressure was exerted on those who chose to buy foreign goods when similar goods were locally produced.

Many factors within the Jewish society and economy were conducive to the growth of manufacturing. These included the large inflow of private capital and the industrial experience of many of the immigrants. Among them were industrialists who were able to transfer their know-how and, on occasion, some of their more experienced workers. They were able to use their previous connections to improve their factories and enhance exports. Workers capable of easily acquiring industrial skills were available. There was also a small consumer market for their products. On the downside, almost all raw materials had to be imported, making production expensive while cheap foreign goods could be freely imported. To make matters worse, the government of Palestine was reluctant to pursue a policy of industrialization and protective taxation, since both were contrary to imperial policy. Nevertheless, the favorable factors outweighed the negative ones, and the manufacturing industry developed steadily. The surveys conducted by the Jewish Agency indicate this clearly.

The rapid growth is clearly evident. The number of establishments increased from a baseline of 100 in 1925, to 395 eighteen years later, while the number of workers, the capital invested, the output and the horsepower used, increased even more rapidly. Thus, on average, each establishment employed more workers, had more capital invested in it, increased its output, and was more intensive in its use of energy. This growth, consistent throughout the Mandatory period, was marked by two dramatic leaps. The first occurred during the prosperity of the 1930s, and the second and more dramatic one, during the Second World War.

Table 4.1. Rate of Development of Jewish Industry, 1925–1943
(Base year 1925 = 100)

Year	No. of establishments	Persons engaged	Capital invested	Gross output	Horsepower
1925	100	100	100	n.d.	100
1926	109	117	120	n.d.	120
1930	116	155	138	100	173
1933	180	270	336	222	870
1937	290	449	729	379	1283
1943	395	920	1353	1744	n.d.

Source: Compiled according to *Survey of Palestine,* prepared by the Anglo-American Committee of Inquiry (Jerusalem: Government Printer, 1945–46), pp. 500–502, based on the censuses taken by the Jewish Agency for Palestine.

Arab Industry

Arab industry faced a far more complicated and problematic set of circumstances.[3] Those factors that were conducive to Arab industrialization included the growing demand for industrial products, the high profit level, and the low wages of Arab labor. However, the factors working against industrialization were stronger. It was viewed with ambivalence, even hostility, by the Arab elites, many of whom felt that industrialization threatened their traditional, rural, Arab way of life and hence their interests. For them, industrialization was integral to British and Zionist colonization and therefore suspect.[4] This attitude contrasted starkly with that of the Zionist leadership that assumed industrialization to be central to the growth of a modern Jewish entity. A smaller group, who hailed mainly from the expanding coastal towns, did try to advance Arab industrial development as a means of increasing Arab autonomy. They belonged to the Arab elite and were landowners who had expanded into commerce, construction, and finance, to which they added industrial enterpreneurship. They, however, did not give first priority to the manufacturing industry and their capital investment was limited. The Arab sector, moreover, lacked the skills and the knowledge of modern methods of production.[5] In addition, the smallness of the consumer market, the limited government support, and the competition from the expanding Jewish industry made industrialization extremely difficult. The detrimental impact of Jewish industry on Arab industry will be discussed later.

And yet, Arab industry did develop. While traditional industries producing soap, olive oil, flour, cloth, and religious memorabilia were stagnant and at times even declined, new industries emerged. The most important of these were tobacco and cigarettes, cardboard boxes, and mechanized metal workshops and foundries. We can gain a picture of this development from the growth figures given by Abramovitz and Gelfat. Over a period of close to twenty years, from 1921 to 1939,

Table 4.2. Development of Arab Industry, 1921–1939

Year	Number of enterprises	Number of workers	Capital invested	Value of annual produce	% of workers in crafts and industry
1921	1,100	6,000	600,000	1,200,000	8–7
1927/28	2,400	10,000	1,100,000	2,140,000	9.4
1939	n.d.	18,000	2,500,000	4,000,000	10–10.5

Source: Abramovitz and Gelfat, *The Arab Economy,* p. 61.

the number of workers in manufacturing multiplied by 3.5, their relative share of Arab labor increased from 7 to 10 percent, and the capital invested increased fourfold.[6]

Mutual Impact

Although it is difficult to compare Arab and Jewish manufacturing, enough data are available to clearly demonstrate the Jewish predominance in the overall size of the manufacturing industry, the pace of growth, the size of enterprises, and their sophistication. Jewish industry also had many more large, capital-intensive and mechanized enterprises. This trend was evident as early as 1928 when the first government survey was conducted.[7] Smith concludes that by the end of the 1920s "the nucleus of a modern industrial sector had already formed, a sector dominated by the Jewish community, while in contrast, Arab participation in industrial activity remained restricted to a growing plethora of small workshops and a low level of capital investment."[8.]

From 1922 to 1939, the value of products produced by the Jewish sector constantly increased relative to Arab industrial production.[9] The accelerated growth of both Arab and Jewish industry during the war years further increased the gap between them because despite the marked growth of Arab industry, Jewish industry surpassed it.[10] The expanded local market brought about a rapid growth in the number of Arab establishments. They increased from 339 in 1939 to 1,558 (!) in 1942, raising their share from 28 to 45 percent of all industrial and craft enterprises.[11] However, in all other criteria indicative of the level of industrial development—gross output, capital invested, and horsepower used—Jewish enterprises predominated. Thus, by 1942, 55 percent of all enterprises were owned by Jews. The Jewish share in the industrial and handicraft labor force, in wages paid and in gross output, was far larger and varied from 82 to 94 percent.

The Jewish manufacturing industry clearly predominated. It is thus not surprising that in the case of the manufacturing industry it was the Arabs, rather than the Jews, who felt threatened. From the Jewish perspective, Arab industrial enterprises had little impact on Jewish industry, or on the fortunes of Jewish labor. There appeared to be little penetration of Arab labor and little competition from Arab products. From the Arab perspective the relationship between the sectors looked quite different. They saw Jewish industrial development as a major (at times, *the* major) factor impeding the growth of Arab industry that, apart from a few specific niches, could not compete with the Jewish advantages. Thus, while there were not the direct confrontations found in construction and agriculture, the Arab elite perceived any advance in Jewish industry to be at the expense of Arab development.

Both Jewish and Arab spokesmen directed their complaints to and at the government. The Jewish leadership and industrialists called for a more active protectionist economic policy. At the time this was common practice in many countries and even in some colonies. They claimed that more generous government protection for the young—but promising—Jewish industry, was essential for its development.[12] At the same time, spokesmen for the Arab community and Arab bourgeoisie claimed that the protectionist policy pursued by the government, in response to Jewish pressure, was far too generous. They argued that the policy of reducing customs on the raw materials needed for local industry, and the taxing of competing imported commodities, was a direct support for Jewish industry since it could best take advantage of these benefits. The residents of Palestine, the majority of whom were Arabs, had to pay the higher price for the taxed imported commodities. Furthermore, it has been argued by Palestinian scholars that the low level of industrialization, for which Jewish industrial development was considered responsible, impeded class development within the Arab society. It restricted the consolidation of a bourgeoisie and of a working class that develop as part of the process of capitalist industrialization and that usually play a leading role in movements of national liberation and social change.[13]

The impact of Jewish industrial development, understood so differently by Arabs and Jews, became a major theme in the controversy over the Jewish National Home. While the Jewish leadership hailed the benefits obtained by all from Jewish modernization and industrialization, the Arabs attributed the slow pace of Arab industrialization almost solely to Jewish competition. They saw the rapid growth of Jewish industry, aided by what they considered generous government support, as a major factor in the consolidation of Jewish economic separatism and a major impediment to Arab development.[14] Seikaly argues:

> The contribution of Jewish industry was the introduction of a wide range of new enterprises, backed by private and institutional capital and manned by a western industrialized proletariat. The fact that this industry was transplanted along with European capital, imported machinery, raw and semi-manufactured materials, as well as with a labour force that maintained a western standard of living, contributed to the difficulties it created for the whole population in Palestine.[15]

Thus, while Jewish leadership claimed that its industrialization quickened the pace of economic activity in general, benefited the population of Palestine, and displaced no one,[16] Arab leadership focused on the indirect damage caused the Arab community by the inhibiting competition of the Jewish industry. In the case of construction the Jews felt threatened and responded by attempting to "close the shop" against Arab workers; in the case of industry the Arabs felt similarly threatened and responded by attempting to "close the market" and boycotting Jewish products.

Haifa, a center of both Jewish and Arab industry, was the major arena in which these developments and relations were played out. Many of Haifa's Jewish workers moved into industry where they faced little competition from Arab workers. They worked in Jewish-owned factories and rarely encountered Arab workers. Arabs employed in manufacturing worked in the small Arab industrial sector, particularly in the labor-intensive tobacco and cigarette industry. Thus the two groups of workers were employed in different industrial settings. They developed alongside one another, each in his own environment, and yet they were not completely isolated from one another. Various forms of contact did exist, as we shall see in the following section.

HAIFA — THE CENTER OF HEAVY INDUSTRY

General Trends

Haifa was the center of large and heavy industry.[17] The most important steps in the Jewish industrialization of Haifa were taken in the 1920s, when both the Mandatory government and Jewish private entrepreneurs predicted that it would become one of the major economic and industrial cities of the Middle East.[18] Haifa never lived up to this prediction and Tel Aviv soon had more industrial enterprises and employees. It did, however, become the major center of large, heavy, and capital-intensive industry. These enterprises were located in a planned industrial zone with a well-developed infrastructure.[19] The major heavy industries were chemicals (mainly soap and oil products), stone, and cement. Approximately 50 percent of all value was produced by them and 63 percent of all capital was invested in them. The light industries—textile, clothing, and paper—produced only 4 percent of all value and 4 percent of all capital was invested in them. In Tel Aviv this proportion was reversed; the heavier industries—stone, cement, and chemicals—produced 10.5 percent of all value and 14 percent of all capital was invested in them, while the light industries produced 48 percent of all value and 32 percent of all capital was invested in them.[20]

Haifa's Jewish industry developed in three phases:

1. The 1920s—1922–1926
2. The 1930s—1932–1936
3. The 1940s—The Second World War

1. *The 1920s (1922–1926).* A number of large enterprises that set the pattern for Haifa's industry were established.[21] These included the flour mills—the grand moulin, the oil and soap factory—Shemen, and the cement factory—Nesher. The electric company established in Haifa in the early 1920s by Pinhas Rutenberg should also be noted, for it facilitated this industrial development.

2. *The 1930s (1932–1936).* The opening of the Haifa port and the development of the Haifa Bay industrial zone created the conditions conducive to industrial development. Many new immigrants from central Europe with industrial expertise, experience, and some private capital were therefore attracted to Haifa. A large number of different enterprises were established. These included metal works and firms producing chemicals, paints, and clothing.[22]

3. *The 1940s—the years of the Second World War.* When the Second World War broke out, Jewish industry in Palestine was ready and able to take advantage of the new opportunities it created. Industry expanded to provide not only the needs of the local population who had been cut off from their previous sources of supply, but also to meet the demands of the British army. Haifa in particular answered the needs of the military, and thus further reinforced its position as the center of heavy industry.[23]

The Jewish manufacturing industry that developed in all of Palestine and particularly in Haifa took full advantage of the attributes of the Jewish immigrants, which the local Arab population could not equal. Skills, experience, know-how, professional and commercial connections, large-scale capital, institutional and political support, and a consumer public were the important assets of the Jewish community. Most of the consumers came from within the Jewish community. Only one-quarter of all enterprises included in the 1937 Census of Jewish Industry and Handicrafts reported having Arab clientele. This percentage was lower in Tel Aviv (16 percent of all enterprises) and higher in Haifa, where just over a third of all enterprises had Arab customers.[24] However, the value of their purchases was a low 14 percent.[25] Thus, for the most part, the Jewish manufacturing industry developed independently of the Arab population and of the Arab manufacturing industry.

Shemen and Nesher—Nahum Wilbush and Michael Pollak

In contrast to most Jewish enterprises, Shemen oil and Nesher cement did interact with the Arab community and its economy. The rural Arab community provided some of the raw materials for the production of edible oil, and some of the manpower necessary for excavating the stone from which the cement was made. Both firms had a considerable Arab clientele inside Palestine and they also exported their products to neighboring Arab countries. At the same time both Shemen and Nesher—the two largest Jewish-owned enterprises—played a major role in the development of Jewish industry, particularly in Haifa.

Shemen oil was registered in London, in 1919, as a shareholding company with a capital of 140,000 £P.[26] It was the major project of Nahum Wilbush (Wilbushevitz), an industrial engineer and the son of a large and wealthy family from Grodno in Russia. He arrived in Palestine in 1903 to study the options for the development of modern industry. He surveyed the land, its rivers, its raw materials and agricultural products, and the existing industry—the local Arab industry of olive oil, soap, and flour mills, the Jewish-owned wine cellars and metal workshops, and noted the German settlers' first steps toward industrialization. He concluded that the production of oil from olive waste had profitable prospects.[27]

After early attempts at the extraction and production of oil in Ben Shemen, Wilbush moved to Haifa in 1905. The town had just been connected to the Hijaz Railway and appeared to have a grand future. He established the Atid factory for the production of oil products and machinery together with several highly dedicated Zionist engineers and entrepreneurs who had immigrated from Russia. The partners all became leading figures in Haifa's new bourgeoisie. Shmuel Pevsner became the largest importer. The engineer Shmuel Itzkovitz, the son of an industrialist from Baku, Russia, and the engineer Tuvia Dunia became important contractors. They were all founding members of the Hadar Hacarmel neighborhood.[28] The company ran into financial difficulties that were exacerbated by the outbreak of the First World War. After the war it resumed activities under the more promising conditions of British rule. Before beginning the construction of the new plant in Haifa, Wilbush signed an agreement with the World Zionist Organization, in which the company pledged to abide by the principles set down by the Zionist Organization, to purchase land through its institutions, and to employ Jewish labor wherever possible.[29] Gdalia Wilbushevitz, Nahum's older brother, who was also an engineer with much experience in building and industrial development, supervised the construction. In December 1924, the High Commissioner, Sir Herbert Samuel, was given the honor of inaugurating the machines.

Shemen was one of the largest and most modern factories in the Middle East. It had three major departments: an oil press for the production of olive oil, sesame seed oil, and linseed oil; a distillery for the distilling and chemical processing of oils; and a department for laundry and cosmetic soaps.[30]

Unlike most of the Jewish industrial enterprises, Shemen did not develop independently of the Arab community and economy. It bought some of its raw materials—mainly olives and olive waste for the extraction of additional oil—from the Arab villages. It sold its products—soap and vegetable oils—to the local Arab market, and it competed with Arab products in the markets of the neighboring countries to which Shemen exported as much as 40 percent of its output.[31]

Soap and oil were traditional industries of the Palestine economy. Nablus was the largest and best known center for soap production.[32] Nablus soap was famous in all the neighboring countries for its superb quality. It was produced from olive oil only, and had no pig fat added to it, an attribute that was of great importance to Muslims. From the mid-nineeenth century it exported large quantities of soap to neighboring countries and was thus one of the few industries to enter foreign markets.[33] The second center that produced soap was Jaffa-Ramla. Its soap was cheaper and was made primarily from oils such as linseed, coconut, and peanut. During the 1920s and 1930s, the number of soap factories in Jaffa-Ramla declined. These were usually small, employing an average of eight persons each. In 1931, Egypt imposed a customs tax on imported soap. This was a major blow to the Jaffa-Ramla Arab soap industry.[34] The Nablus soap industry was, however, able to retain its market and even expand because of the special quality of its soap. As for the oil industry—there were about 500–600 oil presses for the production of olive oil, and another 45 for the pressing of sesame seeds—these were mainly in the villages. The number of presses remained more or less constant over the period. Some mechanization was introduced and the output increased.[35]

It is difficult to assess the impact of Shemen, this large and highly mechanized oil and soap factory, on the market of Arab products in Palestine and in the countries to which these products were exported. For the most part, the products were not identical. The Shemen soap, although cheaper, was not a substitute for the famous Nablus soap. Nevertheless, there are indications of direct competition. Shemen presented its soap as being—"refined as the Nablus soap,"[36] and dyed it red to make it similar to the Arab-produced soap that was dyed with the red dust left over from brick making.[37] The "Menorah," trademark of Shemen on the soap it manufactured, was accepted as a sign of the product's purity and the absence of pig fat which, as noted, was an important asset of the Nablus soap.[38] The Jaffa-Ramla soap industry was probably more seriously affected. Shemen sold oil and soap to Egypt, the main client of the Palestinian soap industry, and its soap even traveled as far as Saudi Arabia. According to Graham-Brown, the economy of size and the multiplicity of products, together with the lifting of the import duties on olive oil and sesame oil, enabled Shemen, by the late 1930s, to undersell the Nablus soap.[39] It was the lifting of the import tax and the protective tariff policy adopted, in response to Jewish pressure, by the government that created strong Arab opposition. According to this policy, competing imported products were taxed while imported raw materials were exempted. This policy and its effect on Shemen were summarized by the Anglo-American Inquiry Commission:

> Protection was afforded to the activities of the company, the import duty on all edible oils being raised from £P 8 per ton to £P 10 per ton, with the exception of the duty on cotton seed oil which was raised from 8 to 15 (pounds sterling) per ton. Seeds used for the extraction of edible oil were, with the exception of sesame seed [locally produced— D.B.], exempted from import duty so that the primary material used for the expressing of edible oil could be imported duty free, while the import duties were increased on those oils which could be used as substitutes for the oils locally produced.[40]

This protective policy aroused great resentment. It appeared to the Arab elite that the Mandatory government was encouraging the Jewish manufacturing industry at the direct expense of the Arab community and its economy. They were affected by the increased price of imported goods and by the loss of government revenue incurred through the customs duty exemption. The issue of protective taxation and exemption was even more controversial in the case of the cement industry and the Nesher Portland Cement Company.

Nesher, the largest private company in Palestine, was founded in 1923 and began excavating the raw materials and producing cement at the end of 1925. It was Nahum Wilbush who discovered the soil rich in raw material for producing cement, outside of Haifa. In 1919, Boris Goldberg, a chemical engineer, and one of the leading Zionists in Russia, established "the Syndicate for Portland Cement in Palestine" that included seven wealthy businessmen, who had emigrated from Russia after the revolution and settled in Britain. In 1921, Pollak, who had lost the fortune that he had made in oil at Baku but had valuable shares saved in the Rothschild bank in Paris, decided to invest in the cement industry. After the untimely death of Boris Goldberg, Pollak was chosen to head the syndicate and from that time on his name was synonymous with the development and management of Nesher Portland Cement.[41] Of the £225,000 initial capital with which the company was founded, Pollak and his brother invested £50,000, Baron E. Rothschild invested another £50,000 via PICA, and the additional £125,000 was put up by several smaller private investors, wealthy Jews from Britain, Zionists, and non-Zionists.

Pollak recruited an expert managerial and technical staff. Isaac Schneerson who had managed a construction company that laid railways in Russia before the revolution, became the secretary of the syndicate. Bela Spiegel, who had managed a coal mining company in Hungary that also owned a Portland Cement Company, was appointed the chief chemical engineer. Arpad Got, an engineer, supervised the building of the factory and Eliezer Levine, a lawyer, became the administrative manager. Many other skilled technicians and scientists joined the staff. Some were recruited from the Jewish immigrants to Palestine, who had been trained in the universities of Italy, Austria, and Germany before immigrating, while others were especially brought over from Europe by the company.[42]

The workers employed in the construction of the factory and, from 1925, in its operation, were mainly Jewish men of the Third Aliya (1919–1923). Like the workers of Shemen, most were young and single and had gravitated to Haifa during the unemployment of 1923. Many were members of the workers' parties and of the Histadrut and were affiliated with the Haifa Labor Council (HLC). They were able to organize and, over time, secure good, or at least adequate, labor conditions. They began working on the construction of the factory at 200 mils (or 20 piasters, *grush*) a day, and a few months later this wage was raised to 250 mils. This increase notwithstanding, the workers sought to improve their earnings and working conditions before the construction ended and production began. They presented the management with their requirements. The workers of the two other large, privately owned enterprises, Shemen and the Grand Moulin, joined the Nesher workers and made similar demands. In February 1925, the workers of all three enterprises went out on strike. They were supported by the HLC and the Histadrut Executive.[43] The striking workers demanded an increase in their wages, improved working conditions, and the right of the Histadrut, via the local labor council and the workers' committee in each workplace, to intervene in matters of employment and dismissal.[44] The workers of all three enterprises won their basic demands.[45] De Vries has argued that the strikes had a definitive impact on the Haifa labor market. They secured the HLC as an accepted authority, able to intervene in all matters concerning employment, wages, and conditions of work. They also established the conditions that the workers had won as the norm for other Jewish workers.[46]

The labor force at Nesher differed from that of Shemen and the Grand Moulin, and almost all other Jewish-owned industry, in that it included both Jewish and Arab workers. Pollak, intent on entering the markets of the neighboring Arab countries, insisted on employing Arab workers, along with the Jewish workers.[47] Despite pressure from the Jewish workers of Nesher and from Histadrut institutions, Pollak would not yield and employed Arab workers until well into the Arab Rebellion in 1938. From 1925 to 1936, there was a clear division of labor between the Jewish and Arab workers. The Jewish workers (250–500) worked in the factory, and the rural migrant Arab workers (100–250) worked in the quarry excavating the raw material from which the cement was processed. Their conditions of employment also differed. The Jewish workers, members of the Histadrut, were employed directly by Nesher, at the beginning wage of 300 mils, and by 1935, 448 mils per day for an eight-hour workday. The skilled and experienced workers earned 700–750 mils per day. This was supplemented by benefits such as an annual paid leave, a library, and other recreational activities.[48] The Arab workers were employed by a subcontractor, who paid them between 100 and 125 mils per work day, which lasted from sunrise to sunset.[49] The relations that developed between the two groups of workers are discussed later.

The output of Nesher increased rapidly and it provided a major share of the cement used for construction in Palestine. As a result cement imports were drastically reduced. Despite its success, Nesher faced severe financial difficulties, particularly at its inception, because of the conditions that characterized all industrial development in Palestine. Most of the raw materials had to be imported and the industrialists had to bear the cost of the customs tariffs. They also had to compete with imported cheaper products that often flooded the Palestine market. This problem was exacerbated by Britain's obligation to keep the markets of the territories under its mandate, open to all members of the League of Nations. Nesher and Shemen argued that these conditions made a protective tariff policy imperative for their survival. Nesher led the fight to change the government's policy. It went directly to the High Commissioner, in a campaign that involved the World

Zionist Organization, the Zionist Executive, the Palestine Administration, and the Colonial Office.[50] They persuaded the High Commissioner and the Director of Customs that Palestinian industries could not survive without positive official support. The anti-protection colonial policy notwithstanding, the Mandatory government did implement a protective tariff policy that favored Nesher. The Report of the Anglo-American Inquiry Commission of 1945–46 summarized this policy:

> Most of the machinery imported for the installation of the factory and the coal used in the production of cement are exempted from import duty, as are also barrels, hoops, staves, sacks and paper bags. While the factory was being established, competition was severe and it was necessary to further protect the "Nesher" company by increasing the duty on imported cement from 200 mils per ton to 600 mils per ton. Later, in 1929, the competition from the imported cheaper Italian cement forced them to increase the duty to 850 mils per ton.[51]

The importance of industrialization for the Jewish National Home was not lost on the Arab leadership, who were therefore especially concerned about the the support granted Nesher.[52] Tawfik Canaan, a contemporary researcher of Arab society and of the Arab village and an outspoken public figure, claimed the protective tariffs for Jewish factories that employed only Jewish labor were tantamount to a taxation of the whole Arab population who were obliged to become consumers of Jewish produce. They were thus compelled, he contended, to help maintain Jewish enterprises in which they were not granted work.[53]

Sir John Hope Simpson, sent to Palestine to inquire into the hostilities of August 1929, dealt, among other things, with the policy of protective tariffs. He accepted the Arab position and reported:

> It is clear that the Company (Nesher) would have made a loss in place of a profit had the whole production been sold locally at the Syrian price. Also that the industry could not be maintained were it not for the protective tariff. The sole good reason in favor of the tariff is that it enables the Company to employ 260 Jews and Jewesses and 130 Arabs who might otherwise have been without employment. This argument is not convincing to the purchaser in Palestine, who ultimately has to pay the protective duty in the price of his cement.[54]

To conclude, while Jewish manufacturing industry was relatively independent in relation to the Arab economy, it was by no means neutral. On the one hand, Arab elites resented the support given to Jewish industry since they felt that the Arab population paid the price without sharing in any of the benefits. On the other hand, some Jewish factories exported a significant share of their products to the neighboring Arab markets and suffered when Jewish products were boycotted on political grounds.

There was little direct competition between Arab and Jewish industry. It is not surprising that there was no Arab-owned cement factory or modern oil factory in Haifa. The resources necessary for such enterprises were available to the Jewish sector but much less so to the Arab sector. The modern Arab industries that did develop, did so precisely in those areas left vacant by the Jewish entrepreneurs. The most important of these was the tobacco and cigarette industry, which was centered in Haifa.

The Tobacco and Cigarette Industry—Mabruk and Hajj Tahir Qaraman

Before 1921 there was no cigarette industry in Palestine. The Ottoman government retained a monopoly on the manufacturing and marketing of cigarettes and tobacco until 1921, when the monopoly was abolished and the industry began to develop. The price of wheat on the world market fell and Arab farmers became interested in the cultivation of tobacco. The government actively supported tobacco cultivation and the Department of Agriculture provided an expert to instruct growers on the best methods for doing so. It hoped that the favorable conditions in northern Palestine would enable farmers to grow high-class tobacco for export.[55] Within two years, hundreds of small shops sprang up in which small tobacco leaf cutting machines were used to make the tobacco products. About twenty larger factories were also established.[56] Much of the industry was concentrated in and around Haifa. Close to three-quarters of the tobacco was grown in the villages around Acre and in the northern districts of Palestine, and the main factories were located in Haifa. The largest of these, owned by Qaraman, Dik, and Salti, was established in 1925. Next in size were the two smaller firms owned by Salim, Najiah, and Khuri and by Aziz Mikati. The firm of Qaraman, Dik, and Salti played a special role in the cigarette industry and in Haifa's economy and society, which warrants a detailed discussion.

Tahir Qaraman, one of the leading figures of Haifa's new "self-made" (*"Isamiyyun"*) elite, was the most prominent of the three partners.[57] He was the largest employer in Haifa, having interests in trade, industry, stone excavation, and, in later years, agricultural experiments. He was a prominent member of important communal institutions and became a member of the Chamber of Commerce in 1929, and of the City Council in 1931.[58] During the Arab rebellion Qaraman was made a member of the National Committee heading the general strike, together with Ibrahim Bek al-Khalil and Hajj Khalil Taha, heads of two of the richest and most distinguished Muslim families. Ibrahim al-Khalil and Khalil Taha were both assassinated during the Arab Rebellion, as were members of many of the rich and notable families. The assassinations were primarily revenge for the contacts of the notables with the Jewish community, and above all for their land sales.[59] Qaraman himself escaped this fate, despite the fact that he had wide-ranging contacts with the Jewish community in Haifa. David Hacohen, a business partner and friend, speculates in his memoirs that Qaraman secretly gave financial support to the rebel bands.[60]

Qaraman arrived in Haifa toward the end of the Ottoman period as a peddler. "Haifa veterans," writes Vashitz, "describe the firm's leading personality as a man who first appeared selling bread on the street and later acquired a small shop."[61] The first step in his career as an industrialist came in 1916 when he formed a partnership with Muhammad Ali Hunayni, a perfume producer from Alexandria, to produce cigarettes. In 1922, one year after private cigarette production became legal, an advertisement for the Qaraman-Hunayni cigarette shop appeared. In that year Qaraman expanded the partnership to include his brother Abd al-Rauf, his cousin Fadl and other merchants, and formed Qaraman, Cousins and Co. to trade in tobacco. Qaraman also joined the tobacco firm of Hasan al-Dik and Farah al-Salti, and provided the financial backing for their technical and administrative expertise.[62] Their factory, Mabruk, became the major producer of cigarettes in Palestine. They benefited from the new tobacco ordinance of May 1925, which facilitated both cultivation and production through its regulation of tobacco growing, processing, marketing, and taxation.

In 1927, Qaraman, Dik, and Salti sold Mabruk to the British-American Tobacco Trust that had set up the Maspero cigarette factory in Jaffa in 1921. The Trust bought Mabruk, intending to turn it into the major supplier of cigarettes for the Arab market, while Maspero would serve the Jewish market.[63] To eliminate competition, the Trust bought out small cigarette factories and shut them down. By 1940, Mabruk, which continued to be managed by Qaraman, Dik, and Salti, was producing 75 percent of the output of the Arab tobacco and cigarette industry. This output increased from approximately 220 tons in 1925, to 450 tons in 1934, and a year later to 540 tons. About 10 percent of this was sold to the Jewish market. From 1936, the output fluctuated, affected, like much else in Palestine, by political rather than purely economic factors. The Arab Rebellion dealt this industry a severe blow.

The Jewish market was closed to it because of the Arab boycott, and the purchasing power of the Arab population dropped sharply. By 1939, output had dropped from its 1935 high of 540 tons to 280 tons. It rose again in response to the demand created during the Second World War and to the reopening of the Jewish market.[64]

Mabruk continued to be seen as an Arab-owned factory, even after its acquisition by the British-American Trust. It became the largest factory associated with Arab entrepreneurship and one of the largest in Palestine. Political, social, and economic significance was attributed to its success, especially among those who hoped that economic development would advance Arab national autonomy. In an article entitled "National Industry," *al-Karmil*, whose editor Najib Nassar, advocated Arab economic enterprise and entrepreneurship, stated:

> For example, the Qaraman, Dik and Salti firm . . . the fact that so many people smoke the products of that firm enables it to employ approximately 300 *"watani"* [natives of the motherland—D.B.] workers and clerks, to advance the cultivation of tobacco in the region of Tarshiha and to retain the capital of the country within its boundaries. . . . Therefore, it is the duty of every individual to support everything that is *"watani."* It is the duty of every Palestinian and every Arab to promote *"watani"* products. And as far as we are concerned, whoever avoids purchasing the cigarettes of Qaraman, Dick and Salti's Company and prefers to smoke foreign cigarettes, is causing harm to the economy of the country . . . is causing harm to the workers of his land, to the tobacco cultivators, to the traders and, more generally, to the finance of the country.[65]

The call for the consumption of *"watani"* products, echoed the call for the consumption of *"totzeret ha'aretz"* by the Jewish leadership. Owners and workers appealed to their national communities to buy their products, in the name of their national cause.

The meteoric rise of Hajj Tahir Qaraman has been explained by Vashitz as that of "an able and enterprising man (who) came of age in a period that accorded his specific talent a maximum of opportunity to realize its potential."[66] This "realization of potential" and "maximization of existing opportunities" included many contacts with the new Jewish community in Haifa. Both he and the Jewish community supported the mayoral candidacy of Hasan Shukri in 1927. He entered into partnership with Solel Boneh, the Histadrut contracting company, to set up the stone and lime excavation company, "Even va-Sid," in which both Jewish and Arab labor was employed.[67] He bought some of the cardboard packaging for the cigarette factory from the Jewish owned

Silverberg Cardboard Box Factory and he bought two paperbag factories from Jewish owners, to supplement the cigarette factory.[68] These
political and economic relations coexisted with informal relations of respect and trust, as David Hacohen writes in his memoirs:

> Qaraman was a man of excellent talents, quick to grasp things, with
> an outstanding ability to unravel complex commercial problems and
> an artist of compromise and rapport with partners so different in cul-
> ture, education and world view. True friendship prevailed between us
> till the day of his death.[69]

So much for the owner of Mabruk—what of its workers? Unlike other
Arab manufacturing enterprises that employed only a small number of
workers, and were more like family workshops, Mabruk employed
between 300 and 900 workers. The numbers varied, reflecting the
growth of the factory and the fluctuation of its output, as well as the
seasonal nature of the tobacco industry. Production began with approximately 200 workers, increased to 300 by 1928 and to 500 workers by
the beginning of the 1930s.[70] In the prosperity of the mid-1930s, the
workforce expanded to about 900, by far the largest number of workers
to be employed in any Arab firm.[71] We have no figures for the years of
the Arab Rebellion, when production fell drastically. Immediately after
the Rebellion, at the beginning of the 1940s, as few as 250–300 workers
were employed.[72]

Women and children made up about half the labor force in the cigarette industry. Their presence caused an already low wage to be further
reduced. Despite slight differences in the sources at our disposal, the
overall wage picture is quite consistent. In the early 1930s, the wages of
male workers ranged from 80 to 100 mils, for a work day of nine and a
half to ten hours. A few experienced and skilled workers earned as
much as 150 mils. In 1935, at the height of production, the wages of the
male workers ranged from 80 to 180 mils, and they probably worked
an eight-hour day. Women's wages were much lower, beginning at 50
mils per day with a maximum of about 100 mils. In 1932, the children
worked as many hours as did the adults and they earned 40–60 mils.[73]
By 1941, the wages and working conditions had improved slightly. According to an HLC survey in July, the male workers of Qaraman, Dik,
and Salti were earning 180 mils, women were earning 120 mils, and the
children 50–70 mils per day for an 8 hour workday.[74] By 1943, according to a further HLC survey, an additional increase could be noted,
whereby experienced male workers in the tobacco industry were earning 350 mils per day, while women and children earned 200–250 mils.[75]

The government wage census for all of Palestine, conducted in 1943, re-ported somewhat different levels of pay, with male workers earning 373 mils per day, women 155 mils, youngsters 183 mils, and children 110–120 mils per day.[76] The increases in wages during the early 1940s could not compensate the workers for the steep rise in the cost of living during the war years. As there was no cost of living allowance in Arab private industry, the real value of the wages dropped.[77]

Labor conditions in this labor-intensive industry were extremely poor. Agassi described the conditions at all three cigarette factories in Haifa, in 1932. Mabruk was the largest of the three, employing 600 workers, about half of whom were under the age of 18:

> The sanitary conditions in these factories are extremely poor. The poi-sonous dust and vapors of the tobacco spread all forms of tuberculo-sis among the adult and young workers, who are then expelled from the factory, regardless of their pleas to remain at work. Other diseases attack the weak bodies of these workers, who are extremely vulner-able as a result of their poor conditions of living and their minimal wages.
>
> These dark conditions of work can exist because of the regime of pressure which extinguishes any whisper of freedom, because of the reign of terror which creates enemies from among the workers, be-cause of the dire need for every piaster and because of the vicious treatment by the lackies of the owner who is hailed and praised by the bourgeois Arab press as a "committed nationalist," a "generous heart."[78]

Despite this "reign of terror" and the knowledge that they could be re-placed by other migrants, the workers did not accept these conditions fatalistically. Just as Nesher and Shemen were the arena for labor con-flict and for setting the norms for Jewish industrial workers, so Mabruk became the arena for the labor conflicts of the emerging Arab working class. Despite the low level of organization, the workers were aware of their basic rights and were outraged when these rights were abused. Any worsening of the poor labor conditions triggered immediate protest. The workers regarded strikebreaking as unforgivable and ex-pected the strikebreakers, who had been brought in by the manage-ment, to vacate the site once the situation had been explained to them. Their refusal to do so led to outbursts of hostility. The workers ex-pected support for improving their work conditions from labor organ-izations and labor unions. Their protests and conflicts were sporadic and, sometimes, spontaneous, and it was difficult for them to sustain an organized conflict for more than a few days.

The first strike broke out in May 1928. The economy was in a depression and both Jews and Arabs were hit by unemployment. Yet Mabruk was doing well and even expanding. On the morning of the 19th of May, the management informed the workers that from that day on they would be working twelve hours a day instead of the nine to ten and a half hours they had been working. Two workers responded that the workers would not agree to such a change and demanded an eight-hour workday. They were dismissed on the spot,, whereupon seventy workers, among them technicians and skilled workers, got up and walked out with them. The Palestine Arab Workers Society (PAWS) had been set up three years before, in 1925, but had not yet initiated any organizational activity. The strikers appealed to the HLC for help in protecting their rights and negotiating with management.[79] The following day sixty to seventy youngsters joined the strikers.[80] But on the third day the balance shifted as some of the skilled workers returned to work, without informing their comrades. The management had begun to take on new workers and no longer insisted on an extended workday. The strike collapsed and many returned to work.

The Arab press gave little coverage to the strike. But shortly after it ended *al-Karmil* devoted a long editorial to it. The newspaper, voicing the position of the Arab national bourgeoisie, criticized the workers for having gone out on strike. It stressed the damage such action could cause an important Arab enterprise that provided employment in a period of depression. But above all, the editorial took issue with the workers for turning to the "Zionist Labor Associations."

> Can't the Arab worker see that the Jewish workers are taking over the jobs in the government offices? If the Zionist Labor Organization genuinely cared about the Arab workers it would leave them a share of the jobs, according to their percentage among the population.[81]

Davar, the Histadrut newspaper, on the other hand, presented the Jewish workers as the supportive allies of the Arab worker in whom the latter had full confidence:

> The Arab worker is just beginning to organize—and already when taking his first steps he finds by his side tens of thousands of class conscious workers, organized in an internally solid and externally influential union—he finds beside him the Hebrew worker . . . out of confidence in him, trusting that the Hebrew worker will not reject him, not despise him or hand him over, the pioneers of Arab labor organization go straight to the Haifa Labor Council.[82]

Davar's glorification of this class solidarity notwithstanding, the Histadrut and the Jewish worker had little to do with the next labor conflict at Qaraman, Dik, and Salti.

On the 11th of January, 1930, the PAWS held its first conference in Haifa. The management of Mabruk warned its workers against participating. Tawfik 'Adma and 120 workers waited till the day after the conference and then approached the newly elected central committee of the PAWS and presented their problems to them. The committee advised the workers to return to work and promised to open negotiations with the management. Some of the workers returned to work while others remained on strike. The PAWS issued a strongly worded declaration in which they accused management of uniting with the Zionists. They called upon all skilled Arab workers to support the exploited workers of Mabruk.[83]

The PAWS in its first public intervention did not attempt any overt action and achieved little. It was, however, made perfectly clear that the Jewish worker and his support were no longer welcome. *Davar*'s declaration of workers' solidarity notwithstanding, the PAWS contended that the Zionists were out to attack the Arab workers' movement. They therefore saw no grounds for partnership and the Arab workers appear to have accepted their leadership.

Over the next few years strikes among Arab workers became more frequent, culminating in the Mabruk strike of 1935.[84] In February of that year forty youngsters (aged eighteen and younger) went out on strike demanding basic changes in their poor conditions of work. The strike ended within a few days with no positive results. Six months later a much larger strike was declared to back the workers' demands for a shorter workday, an increased wage, paid leave, medical expenses, and the recognition of the workers' representatives.[85] The PAWS distributed leaflets around town explaining the workers' demands, and entered into negotiations with the management. They called Rashid al-Hajj Ibrahim to join the negotiations as a mediator. Rashid al-Hajj Ibrahim was one of the leaders of the nationalist party, Istiqlal, and a prominent leader of the Haifa Arab community.[86] At first little was achieved and negotiations broke down. The following day another 250 or 500 workers (the sources differ) joined the strike.[87] The management closed down the factory, and brought in two hundred strikebreakers. Violent clashes broke out between the strikebreakers and the picketing strikers, many of whom were arrested. This did not last long, for the strikebreakers had been brought from the same villages as the strikers and were soon convinced to leave. The following day the management brought in another three hundred and fifty strikebreakers, this time from villages in the Galilee where the tobacco was grown. These workers had no prior commitment to the strikers and had a vested interest in keeping the tobacco industry going. This was a severe blow to the strike. Rashid al-Hajj Ibrahim, however, resumed negotiations and within a few days an agreement, acceptable to both parties, was reached. The strikebreakers were sent home and the strikers were asked to return to work the following day.[88] On the 9th of September the strikers marched triumphantly to the factory gates. Rashid al-Hajj Ibrahim led the march carrying an Arab flag. A band played and bystanders cheered. The Arab workers and the Arab public considered this agreement a great victory and credited the PAWS with its achievement.

The agreement was never implemented. Shortly after the strike ended, the economic situation in Palestine deteriorated. In October 1935, the Italian invasion of Ethiopia sparked an economic crisis in Palestine. The crisis deepened six months later later (April 1936) when the Arab general strike and rebellion erupted. The Arab economy contracted, and so did production at Qaraman, Dik, and Salti. By December 1936, hundreds of workers had been fired. There was no chance of implementing the improvements agreed on a year earlier.[89]

By 1935, the PAWS had taken over the leadership of the Arab workers. The Palestine Labor League, the vehicle of the HLC, had little to do with the struggles of that year. Earlier contacts with Mabruk workers had been singularly unsuccessful. Agassi reviews these earlier contacts and their recurring failures.

> As early as the 19.12.32 we organized the storehouse workers of Mabruk, after a few of them turned to us. They immediately demanded that we improve their conditions of work, but they were relatively few (25 people) and were not enough of a force with which to start a struggle. We therefore refused to enter negotiations with their employer. We explained this to them and called upon them to be patient. As a result they withdrew saying that they could not afford to pay membership dues and wait for better times. Four months later we began developing contacts with a number of supervisors. This became known to the company's management, one of the supervisors was fired immediately, the rest severed their contacts for fear of being dismissed. One of the workers, who remained in contact with the club [the Arab Club run by the HLC—D.B.] for over half a year, asked for a loan from our Savings Fund. At the time it had been decided by the Fund not to grant loans to new members due to delays in the payment of earlier debts. He would not accept this reply and left in anger. In April 1934, a group of youngsters, employed by Mabruk turned to us

wanting to learn English—in response to a notice we had published concerning evening classes. As only very few people had registered for these classes, we were unable to finance the courses. We hoped to find someone who would volunteer to work with this group of youngsters but no such person was found and nothing came out of it.

Agassi concluded:

There were many reasons why the Palestine Labor League remained uninvolved in this strike [of September, 1935—D.B.], but there can be no doubt that if the workers, or the PAWS had approached us for help—as would have been appropriate under the circumstances— both the PLL and the Histadrut would have responded whole heartedly.[90]

The PAWS held the Histadrut responsible for the displacement of Arab workers, and vehemently opposed its attempts to attract Arab workers to its PLL organization. Furthermore, the PAWS strongly opposed the Histadrut's claim to a monopoly over the Jewish labor market. In fact, the PAWS combined political and economic considerations in exactly the same way that the Histadrut did. The workers themselves, who had previously appealed directly to the HLC, refrained from doing so, possibly because of disillusionment, possibly because they had their own movement to which to turn and possibly because of the increased tension between Jews and Arabs in Haifa. Theirs was indeed a class struggle but one that was well rooted within the Haifa Arab community. They were struggling against their employer, who was a prominent leader in the Arab community. They identified Jewish organized labor as an integral part of the Zionist endeavor and therefore perceived it as their national and class rival, not as their actual or potential ally.

WHEN WORKING TOGETHER

Although most Jewish industrialists employed only Jewish labor, there were the exceptions who employed Arab workers as well. How did the physical proximity and the shared desire to improve working conditions affect the relationship of the workers? Did the separating barriers between them come down or were they reinforced? We will try to answer these questions by looking at three firms that employed Jewish and Arab workers for extended periods—the Nesher cement factory and quarry, the Mosaica Tile Manufacturers owned by Mr. Volfman, and the Nur match factory, owned by the brothers, Gershon and Meir

Weitzman. At each of these firms there were conflicts between workers and management over work conditions and there were strikes of both Jewish and Arab workers. There were attempts at each of the firms to organize joint action, but these yielded minimal results. Indeed, the separateness and alienation of the Arab and Jewish workers from one another were reinforced rather than weakened after each strike.

The Nur Match Factory

The Nur match factory was established by the Weitzman brothers, who had owned a large match factory in Vilna, Lithuania. They located the factory in Acre, an Arab town not far from Haifa, probably to avoid Histadrut enforcement of its Jewish labor policy. They employed about 100 male and female workers of whom half were Jewish and half were Arab. Production began in 1925. Wages were low, sanitation and hygiene were poor, and the work with flammable material and poisonous gas fumes was carried out under hazardous conditions. After protracted and fruitless negotiations between the management and the workers over the improvement of labor conditions, the workers declared a strike on the 17th of February, 1927. The Jewish workers organized the strike and immediately called on the Arab workers to join them and so bring about a complete stoppage of work. The strike lasted for five months, from February into June 1927, and was one of the longest strikes of the Mandatory period. Initially the owners attempted to introduce strikebreakers to keep production going, but diligent picketing prevented them from doing so, and the factory was closed.

The Histadrut, through the HLC, organized support for the strikers. Contributions by Jewish workers from other places of work were announced daily in *Davar*, and distributed by the strike committee to both the Jewish and the Arab strikers. The leaders of the strike, all Jewish workers, insisted throughout the struggle that aid and support be shared with the Arab workers.[91] Five months into the strike, the interest of Histadrut institutions waned. Aid to the workers became scarce. Attempts at mediation failed initially, but a compromise was finally reached and signed.[92] The workers gained some of their demands, though much fewer than was victoriously reported in *Davar*, and work was resumed.

Histadrut spokesmen and local Arab leaders hailed the strike as a fine example of working-class solidarity, which transcended national conflict.[93] But this solidarity between Arab and Jewish workers did not last long. One month later, Gershon Weitzman tried to undermine the agreement by reducing wages for all the workers, by excluding the

Arab workers from the agreed benefits, and by substituting Arab for Jewish workers.[94] This lowering of wages in violation of the agreement led some of the Jewish workers to leave the firm, and their place was taken by Arab workers.[95] In August 1929, relations between Jews and Arabs deteriorated throughout Palestine, as a result of the clashes in Jerusalem, and tension increased in Acre as well. The management of Nur, quick to take advantage of the situation, further reduced the number of Jewish workers. Work conditions were back to where they had been before the strike. The long struggle had been in vain. Within two years the management had replaced most of the Jewish workers with Arab workers.[96] These deteriorating work conditions and their inability to resume the struggle, led most of the remaining Jewish workers to leave. Only the clerical and highly skilled Jewish workers remained. They were a clearly differentiated minority in the now predominantly Arab labor force. In 1932 there were 98 workers at Nur—57 Arab and 21 Jewish men; 12 Arab and 8 Jewish women. In 1938, there were close to 200 workers—180 Arab workers and only 15 Jewish workers![97] After the Second World War, in 1946, the workers of Nur went out on strike again, but this time the strikers were all Arab workers and the strike was led by the PAWS. Jewish workers were absent from both the factory and from the workers' struggle. The small number of Jewish workers who had remained were in higher positions and were associated with the management of the firm.[98] Thus, the success of the 1927 joint strike of Jewish and Arab workers was indeed short-lived. Employment in the same workplace had led to joint action, but the political, social, and economic conditions enabled the management to split the two groups of workers and abort their cooperative efforts.

The Nesher Quarry

The Arab workers in the Nesher quarry went on strike in 1930, a few years after the strike at Nur. The management of Nesher subcontracted the quarry work to the large Arab contractor, Misbah Shqefi, who brought the workers to town from the villages in the region of Jenin. He kept the workers under his tight control and severely exploited them. They were compelled to live in extremely poor quarters that he provided, buy their food from the store he ran, and work very long hours for extremely low pay. Their number ranged from 50 to 250. Thus, as in Mabruk, they formed a large concentration of workers that became one of the arenas for recurring strikes.[99] The Arab workers in the quarry, totally dependent on the contractor, were no doubt aware that the Jewish workers at Nesher had organized and won improved work conditions, higher wages, and job security. During the strikes of July 1930, September 1932, and April 1933, the Arab strikers turned to the Workers' Committee of Nesher for help and the Jewish workers responded positively. They put pressure on the contractor, recruiting the help of the HLC, the PLL, and the Histadrut Executive. Three times agreements were signed, but each came to naught.

In July 1930, when the fifty-four Arab workers of the quarry went on strike for the first time, the contractor fired them all and brought in fifty-four new workers.[100] The workers, used to a high turnover rate but not to total dismissal, turned to the Jewish Workers' Committee of the Nesher factory for help. The Committee referred them to the HLC. which negotiated an agreement on behalf of the Arab workers. This agreement ensured their return to work (at 120 mils per day) and some improvements in their wage conditions.[101] However, nothing was implemented. Two years later, despite economic prosperity, the wages of the quarry workers were actually reduced and the contractor controlled his workers as tightly as before. The workers went out on strike. Zvi Grinberg, the secretary of the Nesher Workers' Committee, tried to help them, and involved both Aba Houshi, the secretary of the HLC, and the Histadrut Executive, in the negotiations with the contractor. The rank-and-file Jewish workers of Nesher were more ambivalent in their support of the strike than was their secretary. They were unclear as to how far they would be willing.to go to aid Arab workers, whom they did not want employed in the quarry in the first place. Once again, an agreement was signed with the contractor Shqefi that recognized the committee of the Arab quarry workers, promised a small increase in pay (up from 120 mils to 125, and 150 mils in the future), and a loosening of the contractor's control.

Work in the quarry was resumed. The success of the negotiations under the auspices of the Histadrut led the Arab workers to join the Palestine Labor League (PLL). But even this limited victory did not last long. Within a few months the contractor Shqefi had brought in new workers to whom he owed nothing. In April 1933, he sent all the "veteran" workers home on vacation and refused to employ them on their return. Again, a strike was declared. This time eighty Jewish workers joined the Arab strikers. They rejected the raw material excavated by the new workers. To avoid bringing the whole factory to a standstill, the HLC put pressure on the contractor to accept arbitration and, meanwhile, to continue to employ the previous workers. Six weeks later the arbitrator's decision was announced. He accepted some of the demands put forward by the workers. The contractor was instructed to re-employ the workers he had arbitrarily dismissed and to pay all workers for the

first three days of their strike. He was instructed to raise their wage to
140 mils per day and to fire those who had been hired last. The arbitrator rejected the other demands of the workers. He accepted the firing of
the leaders of the strike and rejected the demand that only organized
workers be employed.[102] The workers were extremely disappointed by
the meager results of their struggle. Not only had the arbitrator rejected
some of their most important demands, but the contractor totally ignored the decisions that had been in their favor. Instead, he "argued,
cursed, pressured, incited the police and unchecked, chased away
workers."[103] Thus the struggle of the Arab workers that began in September 1932, and lasted intermittently till the summer of 1933, ended in
failure. There was not enough Histadrut support for a renewed struggle, and the PLL appeared to the workers, as Agassi wrote in his report,
"helpless in relation to the contractor—which indeed we were."[104]
Under threat of dismissal by the contractor, the workers left the PLL and
their organization disintegrated. Aba Houshi wrote in his final report:

> The failure is attributable in large measure to the stance of the Jewish
> workers of Nesher but even more so to the indifference of the Hista-
> drut Executive and its lack of help.[105]

Again, the essential separateness of the Jewish and Arab workers made
joint action extremely difficult. The commitment of the Histadrut Executive to support the strike of the Arab workers was lukewarm. They had
matters that they considered to be of greater moment on hand. The HLC
was unable to exert effective pressure on the Arab contractor, and the
Jewish rank-and-file workers were ambivalent in their support of the
strikers. The good will and guidance of the HLC and of the local Nesher
Workers' Committee was not enough to prevent the Arab workers' defeat. The Jewish workers in the Nesher factory continued to improve
their work conditions during the years of prosperity, 1932–1935, but the
quarry workers were not able to do the same. In March 1936, when the
next strike broke out, the Jewish workers and the Histadrut were no
longer involved. It was the PAWS that led the strike and there was little
intervention or support from the Jewish workers and their institutions.
Its achievements were no better than those of the Histadrut.

Mosaica Tile Factory

Jewish and Arab workers were also involved in joint action at the Volfman Tile Factory—Mosaica. The firm was established in 1923 with ten
workers, five Jewish and five Arab. By 1933, it had expanded to employ

eighty to ninety workers of whom thirty to forty were Arab.[106] The Arab workers were migrants who were employed by Volfman on a more or less permanent basis. In the 1930s, the Jewish workers were members of *Hashomer Hatzair*, a movement on the left of the Jewish labor movement that advocated establishing close relations with Arab workers.[107] They persuaded the PLL to organize Volfman's Arab workers, even though usually the PLL refrained from organizing Arab workers employed by Jewish employers. Thus both the Jewish and the Arab workers were affiliated with the Histadrut. The Jewish workers were, however, full members of the Histadrut and as such enjoyed all the services provided by the HLC, while the Arab workers were members of the PLL and therefore only entitled to a kind of adjunct status.[108]

In November 1935, the Jewish workers, led by a militant workers' committee, went out on strike demanding an end to the frequent delays in the payment of their wages. At this time the Arab workers faced a completely different problem. Some months before, Volfman had leased land from the Jewish National Fund (JNF) in the Haifa Bay industrial zone, to which he planned to move his plant. The JNF obligated its lessees to employ only Jewish labor and Volfman, therefore, intended to fire the Arab workers. The HLC, the PLL, and the Jewish workers in Mosaica were in a quandary. They were strongly committed to the principle of "Jewish Labor" and struggled for its implementation, but they also felt committed to the Arab workers whom they had organized. The Jewish workers of Mosaica, in an attempt to protect the interests of their fellow workers, demanded of the Histadrut to find employment for the Arab workers in the government sector and to ensure that they receive severance pay on their dismissal from Mosaica. These demands of the Jewish workers were motivated both by their solidarity with the fired workers and by their fear that the Arab workers would be won over by the PAWS and its anti-Histadrut stance. It was not the employer, asserted the PAWS, who called for their dismissal but "the Histadrut, the Jewish workers, who were pushing them out in order to take their place."[109]

Volfman refused the demand for severance pay. The HLC and the PLL therefore called on the Arab workers to join the Jewish workers' strike. Some Arab workers joined the strike, others did not. They had hoped that the Histadrut would protect their right, as organized workers, to remain employed by Volfman, and were deeply disappointed by Aba Houshi's refusal to do so. Most chose to complete their last month of work, take their pay, and return to their village.[110] The strike dragged on with all the Jewish and some Arab workers participating. By January 1936, Aba Houshi had negotiated an agreement with Volfman, in which he met the demands of the Jewish workers and gave a vague promise about the future payment of severance pay to the dismissed Arab workers. The HLC did not provide them with alternative employment. The Jewish workers returned to work and moved to the new site where they resumed the wage conflict. The Arab workers, with whom little contact remained, probably returned to their villages. The HLC's clear bias in favor of the Jewish interests made Arab alienation, anger, feelings of betrayal, and separateness inevitable. While the Jewish workers at Volfman's were committed to the well-being of the Arab workers, the separation between them was structured into the conflict. For a time both Jewish and Arab workers did strike together, but it was a dubious case of "togetherness." Arab workers were being dismissed so as to ensure the future employment of Jewish workers and, despite the possible concern of individual Jewish workers, they did not challenge the exclusion.

TO CONCLUDE

Manufacturing in the Jewish sector differed from construction in that its development was far more independent of the Arab economy and society. There was some selling to and buying from the Arab sector, but its impact was minimal. For the most part, Jewish labor was not affected by the availability of cheap Arab labor and its organization and labor tactics were therefore not devised primarily as a response to such a threat. The impact of Jewish colonization and development on Arab industry was, judging from the Haifa experience, more complex. The direct impact was small, but the more diffuse impact was probably far more significant. Arab labor was probably impressed by the daily example of the Jewish industrial workers and the benefits they had been able to secure. Nevertheless, there was little organizational cooperation between Jewish and Arab industrial labor and their organizations. The wealthy Arab elites were no doubt aware of the Jewish industrial development, but they generally did not invest in industry. Other channels of investment were far more accessible and compatible with their needs. The early development of Jewish industry and the formidable competition it posed was, in all likelihood, one of the factors that diverted Arab entrepreneurs into other forms of economic activity. Thus Jewish and Arab industry developed along different paths, seldom crossing each other, and never merging, even fleetingly, as did happen in both commerce and construction.

The separatism of industry, primarily Jewish industry, was in line with the overall strategy of the separation and separateness of the

Jewish settlement: spatially—a separate planned industrial zone; institutionally—a separate Chambers of Commerce and separate labor organizations; and politically—a separate political network of the Zionist movement both in Palestine and in London. As this policy of separate development became more pervasive, other options were closed. Thus joint labor action, in the rare cases when it was deemed necessary or desirable, met with obstacles that made it all but impossible.

Chapter 5

The Haifa Port—
Entering the Gateway

The government sector created new dilemmas for Jewish labor and led to new strategies in the competition of Jewish and Arab workers. Both the dilemmas and the strategies were clearly demonstrated in the labor market of Haifa. Haifa's strategic position led the British to select it as the site for several enterprises that linked Palestine to the rest of the British Empire. The most important of these were the Haifa port and the Palestine Railways. Our main concern in the two following chapters is with the employment policy of the government in these two large enterprises, and the strategies pursued by Jewish labor to enhance its chances of employment. As with the other industries, the issue of employment at the port and the railways reflected the intricate interplay of the political and economic interests in Palestine. Both Jews and Arabs expected the government employment policy to take their interests into account. The Zionist leadership expected the government administration to employ Jewish workers as part of its support for the establishment of a Jewish National Home. The Arabs expected to be preferred as they were the "sons of the land" (*Ibna al-Balad*) and the vast majority of its population. The British, in developing their employment policy, tried to take into account their overall political interests, their specific strategies concerning Arab-Jewish relations, and their economic priorities.

Competition between Jewish and Arab labor in the government sector was unavoidable. Jewish labor had to deal with the problem of gaining access to the market in the face of much cheaper readily available Arab labor. They could not implement the strategy that had worked so successfully in other industries—the closure of the market to cheap Arab labor. There were no grounds for expecting the government, as employer, to close the labor market to Arab workers. This chapter and the next study the ways in which Jewish labor entered the government sector in two industries, both located in Haifa. Chapter 5 deals with the Haifa port and Chapter 6 with the Palestine Railway (PR). Jewish labor pursued very different strategies in these two industries. I shall argue that the different strategies account for the different working relationships that developed between Jewish and Arab workers in each of these workplaces—separation in the Haifa port and cooperation in the PR.

THE HAIFA PORT AND THE ISSUE OF JEWISH LABOR

The Haifa port with its deep-water harbor guarded the gateway of the empire to the east, as well as the approach to the Suez Canal from the north. It also served to link Europe with Palestine and the Middle East, and was the major channel for the movement of both people and cargo.[1] Into its quiet waters, a protected area of some 300 acres between its two new breakwaters, entered the steamers bringing the new Jewish immigrants and their luggage, as well as foodstuffs and manufactured articles.[2] Boats bearing the raw materials needed for the economic development of Palestine, among them coal, wood, and seeds for expressing oil, anchored at its quays.[3] The railways transported the large citrus export from the coastal valley and the potash from the Dead Sea Works to the wharves from where they were loaded onto the ships. Petroleum was shipped to Europe from the terminal of the long Iraqi pipeline and its oil storage installations. The ships of the Royal Navy frequented the harbor.

The port was the hub of the life of the city. Adjacent to the harbor was a reclaimed area of land created by the filling in of a stretch of the sea, while deepening the harbor to the depth of the approximately 10 meters necessary for the use of large modern vessels. On the reclaimed area large roads were paved to facilitate the approach to the port and the activity surrounding it. The railway, extending into the port, ran through the new railway station, Haifa Central, also located on the reclaimed area. Importers and exporters, customs agents, storehouses and bonded warehouses, as well as banks, travel agents, offices, and shops all crowded onto the newly created stretch of land that would soon be an integral part of downtown Haifa.

In 1933, the improved deep-water port opened with a breakwater and sea wall, quays, transit sheds, and lighter moorings. The deep-water quays provided berthing for four regular-sized steamers or five smaller vessels, and the main breakwater provided mooring for some twelve vessels that could be worked by lighters. The depth of the water also enabled the docking of most of the large cruising liners which visited the port during the winter season.[4] The port was equipped with modern appliances for the handling of goods. Bonded warehouse facilities were provided within the harbor area. Customs transit sheds and about 15 acres of open stocking area were also available. Rail access was provided to the transit sheds and to the wharves as was access to road vehicles.[5] Herbert concludes that, despite some shortcomings, "Haifa achieved a first-rate harbour, which became the lynch-pin in the entire regional system of sea and land communication."[6] Within a year it became clear that the port was too small for all the activity in and around it. The opening of the deep-water port stimulated economic activity. This was augmented by the massive wave of Jewish immigration from central Europe that brought unequaled prosperity and growth. The output of the port in 1926, when the original plans for its improvement were drawn up, was 125,000 tons. By 1934, it had increased to 700,000 tons,[7] and to 930,000 by 1935 and 1936.[8] Plans for expanding the port were delayed because of the Arab Rebellion and then because of the Second World War. Some additional quay and storage space was nevertheless provided.

The Haifa port was under the authority of the Department of Customs, Excise and Trade, and its director as of 1924 was K. W. Stead.[9] The work at the port was mainly loading and unloading vessels and organizing and storing cargo. Much of it was contracted out to contractors and subcontractors who were responsible for recruiting, organizing, and remunerating the workers. Initially the Customs Department contracted out its porterage, the bulk of the work of the port, to a contractor. Later the Customs Department took direct responsibility for the customs porterage and for the workers. The Customs also allowed many of the large importers and exporters to be responsible for their own cargo and they usually contracted the work out to the contractors and subcontractors who thrived on the Haifa port. Thus, while many of the workers were employed directly by the government, via the Customs Department, others were employed privately. This distinction between government and private employment, together with the practice of contracting out whole units of work (e.g., coal porterage, citrus porterage, the lighterage or stevedorage of the port), enabled Jewish labor to break into the port employment market, as will be discussed in detail later on in this chapter.

The port was teeming with workers. Between 1,000 to 2,000 workers filled the quays, boats, open storage space, and transit sheds. Their number varied from day to day, season to season, and year to year. The number of workers depended on the number of ships entering or leaving the port on a particular day. The number also varied between the winter and summer seasons and depended on seasonal cargo, especially the winter citrus export. The work at the port also varied from year to year, rising and falling with immigration, political unrest, and war. In January 1935, for example, at the height of the citrus season, the number of workers fluctuated daily from 2,600 to 3,200. During the winter season of 1935, there was an average of 2,450 workers at the port, while in the summer season the number fell to 1,370 workers.[10] By 1936, 1937, and 1938 there were 1,500, 1,900, and 1,850 workers, respectively, in the busy winter season and 1,100, 750, and 970 workers in the summer season.[11]

The work of the port was largely that of loading and unloading. It was hard physical labor, only minimally eased by the equipment available at the time. Most of the work was carried out manually with only one large crane used in special cases. The stevedores loaded and unloaded the cargo directly from the ships' storage onto the lighters or the wharf. The tallymen counted the cargo as it was being loaded and unloaded. The seamen sailed the lighters from the wharf to the ships anchored at a distance when not enough deep-water anchorage was available at the wharf. The porters unloaded the lighters and stored the cargo in the large transit sheds, carried the citrus crates from the railway cars to the ships, and moved the cargo that the stevedores had unloaded into the storage space. Other workers at the port included the maintenance workers, the customs police, the immigration police, and the clerical workers of the Customs Department and the transit sheds.

The work of the port was a labor-intensive, strenuous process, carried out by an extremely varied workforce. The workers were usually organized into groups controlled by foremen, *ra'isim*, subcontractors, and contractors. A keen observer could easily identify the interrelation between the organization of labor, the nature of the labor process, and the composition of the labor force. Dr. Vidra, the head of the Sea Department of the Jewish Agency, elaborated on the relation between the contracting out of porterage, the nonmechanized means of work, and the employment of Hourani workers. In his letter to the Labor Department of the Jewish Agency he wrote:

> The official porterage of the Haifa Port has been in the hands of the Palestine government for just over a year. Before that, the porterage was in the hands of an Arab contractor, who employed subcontractors,

each of whom was responsible for his team of workers. Naturally, these contractors, including the major contractor, wanted to make the maximal profit. They thus refrained from employing workers from Haifa who demanded a higher wage than the rural porters. When the rural porters also demanded higher wages, the contractors introduced Hourani porters in increasing numbers. Among the Houranis there was also a rapid turnover, as the contractors preferred to employ the newly arrived, whom they paid 8 to 10 grush [piaster, 80–100 mils—D.B.] for an unlimited workday. Except for primitive carts, little equipment was used. As in ancient times the porter carried the crate or sack on his back for 200 or 300 meters. The primitive carts were pushed by hand by tens of porters, and in the winter were likely to sink into the deep mud.

This primitive manner of work required a large number of workers. If a ship arrived in the middle of the day, and had to unload its cargo, the contractor would not take on new workers so as not to lower his profits. Instead he would transfer some of his workers from whatever they were doing to the new ship. As no equipment was used which could increase productivity when required without adding new workers, every increase in the regular work caused a standstill in the port, and ships would wait for days to be unloaded.

To improve conditions at the port the government took on the responsibility for the porterage. It was hoped that the government would bring machinery and mechanize the work process. These hopes were disappointed. The government carried on with the same primitive system which had been used by the Arab contractors. It employed mainly Hourani and Egyptian porters, rejected any Jewish porter and retained the subcontractors, but this time at a regular wage.[12]

Thus Dr. Vidra argued that the absence of mechanization led to the employment of the cheapest workers, the Houranis, to the detriment of both Palestinian Arab and Jewish workers. This was indeed the case. In April 1934, two-thirds of the regular and casual porters employed by the customs contractors and three-quarters of those employed by subcontractors were Houranis.[13] In November 1936, when customs was under direct government control, two-thirds were still Hourani workers, the rest were Egyptians, and there was only a small minority of Palestinian workers.

Jewish labor was determined to break into this cheap, labor-intensive workplace. The Zionist leadership and the Haifa Jewish leadership recognized the importance of the port for the future of the Jewish community. The Jewish settlement in Palestine was closely linked to the Jewish community in Europe from which it received its vital resources of manpower, capital, and, eventually, arms. It wanted to secure some Jewish presence in the port to ensure the flow of these resources and to eliminate the danger of Arab control and possible blockade. Furthermore, the Haifa port was a major source of employment. In the 1920s, before the deep-water anchorage and when only the old piers of the late Ottoman Period were used, Jewish labor tried to enter the port labor force. Small groups of workers were temporarily employed, but were unable to compete with the much cheaper Arab workers.[14] The construction of the deep-water port between 1928 and 1933, and the greatly expanded activity within the port, provided work for hundreds, often thousands, of workers. Jewish labor, so vulnerable to the sharp fluctuations of the Palestine economy and to recurring bouts of unemployment, resolved to secure a "fair share" of this bounty.

When construction began on the new deep-water port, the Zionist leadership tried to define what constituted a "fair share" of jobs for Jewish workers. Chaim Weitzman, the president of the WZO, turned to no less a personage than the Under-Secretary of State for the Colonies, Mr. Ormsby-Gore:

> On the assumption that it will be agreed that a fair proportion of Jewish labour should be employed, the question arises as to what a fair proportion would be. It may be suggested that the proportion should correspond to the ratio of Jews to the total population of Palestine. The Executive are strongly of the opinion that this formula has no application to the present case and would give the Jews much less than their due. As has already been pointed out, the Jews have in the past received considerably less than their fair share of the employment provided by Government and municipal public works. It has also been pointed out that the Jews have contributed, and will continue to contribute, out of all proportion to their numbers to the revenue charged with the service of the loan from which the harbour-works are being financed. There is, moreover, this highly material consideration that the Jews include at least fifty per cent of the workers dependent for their livelihood on industrial labour of the type now required. In these circumstances, the Executive feel justified in asking that the contractors be clearly given to understand that they will be expected to employ Jewish labour to the extent of about fifty per cent.[15]

In his letter to the Under-Secretary of State, Weitzman suggested three criteria by which to determine the share of jobs to be given to Jewish labor. First, the proportion of Jews in the population of Palestine; second, the proportion of government revenue coming from the Jewish community; and third, the proportion of Jewish workers of all wage labor. Each of these criteria would have led to different results. The proportion of Jews in the population of Palestine was approximately 17 percent.[16] Their proportion of government revenue has been calulated by economists as being approximately 38 percent in 1926–27, and 64 percent in 1935–36.[17] And the proportion of Jewish workers in the wage labor of Palestine was assessed at approximately 50 percent.[18] Weitzman clearly preferred the 50 percent criterion.

These Jewish demands were strongly opposed by the Arabs, who stated their own interests and demands. The Jews argued that they were not receiving their proper share in government works and in fact were hardly employed in government works at all. The Arab press and labor spokesmen repeatedly claimed that preference was being given to Jewish labor.[19] The Jews, as Weitzman's letter stressed, argued that their share of employment in government works should be determined by their relative contribution to government revenue and by their proportion of all wage labor. The Arabs rejected both criteria. They claimed that the only criterion should be relative proportion of each group in the population of Palestine. That in itself was considered a concession, as the Arabs did not recognize the legitimacy of Jewish immigration into Palestine and the legitimacy of their increased share of the population.[20]

The hopes and expectations of the Jewish community concerning the development of the Haifa port were met by hesitation and ambivalence on the part of the Arab elite. They argued that the Jews would enjoy most of the labor opportunities created by the construction and functioning of the Haifa port, while the Arab population would be burdened with the repayment of the loan with which the port would be constructed.[21]

During the lengthy debate in the British parliament concerning the Palestine and East Africa loan, and the conditions under which it would be granted, the Arab press published numerous articles opposing the loan.[22] Once the decision had been taken, the emphasis in the Arab press shifted to ensuring the employment rights of the Arabs in the new projects that the loan would finance. Since over half of the total sum was earmarked for the construction of the Haifa port, it became the focus of this concern.[23] The Arab press demanded that the Arabs get their share of the unskilled jobs as well as of the professional and managerial positions, over which the British themselves retained a near monopoly.[24]

Thus the employment of Jewish labor in the construction and functioning of the Haifa port was a complex issue in which political and economic considerations were intricately related. For the Jewish leadership, the demand for the employment of Jewish labor was as much political as economic. Its goal was to ensure a Jewish presence in a strategic position and to gain a new source of employment for Jewish immigrants. The Arabs saw such employment as an additional step in reinforcing the Jewish position in Palestine at the expense of their legitimate rights and therefore opposed it. The British, for their part, acknowledged the political interest of the Jewish community in obtaining a foothold in the Haifa port, but were not willing to bear the cost of the more expensive Jewish workers.

The problem of the difference between the wage expected by the Jewish workers and the economic priorities of the government had to be solved before Jewish workers could be employed in significant numbers. The specific work practices at the Haifa port, whereby some of the work was farmed out to private contractors, facilitated a solution. Many of those using the services of the port were Jewish importers and exporters, some of whom were willing to agree to the employment of Jewish labor by the contractors who carried out their work. The ability of Jewish workers to take advantage of such subcontracting opportunities, as a result of organizational, social, and political factors, is the main story of this chapter.

THE LABOR FORCE OF THE HAIFA PORT — MAJOR TRENDS

Over the decade of the 1930s, the activity in the port increased dramatically. We do not have detailed information about the 1920s, but it seems fair to assume that then too there was some growth.[25] But the most significant change occurred after the opening of the deep-water port, in October 1933. The tonnage loaded and unloaded increased by close to 50 percent in one year and the size of the labor force more than doubled, from 720 workers in the busy season of 1932–33 to 1,670 workers in the first busy season after the opening of the new port (1933–34). In the following two years, from 1933–34 to 1935–36, all indicators show continued growth. This was due not only to the opening of the deep-sea port, but also to the large Jewish immigration and to the general prosperity that ensued. The tonnage of both imported and exported cargo increased. The labor force also increased steadily from year to year and the number of Jewish workers grew numerically and proportionately. Thereafter, in the following two years, 1936–37 to 1938–39, the wave of Jewish immigration from central Europe became significantly smaller and the tonnage of cargo unloaded in the Haifa port dropped. Cargo leaving the port continued to grow, probably due to the growing citrus export.[26] During these years, the years of the

Table 5.1. Cargo and Employment in the Haifa Port, 1930–1939

Year	Cargo[a] Unloading	Loading	Labor Force Total	Arabs	Jews	% Jews
1930	174.8	61.4	n.d.			
1931/32[b] and 1932[c]	n.d.	n.d.	578 (1)	520	58	10
1932/33 and 1933	401.4	71.6	721 (2)	625	96	13
1933/34 and 1934	589.2	99.7	1,671 (3)	1,503	168	10
1934/35 and 1935	787.3	138.4	2,300 (4)	1,980	320	14
1935/36 and 1936	756.7	165.0	2,833 (5)	2,355	478	17
1936/37 and 1937	698.4	296.4	1,875 (6)	1,147	729	39
1937/38 and 1938	502.8	291.4	1,850 (7)	850	1,000	54
1938/39 and 1939	653.1	343.1	2,300 (8)	1,000	1,300	56.5

a. Cargo in 000 metric tons, from Gertz, *Statistical Handbook,* 280.
b. The figures present employment during the busy season, beginning in November of one year through April of the next year.
c. The figures present the cargo during the whole year—January to December.
Sources:
(1) Letter of HLC to the Political Department of Jewish Agency, 30 December, 1931. CZA,S8/2734.
(2) Letter of HLC to David Ben Gurion, 17 January 1933. LA, IV 208-1-608.
(3) Letter of HLC to the Political Department of JA, 19 April 1934. LA, IV 208-1-608.
(4) Letter of HLC to the Immigration Department of JA, 9 January, 1935. LA, IV 208-1-788B.
(5) List of Workers in All Branches of Work in the Haifa Port, 25 January 1936. LA, IV 208-1-788A.
(6) Letter from Vidra of the JA to Meirovitz of the Histadrut Executive, 3 February 1937. CZA, S9/1135.
(7) Data of Jewish and Arab Workers in the Haifa Port, 21 July 1938. LA, IV 250-27-2-322.
(8) Vidra to Meirovitz, 18 December 1938. CZA, S9/1132.

Arab Rebellion and the depression, the labor force decreased and its composition changed dramatically. The number and proportion of Jewish workers increased and the number of Arab workers decreased sharply.

A comparison of the composition of the labor force one year before the Arab Rebellion, in 1934, and during the Rebellion, in 1937, illustrates the change that took place. In that period the Jewish workforce increased from 168 workers to 1,147 and from 10 percent of the total port labor force to 39 percent. During this short period of three years, hundreds of Jewish porters and stevedores joined the workforce. How could this happen at a time when Arab workers, primarily the cheap and hardworking Houranis, were easily available? To answer this question, we will examine the growth of the Jewish workforce in two major activities of the port—citrus porterage and the government custom's porterage.

EXPORTING THE CITRUS CRATES

Citrus was Palestine's largest export. No other reached even 10 percent of its value. Most went to the United Kingdom and a smaller amount was exported to other European countries.[27] Every year more citrus groves were planted.[28] In 1922, there were 10,000 dunams of citrus plantations owned by Jews and 19,000 dunams owned by Arabs. By 1930, Jews owned 60,000 dunams and Arabs 46,000. Nine years later the area had more than doubled to 155,000 dunams under Jewish ownership and 144,000 dunams under Arab ownership.[29] The quantities of citrus exported increased accordingly, as can be seen in Table 5.2. There are no figures specifying the relative share of Jewish and Arab citrus growers until 1930. One can assume that the Jewish share fell well below one-third, as the area owned by Jews was both smaller and more recently planted.

The export of citrus had a major impact on the Haifa port, especially after 1930 when most of it was exported from Haifa rather than Jaffa. The citrus export determined the busy season of the Haifa port. From November through April, the months of the citrus export, approximately twice as many workers were employed than in the quiet summer season.[30] Citrus was thus the export that accounted for many of the jobs and in which Jewish ownership was prominent. It naturally became a major target for Jewish labor, and indeed, the number of Jewish laborers employed in citrus porterage did increase sharply.

Table 5.2 shows that during the 1930s there was a major change in the number of Jewish workers engaged in citrus porterage. During the first half of the decade, the number of Jewish workers employed as porters by Jewish citrus exporters oscillated between 30 and 70—a small proportion of the citrus porters employed by the large Jewish exporters.[31] During the second half of the decade, the number of Jewish porters increased to between 300 and 400. They had gained full control of the porterage of the Jewish owned citrus export.

This dramatic change was brought about by the initiatives of the HLC. As soon as the citrus was directed, in large quantities, to the Haifa port, around 1930, the HLC approached the two large citrus exporting companies—Pardess and the Syndicate of the Jaffa Oranges, known as "the Syndicate" and requested-demanded that they employ Jewish workers. Their central offices were in Jaffa and they were both managed by prominent Jewish public figures of whom the most influential were Yitzhak Rokah and Shmuel Tolkovski.[32] At first the HLC played a primarily mediating role. It distributed the work provided by the exporters to the workers, supplying the exporters with workers

Table 5.2. Citrus Export—Cargo and Workers, 1930/31–1938/39

Year	Cargo (1) no. of cases	Percentage of Jewish exporters	Jewish workers in Jewish-owned export	Jewish workers as a percentage of Jewish export
			Workers	
1930/31	2,500,000	37	n.d.	40-50
1931/32 (2)	3,700,000	37	n.d.	n.d.
1932/33 (3)	4,500,000	48	30	n.d.
1933/34 (4)	5,530,000	51	70	n.d.
1934/35 (4)	7,334,000	58	n.d.	n.d.
1935/36 (4)	5,900,000	60	50–100 (5)	n.d.
1936/37 (4)	10,800,000	60	300–320	85
1937/38 (4)	11,400,000	60	320–400	90+
1938/39 (6)	15,260,000	65	425–450	100

Sources:
(1) Gertz, *Statistical Handbook*, 180.
(2) Aba Houshi to Citrus Bureau, 10 August 1932, LA, IV 250-27-1-295.
(3) HLC to Ben Gurion, 17 January 1933, LA, IV 208-1-608.
(4) HLC, Jewish workers in the Haifa port, 1934–38, LA, IV 250-27-2-322.
(5) The figure of 100 Jewish workers in citrus porterage was given in Aba Houshi's report, 25 January 1936, LA, IV 208-1-788A.
(6) HLC, Hebrew Labor in the Haifa Port, for 1936–40.

and the workers with employment. Later the HLC increased its involvement, and organized the execution of the work assignment. It organized the labor force, determined the labor process, and took full responsibility for the execution of the work serving as a contractor. In 1930–31, the HLC negotiated an agreement with the large Jewish citrus exporters, by which 40–50 percent of the porterage was allocated to Jewish labor. At the time, Muhammad Kamil Namura was the chief contractor of porterage in the Haifa port. All work was allocated to him and he subcontracted it to others. Exploiting this arrangement, the HLC subcontracted 40–50 percent of the work from Hajj Namura, and employed Jewish workers, members of the Histadrut. Namura subcontracted the rest of the work to Arab contractors, who employed mostly Hourani workers. The pay in the citrus porterage was based on a piece rate system. The rate paid by the Jewish exporters to the HLC, in its capacity as a contractor, was 1 mil per crate. This was slightly higher than the rate paid per crate to the Arab subcontractors. It was nevertheless still a very low rate, kept low by the abundance of Hourani workers available to the Arab subcontractors. The HLC calculated that efficient organization would offset the low piece rate and enable the Jewish workers to make a decent wage. This did not happen. During the citrus export seasons of 1930–31 and 1931–32, the Jewish workers earned 120–160 mils per day, well below the norm for unskilled Jewish workers. The division of the cargo between Jewish and Arab workers, argued Aba Houshi, was at the heart of the problem. Because every transport was divided between both groups of workers, there was never enough work for either at any given time. The workers thus all stayed at the port for ten to fourteen hours, dividing the different transports between them, earning a small amount for a very long day of work. Confrontations between the Jewish and Arab workers were frequent as there were more and less desired timings and locations to quarrel over.[33] Aba Houshi proposed alternative arrangements but these were rejected by the exporters and as a result the Jewish workers' share dropped.

The HLC searched for other ways to increase the employment of Jewish workers. Aba Houshi decided to look for experienced Jewish workers who would be able to improve the level of efficiency and productivity. He found such workers in the port of Saloniki. He visited Saloniki several times during 1933 to select Jewish port workers for immigration to Palestine, and convinced the Political Department of the Jewish Agency to allot them immigration certificates.[34]

Another strategy pursued by the HLC to increase the number of Jewish workers in the port was the establishment of a company that would carry out work received on contract. In April 1934, a partnership was formed called Manoff (Hebrew for crane) with three Haifa residents as private investors[35] and two representatives of Histadrut institutions.[36] The firm was to carry out all types of work in the port—porterage, stevedorage, and lightering, and to accept work on contract from government institutions, companies, and private individuals.[37] Manoff initially employed about sixty porters and twenty stevedores, all of whom had immigrated from Saloniki. The company dealt mainly with the porterage and stevedorage of private Jewish enterprises and individual merchants. In the citrus export season of 1934–35, Manoff handled the share of the citrus porterage allocated to Jewish labor.[38] The partnership was dissolved at the end of 1935. The work conditions were difficult. Many of the Jewish traders and customs agents still engaged Arab contractors and many of the workers from Saloniki were tempted by the higher wages of the private market at the time of prosperity.[39] After the liquidation of Manoff, the HLC set up a special department in its labor exchange to deal with port matters.

Before the citrus season of 1936–37, the HLC again asked the citrus exporting companies to allow it to handle their whole citrus transport.

Conditions had changed since late 1932. The HLC had acquired much experience in the work of the port. Its workers were more proficient and better organized. They had also developed ties with some of the Arab contractors. Abdullah Abu-Zeid, the largest and most influential contractor for stevedores and seamen, was the most important of these. Even more critical was the change in political circumstances. The Arab Rebellion and general strike broke out in April 1936. The strike spread slowly, mainly in the eastern sections of Haifa, but the port continued to function as before. The following month strong pressure was exerted on the Arab workers to join the strike and close down the port, the major gateway to Palestine. On the 13th of May 1936, a delegation of the Supreme Arab Council, headed by the Mufti Hajj Amin al-Husseini, came to Haifa to meet with the heads of the seamen, stevedores, and porters and to persuade them, through promises and threats, to bring the work to a stop.[40] The knowledge that the port authorities could easily substitute Jewish workers and other Arab workers for the strikers kept the *ra'isim* at work. Abu Zeid, Aba Houshi's personal friend, played a major role in resisting the pressure to strike.[41] The port remained open and functioning. Only during August 1936, after several assassinations and more threats of terror, did the Arab contractors and their workers stay away from work. But, since Jewish workers were quick to take their places, the Arab workers returned to work within ten to twelve days.[42]

At the end of the summer of 1936, the Haifa port was handling more cargo than it had before the strike, since the Jaffa port had closed down. Arab workers filled the docks as before and Jews and Arabs worked within the port with few outright clashes. Nevertheless, tensions mounted, and the separation between the Jewish and Arab economic sectors deepened. Many Jewish importers and exporters, who had previously turned down Jewish workers, now hired them. Within these changed circumstances the HLC negotiated with the citrus exporting companies to have all citrus porterage handed over to it, taking full responsibility for the execution of the work. After lengthy negotiations, the two large exporting companies, Pardess and Syndicate, were willing to put the HLC to the test. At the beginning of the export season of 1936–37, during the months of October and November, half a million crates were entrusted to the HLC on condition that it employ a significant percentage of Arab workers.[43] The work was carried out to the satisfaction of the exporters who then agreed to entrust approximately 85 percent of the citrus export of that season to the HLC. Despite the previous experience of the HLC, work on such a scale was still a serious challenge, as Aba Houshi wrote later:

Figure 8. Jewish citrus porters, Haifa port, 1937.

The conditions of work were very difficult. Most of the workers were inexperienced, the hours were unlimited (time of work had to be adapted to the movement of trains and ships which was irregular), the wage which had been acceptable to the Arab and Hourani workers for years was not adequate for the Jewish worker. The very fact that Jewish organized workers were doing work previously carried out by Houranis . . . all this created serious difficulties. But, in spite of it all, the work was carried out to the full satisfaction of the exporting companies and of the management of the port, and was seen as a great achievement for organized Jewish labor.[44]

The workers, over 300 of them, were organized in teams. Teams of eight workers unloaded the crates from the railway cars into the transit sheds, while teams of ten loaded the crates onto the ships. Work was organized according to a day shift and a night shift. This limited the number of hours workers spent waiting around the port. The following season, 1937–38, the Jewish exporters had few hesitations and over ninety percent of Jewish citrus export was handled by the HLC. It employed about 320 workers who were organized in thirty-seven teams. Most worked for five to six months.[45] It was a period of unemployment and many workers from all sectors of the Jewish labor force turned to the Port Department of the HLC Labor Exchange. Among them were the veteran workers from Saloniki, members of kibbutzim from the Haifa area, unemployed members of different trade unions,[46] Technion students, and workers who did not belong to the Histadrut.[47]

The wages were satisfactory. The pay differed from team to team and was divided equally within each team. The experienced Saloniki workers earned the highest wage, which was about 13.500 £P per worker, per month (or 500–550 mils per day). Most other teams earned between 6 to 10 pounds a month (250–400 mils per day).[48] Two tenured and one temporary foreman and an accountant supervised the work. The tenured foremen earned 25 £P per month—between two to three times that of the Jewish porters.The temporary foreman earned 10 £P per month, and the accountant 14 £P.[49]

During the following season of 1938–39, the HLC continued to manage the citrus export of the Jewish sector. By this time it employed 400–425 workers. Thus, within three to four seasons, the Jewish-owned citrus porterage had gone over to Jewish labor, despite the availability of cheaper Hourani workers. The contractual system enabled the HLC to play a crucial role in determining the employment of Jewish workers. The HLC did not serve solely, or even primarily, as the representative, or the trade union, of the Jewish workers employed in the port. It served a multiplicity of interrelated capacities—to recruit the workers, to subcontract the work, to manage it, and to determine the conditions of pay. The organizational power gained by the HLC during the 1920s and 1930s enabled it to take on itself this multiple role. The Jewish exporting companies, in turn, were willing to accept such intervention by the HLC as long as it functioned efficiently and entailed no economic loss to them.

IN THE CUSTOMS TRANSIT SHED

Customs porterage was a major part of the work at the port. Initially almost all ingoing and outgoing cargo was transported under the aegis of the Customs Department. As the amount of the cargo increased after the opening of the deep-water port, many of the large importers and exporters were free to employ private contractors and porters. The Customs Department was still responsible for a fair share of the cargo and for the employment of a large proportion of the workers. In 1931,

90 percent of all the port's porterage was carried out by the Customs Department. The Department employed 80 to 100 Arab and 16 Jewish porters in the quiet season, and 200–250 Arab and 30–35 Jewish porters in the busy winter season.[50] After the opening of the deep-water port and the introduction of private porterage, the proportion of workers employed by the Customs Department declined to approximately one-half of the porters of the Haifa port. At the same time, the number of workers employed by the Customs Department was continually increasing as a result of the overall growth in cargo. Thus the Customs employed as many as 500–750 workers, all Arabs, with the number oscillating between the busy and the quiet seasons.[51] Until 1935, all customs porterage was handed over, by tender, on a three-year basis, to one large contractor, who handled all employment. From 1935 onwards, the Customs Department employed the porters directly.

The Jewish leadership made recurring attempts to have Jewish workers employed by the Customs Department. Between 1933 and 1936, the HLC brought in experienced porters from Saloniki, as noted earlier, who had won a fine reputation and were able to earn a fair wage in private porterage. The Customs Department promised a minimum monthly wage of 8 to 9 pounds, but it frequently paid less. In September 1933, Aba Houshi complained to the Director of the Customs Department, K. W. Stead, that the contractors Hajj Namura and Abu Abdullah were not abiding by the wage agreement and were paying only a maximum of 5.800£P. In addition the Jewish porters were subjected to constant harassment.[52] The Saloniki porters eventually left the customs porterage for the better paying private porterage.[53]

Since the Jewish porters, even the experienced ones from Saloniki, were unable to make what Jewish workers considered an adequate wage under the prevailing tariffs, the HLC proposed a change in the system of pay. It proposed that Jewish workers be paid at a piece rate, rather than on a daily basis. In 1936, with unemployment on the increase, the HLC and the Jewish Agency, aided by the Histadrut Executive, tried to impress upon K. W. Stead that Jewish porters were, indeed, capable of "fulfilling their duties in a satisfactory and efficient manner,"[54] and could earn an adequate wage if they were paid by a piece-rate system. Since tension between Arabs and Jews was mounting, the administration was loath to take any step that would aggravate matters. The Chief Secretary therefore rejected the proposal put forward by the Histadrut Executive and the Jewish Agency: "H.E. [His Excellency—D.B.] is satisfied, after careful examination of the Agency's proposal, that it would not be practicable to introduce a system of piece work at Haifa."[55] He added, somewhat ironically, that there would be no difficulty in arranging for the employment of Jewish labor in ordinary porterage and saloon porterage at current rates of pay, on the understanding that laborers who had proved unsatisfactory would not be re-employed.

Despite the curt rejection of the Chief Secretary, within six to eight months the principle of a piece-rate system for Jewish labor was accepted. An agreement had been negotiated, and its final details were being ironed out. It is likely that the outbreak of the Arab Rebellion and the general strike, with the threat to the smooth functioning of the port, made the difference, though this is not stated specifically in any of the records. The Histadrut, through its contracting company Solel Boneh, was to receive part of the customs porterage on contract. Solel Boneh would be responsible for all aspects of the work and the labor force—providing necessary equipment, recruiting, supervising, and remunerating the workers. The Customs Department would pay Solel Boneh 90 percent of what it received from the owners of the cargo and would keep 10 percent. Thus the Customs Department risked no loss from the employment of Jewish workers. Solel Boneh would have to make ends meet. It would have to cover the cost of carrying out the work, of paying the customs its 10 percent, and of paying the workers at the rate acceptable to Jewish workers. Any losses would be borne by Solel Boneh and not by the government authority.

Once the principle of contractual work for Jewish labor on a piece-rate basis was accepted, there were still numerous details to settle. Arab opposition to the introduction of Jewish labor, especially in the aftermath of the general strike, caused much apprehension among the British officials. They therefore tried to establish as clear a separation as possible between Jewish and Arab labor. This was no simple task within the limited and crowded area of the port. Jewish workers were allotted a separate transit shed—number 5—which had just been built. Since Arab workers had not worked there before, the British officials hoped they would not feel that work that they had done previously was being handed over to Jewish workers. There were also negotiations concerning the nature of the cargo that would be handed over to the Jewish porters, its quantity and quality. Each of these issues was a focus of contention. As late as ten days before the Jewish porters were to begin work, Moshe Shertok, head of the Political Department of the Jewish Agency, wrote to K. W. Stead:

> It was my intention to write and thank you for the patience and help-
> fulness which you have shown in the long and intricate discussions
> which have been in progress regarding the introduction of Jewish la-

bour into porterage work at Haifa on a piece-rate basis. . . . You will, therefore, understand how keenly disappointed I was on learning that the offer finally conveyed to our representatives referred only to a portion of general cargo, relegated moreover to a distant shed which may not even be used during the summer, whenever all the ships arriving can be accommodated along the quay. Originally it was contemplated that the Jewish group should handle, in addition to that portion of general cargo, also iron and oil-seeds. These two categories have now disappeared. The volume of work now offered is definitely unrepresentative. Apart from the question of quality, the quantity of the work has shrunk from the original 30% to about 10% of the total imports unloaded at Haifa.[56]

Arab opposition was more articulate than ever. They resented the increase of Jewish labor in private porterage, as many of the Jewish importers and exporters had handed over their work to Jewish porters. At the time that negotiations concerning the customs porterage were being concluded, the private import of cattle had also been transferred to Jewish labor. The Jewish representatives used the riots to justify these changes and thus put the blame on the Arabs. The Arabs felt that the work in the port was slipping away from them and that they were losing ground on all fronts. They attempted to dissuade the port officials from further changes by threats of violence,[57] by numerous memoranda, and by direct personal appeals. Dr. Vidra reported the content of a letter, which he chanced to see, sent by the four chief porters to the senior officials of the Haifa port. They opposed the increased number of Jewish workers in the port, the proposed introduction of Jewish workers to the customs porterage, and, above all, they objected to the superior work conditions being offered them. The letter, as summarized by Dr. Vidra, stated:

> There are already 800 Jews and only 600 Arabs working in the port. In the reclaimed area there are almost only Jewish workers. They rule the port. We heard that you were about to hand over customs porterage to the Jews, and especially to grant a Jewish contractor the unloading of metal and wood, the most profitable work in the port. If you would want to give us the remaining work, we would not be able to accept your offer as that would involve loss. One hundred workers can arrange the unloading of 500 tons of metal in one day, earning 350 mils a day per worker. If you have to take on Jews, then only on a daily basis, earning the same wage as we do, and working under our management. Otherwise there will be conflict and the work will suffer badly. We could not then be responsible for work and order.[58]

In a meeting between K. W. Stead and the major Arab contractors and chief porters, which took place shortly after the letter was sent, Stead inquired whether the introduction of Jewish workers would be detrimental to the work itself, to which the chief porters answered:

> Of course. The Jews are not good porters and could not carry out the work as well as the Arabs. If the Jews were to work together with the Arabs, for the wage of 160 mils per day, as the Arabs do, under the same management, then possibly the work could be organized without interruptions and disorder. It would be extemely unfair to hand over the work to the Jews, by contract, after we put our lives at risk during the strike [the Arab general strike of 1936—D.B.]. If anyone should be given work by contract it is us.[59]

Despite the opposition to the employment of Jewish workers by the Customs Department, and despite violent clashes at the gates of the port on the first day of their employment, the agreement was put into effect.[60] The Jewish workers were concentrated at the Cargo Jetty Shed and the open dump area adjacent to it. Their work consisted mainly of unloading cargo from the lighters into the transit shed, and loading it on to trains and trucks for delivery outside the port. At the conclusion of the citrus export season, with the decline in the number of the citrus exporting ships, room became available at the quays for the importing vessels and the lighters were used less. This reduced the work initially provided for the Jewish workers. They were therefore put to work handling general import cargo directly from the steamers on the main quay, where a special section was allocated to them.

During the first few months the new porters found the work extremely difficult. As Aba Houshi acknowledged, they were hardly used to hauling sacks of 160 kilos and piling them 22 sacks high.[61] "It is found," wrote F. O. Rogers, the British manager of the Haifa port, "that the Jewish porters are unwilling to carry loads—that is, strictly speaking, to act as porters—endeavoring as far as possible to effect all the transportation of goods from point to point by mechanical means.[62] These means, mainly tractors and carts, were provided by Solel Boneh and purchased with the financial aid of the Jewish Agency.[63]

The fluctuations in the daily workload, typical of all ports, caused additional difficulties. Such fluctuations hindered the equitable distribution of labor and income among the workers. Employment of a relatively large number of workers, necessary for those days when the workload was heavy, would leave some with no work on days when the work was less. Such an option would either lower the income of all workers, or differentiate between regular workers, employed on all days, and casuals employed only when additional workers were called for. If small and regular teams of workers were employed, they would avoid the phenomenon of casualization, but would cause delays when the workload was heavy, and—as Rogers pointed out—increase the extent of casual labor among the Arab porters who would be called in to handle the excess cargo.[64]

Despite these difficulties, the Jewish workers, Solel Boneh, and the port officials persevered. By the end of the first year the High Commissioner, Arthur Wauchope, wrote to (no less than) the Secretary of State for the Colonies, Ormsby-Gore, that "Jewish labour has successfully adapted itself to the requirements of the porterage work in the port and the arrangements now appear to be working satisfactorily"[65] Both F. O. Rogers and Aba Houshi attested to the significant improvement in the proficiency of the Jewish workers, their level of pay, and the cost to the port. The Jewish porters of the Customs Department handled more and more general cargo. By the second half of 1937 they were handling 20 percent of the port's cargo—doubling their original workload. Their modernized mechanical equipment, which included tractors, trolley carts, and lorries, raised their productivity.[66] They worked in loading from and to the ships and the lighters. They were, however, excluded from the portering of iron and craned goods as these had to be handled at a particular point in the port and could not be moved to the section allotted to the Jewish workers. "It was not desired," wrote Rogers, "that the Jewish porters should intermingle with the Arab porters but should work separately as a body."[67]

A striking feature of the second half of 1937, wrote F .O. Rogers, was the acceptance of casualization by the Jewish porters.[68] The number of workers fluctuated from day to day to a far greater extent than had been acceptable during the initial period, adapting to the rhythm of work of the port. Thus, for example, in the first two weeks of October 1937, the average number of Jewish porters employed daily was 111, but the actual number working each day fluctuated between 40 to 179 men. Rogers speculated that the Jewish porters accepted casualization because of the severe unemployment in Haifa and not because of a change of heart. "The Jewish labourers and their leaders," he stated, "strongly dislike casualisation, and I am sure that the restoration of the normal demand for labour in the Haifa district will immediately result in inability to obtain Jewish labourers for casual employment on porterage, as was the experience before general unemployment became so acute as it is at present."[69]

The income of the porters increased significantly. During the initial

period, from January to June 1937, the average income of the Jewish
porters was 212 mils per day, far less than that stipulated by organized
Jewish labor. By the second half of 1937 the average wage had reached
350 mils.[70] Despite the increased wages, the government's profit from
Jewish porterage was higher than its profit from the work of the Arab
porters. The agreement between the port authority and Solel Boneh ensured it a 10 percent profit, while Arab porterage brought the port a
profit of 5.2 percent during the same period.[71]

Rogers concluded his report with praise:

> It is a pleasure to record the advance in proficiency in the porterage
> operations attained by the Jewish porters. With greater experience
> their knowledge of the best way to set about the various jobs has in-
> creased, their manual and physical dexterity is greater and their en-
> durance has developed. The regular porters consist mostly of young
> men in their early twenties of slight build and of studious appearance;
> and the beneficial results of their ten months hard work are as marked
> as their efforts and determination have been praiseworthy.[72]

Jewish labor in customs' porterage continued along the same lines.
One hundred to 140 Jewish workers were employed each year. They
constituted a relatively small portion of the porters of the Customs Department, and an even smaller proportion of all the Jewish workers in
the port, as can be seen in Table 5.3. They resented the poor work conditions and the wages paid by Solel Boneh, which were lower than
those in the Jewish market.[73] Indeed, when more bountiful opportunities became available, Solel Boneh had difficulty in supplying workers.[74] Nevertheless, from the standpoint of Jewish labor, the carefully
negotiated scheme that had taken into account both economic and political considerations was most successful. In practice, the handling of
general cargo at transit shed no. 5 became the point of entry into customs porterage in general. From there the Jewish workers moved on to
unloading timber and then to the unloading of coal, which had for
years been the monopoly of the contractor Far'un and his Egyptian
workers. They also hauled and loaded the heavy sacks of potash manufactured at the Dead Sea Works and exported from Haifa.[75] The successful integration of the Jewish worker into the Customs Department
resulted from the Histadrut's perspicacity in exploiting the contract
system of the port and the institutional infrastructure of the Jewish
community. The Histadrut and the HLC negotiated the agreements,
the HLC recruited the workers, Solel Boneh organized and supervised
the work, the Jewish Agency provided mechanized equipment, and

Table 5.3. Jewish Porters in Customs Porterage (C.P.)

Year	Number of Jewish workers	Percentage of Jews among customs porters	Percentage of Jewish customs porters of all Jews working in port
1937[a](1)	120	20%	10.2%
1938(1)	120	30%	8.5%
1939(1)	120	35%	11.2%
1940(1)	100	50%	30.8%
1941(2)	110	20% (3)	19.7%
1942(2)	141	n.d.	16.9%

a. Including the citrus export of autumn/winter 1937–38, similarly in following years.
Sources:
(1) HLC, Hebrew Work in the Haifa Port, 1936–40, 17 March 1941. CZA, S9/1132.
(2) Letter of HLC to Statistics Department of the Histadrut Executive, 18 January 1942. LA, IV 208 - 1-2774.
(3) Dr. Vidra to Meirovitz, 17 November 1941. CZA, S9/1132

the political leadership interceded with the Director of the Customs Department, the Port Manager, the High Commissioner, senior British officials, and even the Secretary of State for the Colonies.

I have described the introduction of Jewish labor to the citrus export and to the customs porterage in some detail in order to illustrate the major strategies and means by which Jewish labor succeeded in breaking into the port labor market. It is the most successful example of Jewish labor penetrating a government enterprise. The major reason for this achievement was the Histadrut's ability to exploit the contract system by which the labor in the port was organized. As a result, Jewish niches were formed within the government-owned port, in which the organizational capacity of the Histadrut, its monopoly over Jewish labor, and the financial and political aid of the Zionist institutions came together to enable hundreds of Jewish workers to earn a fair wage working side by side with the cheapest of Arab workers.

WORKING TOGETHER, ACTING TOGETHER?

For once the physical separation between Jewish and Arab workers was minimal. Hundreds of Arab and Jewish workers worked in the Haifa port, doing similar work as porters, stevedores, and seamen. The possibility of joint action, and even of joint organization, was thus far more real than in any of the industries discussed in previous chapters. And yet, this physical proximity was hardly ever transformed into concrete forms of cooperation between the workers. This is not surprising.

in view of the fact that the major interest of Jewish organized workers was to penetrate a workforce that hitherto had been almost completely Arab. Such a goal was clearly not one around which joint action could evolve. It was pursued through the successful creation of semi-separate niches and sub-niches of Jewish workers who were employed by Jewish enterprises. Thus, again, the structural conditions of employment were not conducive to joint action. Nevertheless, there were a small number of cases in which Jews and Arabs did support one another. The one such case that has been adequately documented is a joint strike of Arab and Jewish seamen, employed by the same Arab contractor. A closer examination of this case will show that it confirms, rather than contradicts, the argument presented above. It was precisely where and when the large-scale introduction of Jewish labor, through separate niches, did not take place that joint action emerged.

In 1932, a strike was declared by the Arab seamen who worked for Reno and Abu-Zeid, the major contractors employing stevedores and seamen. The sailors navigated the boats and barges back and forth to the ships anchored at a distance, sometimes even beyond the breakwaters. In April of that year, when the citrus season ended, the contractors tried to cut their expenses by paying the seamen, local Arabs, on a daily rather than a monthly basis. The seamen, demoted to daily workers, went on strike.[76] Reno and Abu-Zeid also employed six Jewish seamen in response to pressure from the HLC and the Pardess citrus exporting company. The Jewish workers were members of two *kibbutzim* who were stationed in Haifa—*Kibbutz C'* (Gimel) of the *Shomer Hatza'ir* and *Kibbutz C'* (Gimel) of the *Kibbutz Hameuchad*. They worked together— skilled and experienced Arab seamen and young *kibbutz* members, new to the sea, and determined to live up to their new commitment. The young kibbutz members learned the language of the seamen from the Arabs: *"Vera"*—*"Mayna"*—Raise the load, lower it. They passed endless hours together waiting for the ships to arrive. They would listen to the stories of the veteran seamen sitting on the small stools in the cafes by the port, sipping strong coffee—stories of the Persian seas, stories of demons and ghosts, of mermaids who snared the seamen with their alluring songs—till they were all called back to the barges. The Arabs were extremely curious about *kibbutz* life—"Are you communists? Do you live in promiscuity—in free love?"[77] and some, with whom a deeper friendship developed, visited the *kibbutz* camp on their day off.

It is within this context that the Jewish seamen learned that the Arabs had declared a strike and had congregated in a nearby cafe. The employers, hoping to recruit additional workers from the *kibbutzim*, in order to resist the threats of their veteran Arab employees, had not informed their Jewish seamen of the impending change. On learning of the situation, the Jewish seamen, headed by Iz'ia Pesah, who spoke fluent Arabic and was seen as the *ra'is* of the Jewish workers, declared their full support for the strike and joined the strikers. As Avraham (Bumi) Toren recalled many years later, "When we all backed Iz'ia and informed our *kibbutz* and the HLC that we were on strike, there was a great outburst of joy. They carried us on their shoulders through the Arab market, bought us drinks in the cafe . . . they did not know how to express their immense happiness."[78]

The Jewish seamen accompanied their comrades to the offices of the PAWS where they registered and then went on, together with a group of the striking seamen, to Aba Houshi at the HLC. Aba Houshi, wary of possible objections to his representing Arab workers, entered negotiations as a mediator rather than as the workers' spokesman. He met with the Arab and Jewish workers and with representatives of the HLC, and presented their proposals to the contractors as he reported to the Histadrut Executive:

> Various proposals were made by the Arabs. The establishment of a Jewish-Arab cooperative was suggested, as was the normalization of the working hours. The Arabs were willing to return to work, if the contractors would sign a contract stating that after a week or two of working on a daily basis they would once again be paid as monthly workers. They were even willing to work a few days with no pay at all, as long as they would not be expected to work as daily workers permanently. All of these proposals were rejected.[79]

The strike did not achieve its goals. The ambivalence and distrust between the Arab and Jewish officials militated against its success. Hanna Asfour, of the PAWS, tried to undermine the efforts of Aba Houshi who, in turn, was faced with the strong reservations of the HLC executive. In addition, it was the quiet season when there was little work in the port and this greatly weakened the workers. The seamen returned to work after a few days, with only vague promises. Still, they were deeply impressed by the aid of the Histadrut and many joined the PLL, forming a Seaman's Section. The Jewish seamen of the *Shomer Hatza'ir* called for the establishment of a joint Arab-Jewish union, and saw in it an important step toward joint organization. But Aba Houshi followed the model adopted by the Histadrut Executive, by which each national group formed a separate unit, within a common union.[80] Despite Aba Houshi's impressive report, in the summer of 1932, on the various activities planned for the Seamen's Union,[81] it appears to have disintegrated by the winter of 1933, to the extent that it ever actually existed. Aba Houshi reported:

> The trade union organization of the seamen has become more diffi-
> cult. During the winter months it is impossible to meet with them fre-
> quently as they work 14–16 hours a day, and are seldom free for a
> meeting or discussion. It seems that far more time will be needed to
> achieve a minimally consolidated class consciousness.[82]

The friendship between the seamen continued but there was little joint action. During 1933–34, Jewish seamen and stevedores from Saloniki filled the ranks of the Jewish workers. They did not have the commit-ment that the members of the *Shomer Hatza'ir* had to class solidarity and joint action with the Arab workers. Political tensions increased. The HLC became more involved in managing the introduction of orga-nized Jewish labor into the new Haifa port. The conditions that had prevailed in 1932 among a small number of workers no longer existed. A few Jewish seamen and stevedores continued working together with skilled Arab workers in the employment of Reno and Abu Zeid, but they were very much the exception. Most Jewish workers worked under the aegis of the Histadrut, separated from the masses of skilled and unskilled Arab workers.

TO CONCLUDE

The dilemma that faced Jewish labor in the government sector was highlighted in the Haifa port. Jewish workers had to compete with all levels of Arab workers, urban clerical workers, skilled urban and rural manual workers, and, above all, the Hourani casual workers. This was also true of the other large government enterprises in Hai-fa—the Haifa Municipality and the Palestine Railways.[83] Although the problems were similar, the solution devised by Jewish labor at the Haifa port was particular to it alone. The contract system allowed the contractor rather than the government employer to define the work conditions. The Jewish labor movement exploited this opening as-tutely. It became a major contractor, through its contracting company Solel Boneh, recruited labor, determined its conditions of work (via the HLC Labor Exchange), and negotiated the conditions of tender with the management of the Haifa port (via Solel Boneh).

The case of the Haifa port demonstrates the intricate and complex interplay between the economic and political dimensions of the Pal-estine labor market. Indeed, work was contracted out, and Jewish workers did invest immense energy in becoming porters, stevedores, and seamen, as described so eloquently by F. O. Rogers. But this individual effort would not have succeeded by itself, were it not supported by the resources of the world Jewish community. The close links between the Zionist institutions and the British establishment, and between the Histadrut institutions and the institutions of the WZO, were effectively mobilized. Zionist political pressure was exerted. There were extensive negotiations with the most senior political figures like the High Commissioner to Palestine and the Under-Secretary of State for the Colonies. The Jewish Agency contributed money to Solel Boneh, which took on the organization and control of the work. The HLC, under the leadership of Aba Houshi, coordinated the whole operation. This interplay of forces must also be understood in its wider political context. The Arab Rebellion introduced tension, insecurity, and apprehension. Despite the fact that the Haifa port remained in full action, the situation had changed and both the port authority and Jewish importers and exporters were less inclined than before to depend on Arab labor only.

Jews and Arabs did work side by side at the port but the structural arrangements—different contractors, different equipment, different storehouses and different gates of entry—ensured that they worked separately. The organizational separation eased the entrance of Jewish workers into the Haifa port, but it also both reflected and reinforced the existing barriers between the Arab and Jewish workers. Separation in all forms was beneficial for the Jewish workers because it enabled them to advance their interests and improve their position. At the same time it made joint action and common class solidarity between Jewish and Arab workers unlikely and irrelevant.

Chapter 6

The Palestine Railways: "Here We Are All Natives . . ." or the Limits of Cooperation

Side by side with the merchants, consuls and missionaries, the railways forged the way for the European powers into the declining Ottoman empire. Palestine, with its strategic and religious appeal, was of special interest. Railroad lines were built, eventually changing both hands and gauge, in ways that reflected much of the political, social, and economic dynamics of Palestine. The railways initially linked the coastal entrance points with the hinterland and served pilgrims, tourists, and exporters. Soon after, at the end of the First World War, they served the conquering British forces and helped to consolidate British civilian rule between the two wars. During the Second World War they served the needs of the British army linking Palestine with Egypt, Trans-Jordan, Lebanon, and Syria. Within Palestine itself, the railways were less effective in serving the needs of the rapidly expanding population and economy, and had to face strong competition from the far more flexible and adaptable motor transport.[1]

Railway construction began in 1888 when a French company obtained a concession to build a line to connect Jaffa, then the main port of Palestine, with the inland city of Jerusalem. During the First World War, the Ottoman government assumed control of the line, but it was taken over by the British Egyptian Expeditionary Force as it made its way into Palestine. The second important coastal-inland link connected Haifa to Dar'a, which was on the mainline of the Hijaz Railway.[2] The Syrian Ottoman Railway, financed by English capital, had begun to construct a line from Haifa to Damascus in 1892. This was bought out by the Hijaz Railway Administration and incorporated with the planned Haifa-Dar'a extension that was opened in 1906.[3] Other extensions and feeders to the main Hijaz Railway were constructed before the First World War. They connected Acre with Haifa and Affula, southward with Jenin and Nablus, and eastward with Tulkarem and Lydda. The Jaffa-Jerusalem line was extended from Lydda south to Beer-Sheba and Quseima, creating a through connection from Damascus to Quseima.

As the British forces moved into Palestine in 1917, pushing back the Ottoman army, they built a railway line parallel to the seashore, starting at Kantara, in Egypt, extending through al-Arish, Rafah, and Gaza, then eastward to Lydda, which was on the Jerusalem–Jaffa line and from Lydda north to Haifa via Tulkarm. This route bypassed Tel-Aviv, the major center of the Jewish population, and made it well nigh impossible for the railway to serve the needs of the Jewish settlement. It thus triggered the development of the road network and motor transportation. With the transfer from military to civil rule, at the end of the First World War, the government of Palestine bought the Palestine Railway from the British Army for a heavy price. It then invested in improvements to the Kantara-Rafa-Haifa line, as well as in equipment and buildings. The Memorandum prepared by the Government in 1937 for the Palestine Royal Commission detailed the improvements it had made. Lines that were commercially viable were converted to standard gauge and lines that were no longer viable were scrapped. Some bridges were rebuilt and others were added to meet the needs of the heavier traffic. New equipment was installed in the major stations, especially in Haifa and Lydda, together with storage sheds for the citrus crop. The large mechanical repair workshops were transferred to Haifa from Lydda in 1922, and from Kantara in 1932, making Haifa the main workshop center.[4]

The Palestine Railways functioned as a separate economic unit, and not as a government service. It thus had to balance its budget and, if possible, make a profit for the government coffers. Most years the income of the Palestine Railways exceeded its running expenses, but could hardly meet additional costs. As Sawaf has noted, in addition to the operating expenses, the Palestine Railway had to pay interest on the loan with which it had purchased the railway from the army and had to contribute to special funds for the long-term upkeep of the railway. "When loan interest and renewal and sinking fund charges are deducted from the net receipts," wrote Sawaf, "there remains little or no surplus revenue accruing to the Government from the operation of the Railway."[5] This parlous financial situation was reflected in the wages and labor conditions of the Palestine Railway workers—both Jews and Arabs.

The economic activity of the Palestine Railway, which included development projects as well as passenger and goods traffic, fluctuated from year to year. When the railway was transferred from military to civil control many improvements were initiated. In 1923, with the retrenchment of government and government-related expenditure in general, the number of development projects declined. However, traffic picked up in the mid-1920s with the prosperity brought about by the increase in tourism to Palestine, the large Jewish immigration, and the economic activity of 1924–25. It declined once again with the onset of the 1926 depression, which lasted until 1929. The increase of passengers and goods during the 1930s and their fluctuations from year to year reflected the demographic, political, and economic situation in Palestine, and demonstrate how closely the fortunes of the railway were tied to the fortunes of the country.

In 1932–33, road competition began to affect the number of passengers and was countered, according to Sawaf,[6] by reducing fares and improving services. The construction of the Tel Aviv-Haifa road, which was constructed between 1935 and 1937, increased the competition, but this was offset by a sharp increase in the number of of passengers traveling on the Hijaz Railway extension from Haifa to Semah in order to reach the new Jewish settlements.[7] By contrast, goods transport was less affected by the competition from the roads and increased systematically during the 1930s, when building materials and the steadily increasing citrus exports were transported by rail. The onset of the disturbances of the Arab Rebellion, in 1936, led to a decrease in passenger transport and an increase in the transport of goods. Tourism decreased and the frequent attacks of the rebels on the railway made it unsafe, decreasing the transport of passengers. At the same time, due to the closure of the Jaffa port, all exports were directed by rail to the port of Haifa which, as noted in the previous chapter, remained functioning all through the Rebellion. This increase in the transport of export goods notwithstanding, the Palestine Railways suffered financially toward the end of the 1930s. Some of the services were canceled during the Arab Rebellion, and there were additional expenses for security and the repair of damages.[8] Thus during the early years of the 1930s (1930–1933/34) the Palestine Railway was in deficit, during the mid-1930s (1934/35–1936/37) it enjoyed a profit, and from 1937–1940 it again showed a loss.[9]

A sharp shift took place in the Palestine Railway, as in most of the economy, with the transition, in 1940, from the depression caused by the Italian-Ethiopian war and the Arab Rebellion to the activity triggered by the needs of the army during the Second World War. The army became its main client since there was no tourism and little export. The railway provided a land link between Port Said and Haifa. All imports from England were brought to Port Said via a route that circumnavigated Africa and then transported to Haifa by rail. After 1941, the railway lines were extended from Haifa to Beirut and to Tripoli, creating a direct link between Europe and Egypt. During the war, facilities for handling the increased traffic were further developed. The marshaling yards at Haifa and Lydda were modernized and enlarged and all locomotives were converted from coal to oil. During most of this period from 1940–41 to 1945–46 the Palestine Railway showed a profit.[10] With the end of the war the use of the railway by the military declined sharply. Passenger traffic was limited because the motor traffic and the newly developed network of roads answered the needs of short-haul passenger movement more efficiently. Freight transport, on the other hand, was handled mostly by the railway. Grains, provisions, cement and building materials, potash, and citrus were transferred mainly to and from the Haifa port. The last years of the British mandate, 1946 and 1947, were once again years of uprising and rebellion. The Palestine Railways were again a major target for sabotage that caused much damage and endangered passengers and workers. The Palestine Railways again suffered a deficit.[11]

The Palestine Railway was not part of the economy of Haifa in the same way as were, for example, the large industries of Nesher Portland Cement factory and Mabruk cigarette factory or the government-owned Haifa Port. Nevertheless, Haifa played an important role in the Palestine Railway and it, in turn, was important to the economic life of the town. In the early 1920s, the general management of the Palestine Railway was transferred to Haifa, as were the large mechanical workshops for the repair of locomotives, carriages, and wagons. These workshops employed a large number of workers, almost all of whom were skilled. The number varied from approximately 500 workers in the 1920s, to 750–800 from the mid-1930s. Most of the Jewish workers who were employed by the Palestine Railway were located in Haifa. The mechanical workshops concentrated hundreds of workers, both Jewish and Arab, on a regular, long-term basis, within the same location, doing similar work, day in day out. It was therefore the workers of Haifa who organized the railway workers, who established the Railway Post and Telegraph Workers' Organization (RPTWO) and the Arab Railway Workers Organization (ARWO), and who deliberated about cooperation and joint action between Jews and Arabs, attempting to implement it.

TRENDS IN THE LABOR FORCE
OF THE PALESTINE RAILWAY

The Palestine Railway (PR) employed between 3,000 to 8,000 workers, which made it one of the largest employers in Palestine. The workforce was very varied. The senior officials—top management, heads of departments, chief engineers—were all British expatriates. Between 60 and 90 in number, they accounted for 1 to 2 percent of the employees.[12] About 20 percent of the workers were Egyptians, and they were employed mostly along the Kantara-Rafa line that was administered by the Palestine Railway but not owned by it. They are not included in this chapter. Most of the Palestine Railway workers were Palestinian Arabs of whom about 25 percent were Christian and 75 percent were Muslim. Between 8 and 13 percent of the workers were Jews. The workers carried out different tasks and were hired under differing conditions. Many were seasonal, unskilled casual workers while others were skilled workers working on a regular basis, though without the security usually associated with such a status. A few were classified monthly workers whose salaries included various benefits.

Table 6.1 shows the size and composition of the labor force of the PR. It is difficult to give a precise breakdown between Jews and Arabs. The official figures categorize the employees according to their nationality, where both Jews and Arabs might have been included under Palestinian nationality (going by their citizenship), or by religion, where both Arabs and British might have been included under the Christian religion. Nevertheless, the figure for Jewish workers, presented in the official reports, together with the fact that British Christian employees accounted for 2 percent at the utmost, enable us to assume that almost all non-Jewish workers were Palestinian Arabs.

The number of employees shifted according to the needs and activities of the railways. In the early 1930s, the railways employed 3,000–3,400 workers. During the mid-to-late 1930s, the workforce was 4,000–4,500, and during the Second World War the work force numbered over 7,000 workers. In the early 1930s, activity was relatively limited. It picked up with the prosperity of the mid-1930s and flourished during the war. Some slowdowns, such as the decline in activity and profits in 1937/38–1939/40 and in 1946/47 did not automatically lead to a reduction of the workforce. We do read of dismissals during these years in numerous documents, letters, and memoranda of the workers' representatives.[13] Nevertheless, the overall figures do not point to large-scale dismissals. Instead the management chose to respond to its economic

Table 6.1. Employees of the Palestine Railways, 1930–1947

Year	Total no.	Jews	Percent of Jews
1929 (1)	3,000	384	12.8
1930 (2)	3,361	418	12.4
1931 (2)	3,424	443	12.9
1932 (3)	3,454	419	12.1
1933 (3)	3,124	393	12.3
1934 (30	4,093	336	8.2
1935 (3)	4,170	239	5.7
1936 (4)	4,352	365	8.4
1937 (4)	4,581	456	9.9
1938 (4)	4,323	409	9.5
1939 (4)	4,196	343	8.2
1943 (5)	7,780	515	6.6
1944 (6)	7,746	653	8.4
1945 (6)	7,285	605	8.3
1946 (6)	7,701	520	6.7
1947 (6)	7,589	528	6.9

Sources:
(1) 1929—RPTWO to Labor Center, 23 June 1929. LA, IV104-49-238.
(2) Report of General Manager, 1930/31, p. 51.
(3) RPTWO to HE, 11 October 1935, based on Report of General Manager. LA, IV208-1-515a.
(4) Report of General Manager, 1938/39, p. 112.
(5) RPTWO to HE, 26 October 1943. LA, IV208-1-3660, based on information from Report of General Manager.
(6) Report of General Manager, 1946/47, p. 131.

difficulties by vitiating the work conditions. They cut the work week to five days and postponed various fringe benefits.

The shift in the number of Jewish workers in the labor force of the Palestine Railway was more complex. Table 6.1 shows clearly that the number and percentage of Jewish workers was small and remained small. In fact, the proportion became much smaller over the years despite the significant growth of the Jewish population in Palestine. This was in striking contrast to the Haifa Port where, as we showed in the previous chapter, the proportion of Jewish workers increased steadily (see Table 5.1). I contend that the different ways in which labor was organized in the Palestine Railway and in the Haifa port accounted for much of this difference. In both of these very large, government-owned enterprises the wages were extremely low, but only at the port was much of the work contracted out. This enabled private Jewish employers, Jewish public institutions, and Jewish financing to intervene and thereby create a mini-Jewish sector within the government-owned port. Through its system of organization and control as well as its mechanization, this mini-Jewish sector was able to pay its workers higher wages. This option was not available in the Palestine Railway. None of the work was tendered out and the management was unwilling to accept the suggestions of the Jewish institutions that it adopt such practices. All work was carried out within different departments of the Palestine Railway, under the supervision of the head of department and his senior officials and foremen. Railway officials were directly responsible for recruiting the workers. Jewish and Arab workers were employed under the same conditions and paid similar wages. Since the Jewish workers were unable to devise special ways of improving their income, as was the case in the Haifa port, they tended to avoid working in the Palestine Railway.

A second fact to be noted from Table 6.1 is that although the number of Jewish workers was small, it fluctuated sharply, between a minimum of 239 and a maximum of 653 workers. This fluctuation was not identical with the pattern of shifts in the number of workers in the railway. Thus, for example, while the number of workers increased during the prosperity of 1934–35, the number of Jewish workers declined relatively sharply. Between 1935 and 1938, the labor force of the Palestine Railway was relatively stable, but the number of Jewish workers increased. During the Second World War, the workforce peaked in 1943 and then remained relatively stable until 1947, but the number of Jewish workers peaked in 1944 and dropped again in 1946.

These fluctuations reflect factors that were particularly significant for Jewish workers. The first factor, which is primarily economic, concerns other employment opportunities that were available to Jewish and Arab workers. The Arab workers had relatively few opportunities for wage labor, and these paid extremely low wages. The Jewish workers, on the other hand, usually had more and better opportunities open to them. A significant worsening of labor conditions in the Railway, such as a transition to a five-day week, therefore motivated Jewish workers to look elsewhere to a much greater extent than Arab workers. Prosperity within the Jewish economy created new employment opportunities for Jewish workers that attracted them away from the low paying PR. Thus in 1934–35, when the Palestine Railway showed a profit and expanded its labor force due to economic prosperity, many of the Jewish workers left it for better paying jobs in the Jewish sector. This happened again at the end of the Second World War, when wartime restrictions on the movement of workers were lifted and construction work in the Jewish sector recommenced. Many of the Jewish workers who had joined the Palestine Railway during the War chose to leave.

The second factor, which was of an organizational-political nature, concerned the special activity of Jewish institutions. While they could not intervene in the actual carrying out of railway work, they could help workers acquire skills that would facilitate their recruitment. They therefore initiated training courses and provided financial aid for workers on long-term training and apprenticeships. The Zionist institutions also applied political pressure on the railway and government to increase the small proportion of Jewish workers, especially when political circumstances were conducive. Immediately after the First World War, political pressure was needed to facilitate the introduction of Jewish workers.[14] According to Jewish workers, military officials strongly resisted hiring Jews and instigated and exacerbated conflict between the Jewish and Arab workers.[15] This resistance was to some extent overcome by the need of the PR for skilled workers. Jews entered the Railway as apprentices, both in Lydda and in Haifa, for very low pay that Zionist funding supplemented by providing loans and cheap meals.[16] During the Second World War, in 1943, when the railways needed more skilled workers, the Jewish Agency initiated and funded training courses. As a result, the number of Jewish workers rose significantly in 1943 and 1944.

Political pressure was also applied in 1936–37, when both the Jewish Agency and the Histadrut attempted to take advantage of the Arab general strike and rebellion to induce the railway management to hire Jewish workers. The Histadrut recruited skilled Jewish workers, some of whom had previously worked in the Palestine Railway, to substitute for the Arab workers who had gone out on strike. The railway management was very hesitant to take up the Histadrut's offer, lest it further exacerbate political tension.[17] Nevertheless, the number of Jewish workers increased significantly and so did their overall proportion of the workforce.

Thus a complex combination of factors affected the employment of Jewish labor at the Palestine Railway. Central to these were the low wages and the inability of Jewish labor and its institutions to improve them. When other, better paid, opportunities emerged, Jewish workers tended to leave the railways. On the other hand, when work was scarce, Jewish workers attempted to raise their level of skill so as to take advantage of the relatively better paid, skilled jobs of the PR, primarily in the mechanical workshops. It is thus necessary to take a closer look at the internal divisions within the Palestine Railway and their impact on the composition of the labor force.

THE PALESTINE RAILWAY AND
ITS INTERNAL ORGANIZATION

The work in the railway was diverse and called for a complex internal organization and coordination. It included the laying of tracks, when new lines were constructed or when the gauge of existing lines was changed, as well as the maintenance of the tracks on a regular basis and their repair. Stations had to be established along the railway lines and traffic into and out of the stations had to be supervised. The trains had to be kept in good repair, cleaned, and inspected regularly. These different activities had to be coordinated to ensure that the railway functioned efficiently. The organization of the PR was divided into departments—the Engineering Department, the Traffic Department, the Running Department, and the Mechanical Department. All departments were under the direct control of the General Manager and all work was carried out under the supervision of the Palestine Railway with no tendering out to contracting companies, individual contractors, or subcontractors.

The Engineering Department was responsible for the laying and maintenance of the tracks. It was the largest department and employed between one-third to one-half of all the railway workers. They were mostly plate-layers and their work was largely unskilled. They were the lowest paid workers. About two-thirds were regular daily workers and the rest were employed on a seasonal basis as casual workers.

The Traffic Department was responsible for the work to be carried out in the railway stations. The number of workers ranged from 400 to 500 workers and amounted to 10 to 15 percent of the overall workforce. Approximately half of the workers of this department were located in the district of Lydda and the other half in the northern district of Haifa. The stations were heavily staffed. Two hundred and fifty-six workers staffed the Haifa station, as of April 1937.[18] Among them were forty-two officials and nine yard masters. There were shunters, thirty-eight of them, who moved cars from track to track when necessary, there were pointsmen, lampsmen, and signalmen who directed the traffic within the station, there were cleaners who cleaned the station and others who cleaned the carriages (six and eighteen, respectively), there were the gatekeepers (eleven), cooks (five), and ticket examiners, all of whom provided basic services required in the station, and twenty-seven guards, possibly a higher number than usual due to the tense relations between Jews and Arabs during the years of the Arab rebellion.

Table 6.2. Palestine Railways: Workforce According
to Departments

Year	Mechanical workshop	Traffc	Running	Engineering	Total
1929 (1)	738	490	424	1050	2702
1935 (2)	753	402	649	2326	4130
1937 (3)	850	506	659	1317	3332
Percentage					
1929 (1)	27.3	18.0	15.7	38.9	100
1935 (2)	18.2	9.7	15.7	56.3	100
1937 (3)	25.5	15.2	19.8	39.5	100

Sources:
(1) From RPTWO to Labor Center, 23 June 1929, LA, IV 104-49-238. An additional
    300 workers were listed as clerical workers (77 British, 26 Jewish, and 195 Arab
    clerical and storehouse workers).
(2) RPTWO, Jewish and Arab Workers in the PR, 11 October 1935. LA, IV
    208-1-815A.
(3) Abramov to Histadrut Executive, 19 April 1937. LA, IV 208-1-1325.

The Running Department was in charge of the heart of the matter—
the running of the trains. The relative size of this department seems to
have increased with time.[19] A team consisting of a driver and stokeman
ran the train. In 1937, 117 drivers and 117 stokemen were employed.
Many other workers, with differing levels of training and expertise,
attended to the engines. Among these were the steam raisers, coal-
checkers, pump-men, tube-cleaners, and engine cleaners. Other workers, including the examiners and oilers, tended to the wagons and carriages. The boiler smiths, the blacksmiths and coppersmiths, the
electricians and carpenters, the fitters, and the carriage and wagon re-
pairmen carried out those repairs that did not require the removal of
the engine or the carriage from the track to the workshop. All these
trained and skilled workers were aided by 111 unskilled laborers from
whom candidates for training in the skilled jobs were chosen.

The Mechanical Department, headed by the Chief Mechanical Engineer (C.M.E.), was responsible for the large workshops that repaired
locomotives, carriages, and wagons. New workshops were built in the
early 1920s, near the outlet of the Kishon River in Haifa Bay. In 1922,
the Lydda Workshops were transferred to Haifa, and in 1933 the workshops in Kantara were also relocated to Haifa. The Mechanical Department was extremely large, second only to the Engineering Department.
This was the only department whose staff was concentrated in one
place. They all worked in the large sheds of the Mechanical Workshops

where there were sections for repairing the locomotives of the standard gauge (1.43 cm.) tracks and those of the narrow gauge (1.05 cm.) tracks. There were also sections for building and repairing wagons and carriages. About three-quarters of the workers were skilled workers. An additional two hundred or so workers were untrained laborers who were recruited as apprentices when the need arose. Most of the work required skills in metal work so there were blacksmiths, coppersmiths, tinsmiths, boilersmiths, fitters, welders, and engravers. There were also electricians, painters, carpenters, upholsterers, and clerical workers.[20]

The few hundred Jewish workers were not distributed equally in all departments. They were concentrated primarily in those departments that required skills. Very few worked in unskilled jobs.

About half of the Jewish workers were employed in the Mechanical Workshops. This was a highly skilled department that concentrated its workers in one place, Haifa. The Jewish workers were therefore close to a large Jewish urban center with a highly organized labor movement. Both the Traffic and Running Departments had a fair amount of skilled work, in which the Jewish workers were employed. But the work of these departments was far more dispersed, and their recruitment policy

Table 6.3. Ethnic/National Distribution of Workers in the Palestine Railways

a. Departmental Distribution of Jewish and Arab Workers in PR

Year	Workshop			Traffic			Running			Engineering		
	J	A	T	J	A	T	J	A	T	J	A	T
1929 (1)	192	546	738	64	426	490	93	331	424	9	1041	1050
1935 (2)	120	633	753	22	378	400	75	474	549	121	2314	2435
1937 (3)	120	730	850	52	454	506	94	565	659	43	1274	1317

b. Distribution of Jewish Workers in Departments of PR, Percentage

Year	Workshop	Traffic	Running	Engineering	Total
1929	54	18	26	2	100
1935	50	9	31	10	100
1937	39	17	30	14	100

Sources:
(1) From RPTWO to Labor Center, 23 June 1929. LA, IV 104-49-238. An additional 300 workers were listed as clerical workers (77 British, 26 Jewish, and 195 Arab clerical and storehouse workers).
(2) RPTWO, Jewish and Arab Workers in the PR, 11 October 1935. LA, IV 208-1-815A.
(3) Abramov to Histadrut Executive, 19 April 1937. LA, IV 208-1-1325.

seems to have discouraged the hiring of Jewish workers at the departmental and workplace level. The Engineering Department, most of whose workers were the unskilled plate-layers, had very few Jewish workers and they worked in the few skilled engineering jobs.

A more detailed account of the Jewish workers in each department was drawn up from time to time, usually by the secretaries of the Railway, Post and Telegraph Workers' Organization (RPTWO). Michael Grobman, the first secretary of the RPTWO, reported that the Engineering Department had no Jewish workers among the plate-layers who made up by far the largest group of workers in the largest department of the railways. He attributed this to the extremely low wages of the plate-layers and to the inhospitable attitude of the foremen and senior officials.

> All foremen are Arabs and their attitude towards the Jewish worker is not especially good. It is extremely difficult for individuals [individual Jewish workers—D.B.] to be in such an atmosphere. The senior officials in this department, while they do not theoretically distinguish between religious and national groups in the recruitment of workers, do in fact refrain from taking on Jewish workers.[21]

Both the Traffic and Running Departments could be expected to have more Jewish workers than the Engineering Department, as their wages were better. Nevertheless, wrote Grobman, there were occupations in which there were very few Jews for no good reason. For example, there were only six to seven Jews among the thirty-six signalmen or three to four Jews among the twenty-five train guards.[22] Grobman attributed this primarily to the employment policy of the Arab or British official in charge. Additional difficulties arose within the Wagon Department, which had been a separate unit but was later attached to the Mechanical Workshops. "A few years ago," wrote Grobman in 1929, "the number of Jewish workers in this department was satisfactory, but over the last few years it has become almost completely Arab-Syrian. Many of the Arabs working in this department are Syrians from Damascus who bring in members of their families whenever new workers are recruitied. All foremen in this department are Syrians and they are in full control."[23] The only significant exception, wrote Grobman, was in the Mechanical Workshops, where there was a concentration of Jewish workers. This was due to the difficulty in finding expert skilled workers among the Arabs, and to the fact that the foremen who managed the Workshops were Jewish. They had the authority to hire workers and could set their wage at any point between the minimum and maximum levels defined for each position. They appear to have given some advantage to Jewish workers, though Grobman claimed greater preference could have been extended.[24]

By 1937, eight years later, the distribution of Jewish workers had not changed significantly. There were still relatively few Jewish workers in the Engineering Department, though both their number and proportion had increased. The forty-three Jewish workers in this department were employed in professional engineering work and in clerical work. None of them worked in the laying or maintenance of the tracks.[25] In the Traffic Department, forty-two of the Jewish workers worked in the train stations of the Lydda District. Twenty-one were assigned to the station of the Jewish city of Tel Aviv and ten to the Haifa station. An occupational breakdown was given for the Haifa station only. Of the 256 workers only ten were Jewish. Six of the ten were classified as clerical workers (out of thirty-three); two were "checkers" (out of thirty-two); one was a carriage cleaner (out of eighteen), and one was a guard (out of twenty-seven).[26] There were more Jewish workers in the Running Department. They worked in many of the occupations. There were twenty-one fitters, three steam raisers, four boilersmiths, three carriage and wagon repairers, two carriage and wagon examiners, two blacksmiths, and a single engine cleaner, pump-inspector, shedman, weighbridge inspector, electric chargeman, leading hand fitter, turner, carpenter, coppersmith, and electrician. There were conspicuously few Jewish workers in the important positions of train driver and stokeman. Jewish documents frequently refer to the small number of Jews in these strategic positions. In 1937, seventeen of the 117 drivers were Jewish, as were seven of the 117 stokemen.[27] This number decreased because several Jewish drivers were killed in attacks at the railway service, and specifically at moving trains.[28] The number of Jewish locomotive drivers did not increase even during the Second World War. Of the 500 drivers employed during the war only sixteen were Jewish![29]

The number of Jewish workers in the Mechanical Workshops remained more or less constant, though their proportion of all workshop workers dropped significantly. More Jewish skilled workers were concentrated in the Mechanical Workshops than in any other department and it was the one place where a relatively large number of Jewish workers worked together in one location, albeit among the different work sheds.

This departmental and occupational distribution meant that Jewish and Arab workers often worked side by side. This was the case in the mixed train stations of Lydda and Haifa, on the trains themselves, and in the Haifa Mechanical Workshops. We have very few reports of the

Figure 9. Arab and Jewish railway workers, mechanical workshops, Haifa, circa 1925.

relations between workers as they worked together, day in and day out. However, the extent to which friendship between Jewish and Arab workers was sustained during periods of violent clashes indicates a basic trust and mutual concern that must have developed over the years. As Ephraim Shwartzman recounted, joint organizational activity (to be discussed later on in this chapter) all but ceased during the years of the Arab Rebellion (1936–39) but personal contact continued.

> Even during the riots there were many cases when Arabs, train workers, saved Jews, from extremely difficult situations. I, for one, was saved twice by Arab friendship at work. Such friendship did not cease.[30]

To conclude this discussion of the occupational and departmental distribution of Jewish workers, it is important to note the relation between this distribution and the level of wage in the PR. In other arenas of work, Jewish labor had been able to obtain significantly better wages and labor conditions than Arab labor. Within the Jewish economic sector, this had been achieved by a policy of closure that prevented cheap

Arab labor from competing for work and pre-empting the jobs of Jewish workers. This strategy was not applicable within the government sector, which was too important a source of jobs to be ignored. The strategy adopted in the Haifa port of creating semi-isolated niches within the government service could not succeed in the Palestine Railway. Thus the only option by which Jewish labor could retain a level of wages similar to that which it had obtained in other industries was to concentrate on the skilled positions that were better paid. The departmental and occupational distribution presented so far indicates clearly that they succeeded in this. This is a common strategy for higher-priced workers where closure of the labor market is not possible. As Bonacich writes, under such circumstances, the higher priced workers attempt to create a "caste system" in which they monopolize the better paid skilled jobs. In this way they retain their advantage and protect it.[31] In the case of the Jewish workers in the Palestine Railway, this option was only of limited applicability. Although Jewish workers could enter skilled positions, they most certainly could not monopolize them. They had neither the political strength nor the organizational power to block Arab workers from any position. On the contrary, Jews found it difficult to enter many of the the skilled occupations. Thus the Jewish workers remained a small minority, concentrated in the skilled occupations but never dominating them. They worked side by side with Arab workers of the same level of skill and earned the same wages.

WAGE AND CONDITIONS OF SERVICE

The Palestine Railway paid its workers, Jewish and Arab, according to the wage scale current for the Arab workers in the Arab sector of Palestine's economy. The lowest paid workers were the "regular laborers" and the more experienced workers known as "skilled laborers." Their daily wage ranged between 150 and 120 mils. Sometimes they earned even less. During the later 1920s and early 1930s, the platelayers earned 120–130 mils per day as did various categories of cleaners such as machinery-cleaners and tube-cleaners.[32] During the prosperity of 1934–35, after much pressure by the workers' organizations, the PR management agreed to raise the wage of the plate-layers from 120 mils per day to 140 mils, but during the slowdown of the late 1930s they lowered the wages to 120 mils and below.[33] By the early 1940s, the cost of living had increased sharply, but the wages had not. In some cases they had even been reduced. In June 1942, a memorandum of the Central Committee of the RPTWO stated that the basic wage of engine cleaners had been reduced from 150 to 130 mils per day and that of laborers from 120 to 100 mils.[34] It was further argued that railway wages were in many instances lower than wages paid for the same occupations in other government departments.

> In this connection we should especially like to emphasize the wage rates of laborers. The railway minimum for that job is 100 mils. At present the Post & Telegraph is paying 150 mils and we should mention here that wages of all the laborers in the Engineering Branch of that Department have recently been raised to 250 mils. . . . We contend that as in the P.&T. department, railway laborers are not engaged in work of a purely unskilled nature.[35]

During the summer of 1942 the workers won a slight raise. By September of that year, the railway was paying its laborers the minimum basic wage of 120 mils per day and an additional 40 mils as a Cost of Living Allowance (CoLA). Other low-level workers in the railways were receiving a wage of 200 mils (basic wage plus CoLA), which was also less than that paid by other government departments and international firms. It was only when laborers began to leave the railways for better paying jobs that the General Manager petitioned the Controller of Manpower to raise the wages.

> I have ascertained that the rates in operation for the C.R.L. [Consolidated Refineries Ltd.—D.B.] and I.P.C. [Iraq Petroleum Company—D.B.] are at present a total of 210 mils per day, that is 120 basic plus 90 cost of living. This rate is now being reviewed and it is expected that there will be an increase of at least 10 mils per day and probably an increase to a total of 230 mils per day.
> My own view is that 230 mils is likely to be the rate which will have to be adopted and I am giving authority for casuals in the Railway Department to be engaged up to this figure.[36]

It took the general strike of all government workers in April 1946 to win an increase of the basic wage of the laborers to 200 mils per day, to which a CoLA was added.

Many of the railway workers had jobs that required particular skills. Their wages were higher than those of the laborers, but the differential was not commensurate with their long years of training and of service. In 1929, metal workers, engravers, boilersmiths, carpenters, and painters earned between 200 and 500 mils per day and in 1937, fitters, turners, blacksmiths, coppersmiths, and electricians were earning the same wage.[37] Workers employed in a large number of occupational grades earned a similar wage on a monthly basis. Among these were stokemen, train guards, signalmen, conductors, carriage and wagon examiners, coal checkers, steam raisers, and head-laborers.[38] Locomotive drivers, crane drivers, pump-inspectors, weighbridge inspectors, electric chargemen, and leading hand fitters earned slightly more.[39] Surveys of wages actually earned showed that most of the daily workers earned 300–400 mils[40] per day and most of the monthly workers earned 8.5–10 and 10.5–13 £P per month. As with the laborers, these levels of wages of skilled workers were increased somewhat in the mid-1930s and reduced toward the end of the decade. For example, the basic wage (not including cost of living) dropped from the increased minimum of 260 mils per day to 200 mils, for the wide range of metal workers.[41] The median wage continued to range between 300 to 400 mils per day for painters, fitters, electricians, carriage and wagon examiners, and riveters. Only a few occupations—welders, tinsmiths, and boilersmiths—were paid slightly above the 400 mils, while the wages of occupations like guards, signalmen, shunters, stokemen, and repairers fell below 300 mils.[42]

A brief comparison between the wages of the Arab and Jewish railway workers and those of other industries (e.g., in the Nesher quarry, in private construction, and in the government Department of Public Works) is revealing. Until the late 1930s and early 1940s, unskilled Arab workers in the Nesher quarry, in construction, and in other government departments (e.g., Public Works Department) earned between 100 and 150 mils a day, usually 120–125 mils. This was also the wage paid by the Palestine Railway. By contrast, unskilled Jewish workers in the Jewish sector earned about 250–300 mils per day, and much more than that in a highly organized and flourishing enterprise such as the Nesher cement company. The disparity between the wages of Arab and Jewish skilled workers was much smaller than that among the unskilled workers. Nevertheless, in many cases, though certainly not in all, the wages of the skilled Arab worker were lower than that of his Jewish counterpart. Similar differences can also be seen in the construction industry, despite the greater experience of the Arab workers. The skilled railway workers earned more or less the same as the skilled Arab workers in construction. At times their wages fell below even that level.

The wage level at the Palestine Railway was more constant and tended to fluctuate less than did wages in the private sectors. During periods of prosperity the rising salaries in the other industries widened the gap between the railway workers and their counterparts. This was true for all skilled workers, particularly the skilled Jewish workers. Wages remained more or less constant in the railway, while they rose sharply in construction and in the Nesher cement factory. In 1943, the workers in the private sector enjoyed a far more generous cost of living allowance than the railway workers. The low income of the railway workers was exacerbated by the absence of systematic increments. The workers complained about this constantly.[43] Such increments would have rewarded increased experience and expertise and recognized the changed needs of the workers over the years. Wages for each occupational grade were determined by a wage scale that set the minimum and maximum levels. The workers accepted the wage scale as a system, but were dissatisfied with the way it was implemented. The increments were granted so infrequently that the workers seldom reached the higher wage levels of their occupational grade. The RPTWO complained to the General Manager in June 1942:

> We believe that it is fair to assume that the railway employees are entitled to normal advancement in wages (within the limits of the existing wage scales) by reason of the increased benefits derived by the Department from their expertise. Such increments would partially meet their growing needs. . . .
>
> The progress from the minimum wage to the maximum is currently by small and irregular increments such that the maximum is not reached until an advanced age. Some examples will illustrate this:
>
> Today a driver (regarded as good and efficient) after 14 years in that capacity—22 years of service in all—receives 12.500 £P. With the present rate of advancement he may reach his maximum of 18 £P.—after another 22 years.
>
> A Guard earning £P 7.600 after 7 years will have to wait another 28 years to attain his maximum of £P 10.[44]

In response to strong joint pressure from Jewish and Arab workers during the prosperity of 1934–35 (to be discussed later in the chapter), the General Manager promised to pay annual increments to one-third of all workers every year. This practice was halted during the railway's economic difficulties in 1938, and then resumed in 1940.[45] Only in 1943, after additional joint action, did the new General Manager promise annual increments to all workers, albeit not as a matter of course but conditional on their proficiency and efficiency.[46]

At times, the Palestine Railways actually reduced workers' income by changing the conditions of work. During seven months of 1926–27 and again in 1928 the work week was cut to five days.[47] Wages were effectively lowered by changing the name of occupational grades, by hiring workers at lower minimum rates than had been the practice, or by requiring workers to carry out work of a higher occupational grade without increasing their pay.[48] Furthermore, while the number of days per week was cut, workers were at times required to work longer hours for which they received no extra pay.[49]

By the early 1940s the sharp rise in the prices of goods and services, caused by war shortages and full employment, had made the cost of living the most urgent and pressing issue. As the workers wrote to the General Manager in June 1942, the retail prices of foodstuffs had increased between the summer of 1939 and the winter of 1942 from a baseline of 100.0 in August 1939 to 284.6 in the Arab markets and 210.3 in the Jewish markets. The workers' cost of living allowance came nowhere close to compensating for such a rise in prices. Added to their basic pay, which remained unchanged, the wage of 1942 resulted in a loss of between 20 to 40 percent in the value of their real wage.[50]

Issues of income—low wages, lack of increments, and insufficient cost of living allowance—were not the whole story. They were only a part of what made the worker feel that he was being exploited. His unsatisfactory wage was exacerbated by poor sanitary and medical conditions and by the contemptuous attitude of the supervisors and senior officials. The publications of the RPTWO, which appeared during the 1920s under different names such as—*Ha-Katar—The Locomotive*,[51] *Hed Ha-Katar—Echo of Locomotive*,[52] *Ed Ha-Katar—Steam of Locomotive*,[53] *Al Ha-Mishmar—On Guard*,[54] *Hedim—Echoes*,[55] printed numerous articles and letters by members describing the difficult conditions in which they were working. One extract from 1923–24 will suffice:

> The workers of the Railways enjoyed an 8 hour work day. But now? How long do the mechanics and stokemen work? An official regulation allows them to work 12 hours a day but in practice the management does not pay attention to any regulations whatsoever. It forces the worker to work fifteen and sixteen hours a day—and at such heavy and responsible work! The worker exhausts himself, wastes his health and strength and within a short time he becomes an invalid. Hopeless, he feels bereft of the strength to work and the strength to live. And if not? If he refuses to dissipate his strength in this way, the management has only one answer: get out!
>
> In these difficult circumstances, with such hard work, we are never sure what the morrow will bring. The "retrenchments" continue. If they fired only those who were really not needed . . . but in practice this is not the case. In the course of the last year, with its many dismissals, 500 people were fired in the locomotive department alone! A third of the work force! Yet, immediately after this they forced the remaining workers, especially the stokemen and mechanics, to work more than 8 hours a day. In addition they stopped a number of essential operations. They halted repairs of locomotives and coaches and much more!

All this causes damage to the operation of the trains and huge losses can be expected in the future. But for the present it achieves "retrenchment!" Furthermore, in the name of retrenchment the management has fired workers who have been working for some time, sometimes even heads of families, workers who earn 25 grush for a day's work, and replaced them immediately with new workers. These new workers are children who work for 12 grush a day! . . . a private employer would not dare exploit his workers in such a way, but the railway management, which is appointed by the government of the country and which ought to concern itself with improving the general good, allows itself such liberties.[56]

By the early 1920s, it had become clear to the Jewish workers that as a small minority among the railway workers they had no chance of changing their work conditions. There was no way, under the prevailing conditions in the railway, that they could significantly increase the number of Jewish workers nor could they secure higher wages for themselves alone.

The article in the railway workers' journal continued and pointed to the course of action that should be pursued:

The workers must begin thinking about how they can improve their condition. It is not only a question for Jewish workers alone or Christian or Muslim workers. We can all expect to be fired. We all earn the same wage. We all do the same hard work. On whom should we pin our hopes? On the management? But it does not heed a thing. The Muslims, the Jews and the Christians have many clubs, associations and organizations. But it is only the labor organizations which truly care about our situation. It is our workers' organization [the RPTWO—D.B.] which came to the defense of the workers when they were fired and which has defended us on the issue of a day of rest. The RPTWO has tried to prevent our situation from deteriorating. But the government has but one answer: "Why should we listen to you? Why should we fear you when only a small fraction of the railway workers supports you?" And truth to tell, of the thousands of railway workers, most keep their distance from our labor organization. Most do not join. If all of us were to support one another, if we were all members of the RPTWO, the picture would most certainly be different. The worker is strong when he is united. What can the employer do then? When a single worker displeases management, what will they do? They will throw him out and find another to replace him, or they will simply work with a smaller number of workers by forcing the remaining ones to do the work of he who was fired. Is that not what they have done all along? But what will they do if all the

workers support one another? Will they manage the work without
any workers? That is surely impossible. They most certainly need the
workers! Without workers the train will not move![57]

To refer back to Bonacich's theoretical model, the Jewish workers could
neither close the Palestine Railways to Arab labor nor could they
monopolize the better paying skilled positions. They were left to pursue strategies of equalization by finding ways in which they could improve the work conditions of both Jewish and Arab labor. The only
hope of achieving this goal lay in joint action and joint organization.
Therefore it was in the Palestine Railway that the conditions evolved
that enabled and indeed *necessitated* class action and that transcended
national differences. Yet class interests did not exist in a vacuum. The
Jewish and Arab workers, and especially their leaders, could not disengage themselves from the pervasive impact of Jewish colonization,
Arab opposition, and the ensuing national conflict. For close to three
decades, various forms of cooperation were indeed pursued. But time
and again national interests intervened and created obstacles that the
workers were unable to overcome. Time and again bread-and-butter
class interests emerged and necessitated joint action. Such cooperation
often disintegrated, but it was never absent for long.

JOINT ACTION AND JOINT ORGANIZATION

"Comrades!" cried a Jewish worker in August 1934 in a mass assembly
of hundreds of workers:

> We have gathered together here for one purpose: To discuss our or-
> ganization problems. How can we create one organization out of all
> the workers of the railway, out of all the nationalities and religions?
> Each one of us knows that the strength of the railway workers is in
> our unity. But to actually bring this about? It is always left up in the
> air. Comrades! Our intention is to organize ourselves on a profes-
> sional basis with no high politics, because politics takes from us the
> essence of our cause—The issues we encounter daily for which we
> need to fight with all our might.
>   How long will we remain so very oppressed at the railways? Right
> now, at other places like Nesher, Shemen and Rutenberg, the worker
> is treated so much better than at our place of work.
>   Are they all wise and we fools? No, friends, we must unite in one
> organization and fight for our day to day interests without any poli-
> tics or philosophies.
>   Friends, we have common interests at the Railways and I think that

12 years is time enough to know one another and to trust one another. Our interest is the interest of all the workers at the railways, our interest is to improve our situation so that the management will not be able to do whatever they wish with us.[58]

In no place was the issue of joint organization and joint action as pertinent as in the PR. It was the one place in which common action was essential to further the interests of both the Arab and the Jewish workers. It was the only workplace where the necessary conditions existed that could make such cooperation possible. These included a relatively stable labor force of skilled workers, both Jewish and Arab, who worked in the same place, under the same conditions, and were employed by the same management, a colonial government employer. But these workers were enmeshed with their national communities, national movements, and national labor organizations. Would they be able to disregard "politics and philosophies"? No, not really. Their class interests were, however, not totally submerged by the agenda of national conflict. The tension between the two, between class interests and national priorities, was ever present. It shaped the form the cooperation took. At times this tension impeded cooperation. At times it triggered it.

Together Within a Histadrut-Oriented Organization, 1919–1927

In the early 1920s, when the Histadrut was being consolidated as an exclusively Jewish national labor organization, a leading force of Zionist colonization, the workers of the PR attempted to bring about a different form of organization. They established an organization composed about equally of Arab and Jewish workers. The membership was to include all railway workers regardless of religion or nationality. Indeed for a short moment the railway workers conceived of this as the form of organization most appropriate for all the workers of Palestine. They proposed it as the model for the General Federation of Jewish Workers—the Histadrut. This would have completely transformed its organizational, ideological, and political character. By 1927, this proposal had been dropped and national divisions were again accepted as the formative organizational principle. Common action among Jewish and Arab PR workers continued, in itself a striking exception to the general rule in Palestine, but it had been drained of its transformative potential.

In 1919, shortly after Jewish laborers began working in the Palestine Railway, they formed the Organization of Railway Workers of Palestine, preceding the Histadrut. Within a few months the Jewish workers employed in the Postal, Telegraph and Telephone services joined them and they changed the name to Railway, Post and Telegraph Workers Organization—RPTWO. When the Histadrut was established the following year, they joined it, but retained their autonomy within it. The organization, in its earliest phases, was informed by two guiding purposes. First, the improvement of working conditions—wages, sanitary conditions, lodgings—for all workers and, second, "the increase of the Jewish element at the Railway works."[59] Within a short time improved working conditions became the dominant issue. By 1922, it had become clear that for the organization to be effective it would have to include Arab, as well as Jewish, workers. The small Jewish minority among the railway workers could do nothing on their own. If they were to have any chance of succeeding, they needed to persuade the Arab workers to join them.

A resolution to this effect was passed that year, in the Fourth Convention of the RPTWO, convened on 24 February 1922. During the following year the Jewish workers devoted much effort to recruiting their Arab colleagues. Michael Grobman, active in the organization from its foundation and its secretary for many years, described this process as the development of class consciousness by the Arab workers, guided by their Jewish comrades. Once such understanding had been reached, and once the manipulative incitement of the British officials against the Jewish workers was overcome, he wrote "The Arab worker extended his hand to his Jewish brother. The ground had been prepared for an international trade organization."[60] It should be noted that the term "international" was used to refer to the joint membership of the two national groups—Jewish and Arab.

Between 1923 and 1925, many Arab workers joined the RPTWO. By the end of 1925 the RPTWO had four branches—Lydda, Jerusalem, Kantara, and Haifa. There were 938 members, of whom 440 were Jews and 498 were Arabs. The Haifa branch was the largest. It had 300 Arab members and 150 Jewish members.[61] Never again would the RPTWO reach such a large and mixed membership.

The success of what Grobman described as a one-directional process of consciousness raising created a serious dilemma. When the Arab workers joined the RPTWO, they were joining an organization that was affiliated with the General Federation of Jewish Labor—the Histadrut. How could Arab membership and Jewish exclusivity exist concurrently? And yet, how could it be otherwise? The affiliation of the RPTWO with the Histadrut was vital for the Jewish railway workers. At the individual level, the Histadrut provided the social framework within which the Jewish workers lived their lives. It provided essential services—health service, a loan in case of need, employment via the HLC Labor Exchange, and a channel to the political life of the Jewish community. At the organizational level, the Histadrut was essential as the go-between for the RPTWO in approaching the PR management, since the Palestine Railway did not recognize the RPTWO as a formal representative of the railway workers.[62] At the same time, the essence of the Histadrut, its Jewish exclusivity, contradicted the strategy pursued by the RPTWO. The central goal of the Histadrut was the transformation of Palestine into the Jewish national home—the conquest of the land through Jewish colonization, the conquest of the land through Jewish labor. Here, there was little room for the Arab worker!

The RPTWO recruited Arab members, but was deeply divided as to how to cope with the dilemma that inevitably arose. The strong constituency of left-wing workers, members of the Palestine Communist Party (PKP) and of *Poalei Zion-Smol* proposed far-reaching changes in the structure of the Histadrut, whereby workers would be organized without regard to their national affiliations.[63] The dilemma would thus be solved by removing Jewish exclusivity from the Histadrut and by separating class struggle from national community building. The mainstream Jewish members of the RPTWO did not support such radical changes. They advocated a "flexible incorporation" of the Arab members into the Histadrut. By this they meant that the Arab members of the RPTWO would, indeed, become members of the Histadrut, but this would not entail a structural and ideological change of the Histadrut into a binational labor organization. The Histadrut Executive (HE), for its part, would neither contemplate relinquishing its leading role in the national movement, nor did it want to set a precedent by allowing full Arab membership. It called for the separation of the Jewish and Arab workers into two distinct national units, within the same organization. This was the only form of Arab membership that the Histadrut Executive would consider. Both the left-wing and mainstream members of the RPTWO rejected the division of workers into distinct national units. They felt that it would make it more difficult to recruit Arab members and it would impede the consolidation of the organization. The rift between the RPTWO and the HE widened.[64]

The Arab workers, who had joined the RPTWO, were in at least as much of a quandary. While they accepted the importance of organization in general and of joint organization in particular, they did not want to be affiliated with the Jewish-Zionist national project. They were also split between two main courses of action. Some hoped to shape the RPTWO as a class organization, with no reference to the nationality of its members. This could be achieved, they argued, through joining forces with those Jewish workers who supported the transformation of the RPTWO and of the Histadrut into a class-oriented organization. Together they would constitute the majority of the membership and would therefore be able to determine the nature of the organization. Other Arab members soon came to the conclusion that such an internal change was highly unlikely and chose to leave the RPTWO. They called on their Arab comrades to follow them.

These different orientations among Jewish and Arab workers came to the fore in a dramatic meeting that took place well into the night of the 20th of November 1924. The Central Committee of the RPTWO, made up of both Jewish and Arab members, convened for its first meeting. After the issues on the agenda were concluded, Hasnin Fahmi, one of the Arab members of the Central Committee, requested leave to present a number of questions to the Jewish members, "on condition that no one gets angry."[65] He then requested a reply to the following two questions: (1) Was there any connection between the RPTWO and the Zionist idea? (2) Were the Jewish members of the Central Committee themselves Zionists? He added that, since he was aware that not all Jews were Zionists, he wanted to know how the Jewish members of the Central Committee identified themselves. What happened next was later described by the different parties. Grobman reported to the Histadrut Executive that "after a short consultation" the Jewish members replied "in a resolute, straight forward manner" that the RPTWO was a class-based organization, and as such had nothing to do with the Zionist idea. The political views of the individual Jewish members, continued the reply, were not the concern of the Arab members who, in turn, were not asked about their own political views. According to Grobman, the Arab members were somewhat taken aback by the assertive, non-apologetic tone of the answer. Having been told that they could inform the Arab press that the RPTWO had no connection to the Zionist idea, "they went on their way."[66]

The same incident was reported in the Arab press. Repeating the questions put forward by Hasnin Fahmi, the response was described as follows:

> After these two questions the [Jewish—D.B.] members became angry and did not utter a word. After a deep silence their answer was that they would reply in an hour. It was then midnight. The Arab members left, Hasnin Fahmi leading the way. When 1 o'clock struck the secretary Khalfon appeared[67] and answered Fahmi as follows: Reply A. Our organization is called an organization of class struggle. B. Hasnin does not have the competence to present such a question . . . [a number of

unclear words—D.B.] Hasnin sighed at the waste of his time and the time of his friends at receiving such useless answers after they had thought that the organization had no national or religious affiliation, and they announced their resignation.[68]

Other Arab members quit the RPTWO together with Hasnin Fahmi. Within a few months, they formed the Organization of Arab Railway Workers (OARW), and called on all Arab railway workers to join them.[69] The OARW was the nucleus of the Palestine Arab Workers' Society (PAWS), which was set up later that year (1925). Many other Arab workers still hesitated. They shared the view that the RPTWO was indeed run as a Zionist association, which was in total contradiction to the workers' interests. But they were still committed to a mixed trade-union-like organization, one that would focus solely on the problems that concerned the railway workers regardless of religion or nationality. They were still of the opinion that the RPTWO could become such an organization and that an alliance between the Arab members and the Jewish left-wing members could bring about a different leadership. The time had not yet come to quit, they argued.

> We must work to take over the management of the association and turn it into an organization which will defend the interests of all the workers—Arabs and Jews. There is a large number of Jewish comrades who are highly experienced in the running of the association and who are sincerely and devotedly willing to help us. . . .
>
> By withdrawing from the organization we are reinforcing the position of the Zionists who are interested in our withdrawal, as they do not want any opposition to their political work.[70]

Another worker took a similar line:

> The organization itself is not Zionist. Indeed, there are among the leaders some who are enthusiastic about Zionism, while the rest are far from being Zionists. Such is the battle today within the association, and it is a violent struggle between the loyal workers, people of principles and integrity who are willing to sacrifice themselves for the existence of a common association and for the rights of the workers, and the deceitful Zionist leaders. Is it fair to leave these loyal comrades to pursue their sacred duties on their own, without your help?[71]

For a time, many of the Arab members remained within the RPTWO. On the 9th of January 1925, shortly after the above confrontation, the General Council of the RPTWO convened for its biannual meeting. It adopted a resolution that was by far the most radical that it had ever adopted or would adopt in the future. It declared the RPTWO to be an international trade association, which would include all railway workers without regard to religion, race, and or nationality. It further resolved to

> Demand of the General Convention of the General Federation of Jewish Labor that it organize all its trade associations on an international basis, and establish a country-wide, international trade association, to which the RPTWO would belong.[72]

In essence this resolution called for a total restructuring of the Histadrut and rejected its basic principle of Jewish exclusivity. It posited a federation of Arab-Jewish trade unions as a substitute for an overall association of Jewish labor concerned with promoting all forms of Jewish national colonization.

This was not to be. The following two years witnessed a weakening of the RPTWO. By the time the General Convention of the Histadrut took place, in June 1927, little remained of the radical spirit of 1925. The economic difficulties faced by the PR during 1926 and 1927 led to the deterioration of working conditions. Many of the Jewish workers left the railway, thus depleting the ranks of the active members. Many of the Arab members, disappointed by the lack of change within the RPTWO, left the organization. Some joined the newly formed Organization of Arab Railway Workers.[73] The decline of the RPTWO was exacerbated by its failure to gain the recognition of the PR management despite its extensive efforts to do so. Time and again the Railway management and the Palestine Administration posed obstacles to the recognition of the RPTWO. Time and again the RPTWO overcame them only to be presented with other claims and demands.[74] By the end of 1926, it was clear that the RPTWO had little chance of being recognized as the representative of all railway workers. Its potential advantage faded and the commitment of its members weakened.[75] Thus by 1927, it was clear that the RPTWO stood little chance of successfully challenging the Histadrut and bringing about its transformation.

The General Convention of the Histadrut, in June 1927, passed a resolution that determined how Arab workers would be associated with it. They were to form a separate national unit, which would be federated with the Jewish national unit, the exclusively Jewish Histadrut. Both national units would together form an overall, binational, labor organization—the Palestine Labor League.[76] This blueprint was then adopted by the RPTWO. Rather than transforming the Histadrut into an international trade association, as it had set out to do, the RPTWO itself accepted the division of its members into two national units. Instead of transcending nationalism, it reintroduced it as a structuring criterion of organization. The effect was immediately evident. In the coming convention of the RPTWO, which was to take place the following month in Haifa, there were no Arab delegates. Arab railway workers were still, formally, members of the RPTWO, but they no longer appear to have been actively involved. It was a convention of Jewish delegates, representing a primarily Jewish membership. An Arab worker, Ali Batl, a member of the Central Committee of the RPTWO, was one of the speakers to greet the assembly, but neither he nor any other Arab worker appears to have spoken during the three days of debates.[77]

Not all the Arab members left the RPTWO, and others did join from time to time. The RPTWO still declared itself to be an "international" organization. It still strove to represent both Jewish and Arab members. But this intention, or pretension, was to become a divisive rather than a uniting force in the years to come.

The Joint Committee, 1928–1936

At the opening of the Sixth Convention of the RPTWO in July 1927, Eid Salim, one of the most active Arab railway workers, addressed the assembly. He had joined the RPTWO earlier on, and left it it to become one of the founders of the Organization of Arab Railway Workers and of the PAWS. He was now bringing the greetings of his organization to the Convention of the RPTWO. Thus, although many of the Arab workers left the RPTWO and joined the OARW, they did not sever their relations with it. Instead they attempted a new form of cooperation in which the two separate organizations worked together.

The Joint Committee, composed of an equal number of representatives from the Organization of Arab Railway Workers (OARW) and of the RPTWO, was set up toward the end of 1927. By the beginning of 1928, the committee had formulated its platform. The platform stated that the RPTWO and the OARW would each continue to exist but would not act unilaterally on matters affecting all the railway workers. Where there was disagreement, two additional members of each organization would be called in for further negotiations. Only if this failed were the organizations free to pursue their separate courses, in the best interests of their members. "The Committee will attempt to bring about understanding among the workers, and strengthen their social relations in order to increase its activities for the maximum benefit of all," concluded the Platform.[78] The committee met for about half a year and disbanded in June 1928. It was reconstituted in 1934.

Meetings were held twice a month and dealt with concrete issues that concerned the workers. These included individual problems, such as that of the worker who had been fired for having smoked at work,[79] as well as general problems such as the need to improve the medical care and the sanitary conditions provided by the PR, the need to ensure payment for overtime, and the need to ensure that the days of leave owed to the workers would indeed be granted them.[80] The Joint Committee was represented by an Arab and a Jew when negotiating with senior officials over matters that were of concern to all railway workers.[81] Issues were aired and debated at the Joint Committee, and there seems to have been no significant disagreements concerning the actual needs of the railway workers. Nevertheless, the very existence of the Joint Committee was a source of serious contention among both the Jews and the Arabs. Each feared that its cooperation with the other in the Joint Committee would legitimize and strengthen the other party.

The RPTWO continued to claim that it was the one organization that represented both Jewish and Arab workers. It appealed to the Arab railway workers to join its ranks, and called on the PR management to recognize it as the representative of all railway workers. The Central Committee of the RPTWO and the HE feared that cooperation with the OARW would reinforce the latter's legitimacy as the representative of the Arab workers, and weaken the RPTWO's claim to represent *all* workers. They argued that the Joint Committee endangered whatever incentive individual Arab workers had for joining the RPTWO, by providing an alternative channel for cooperation. Every step taken by the Joint Committee was weighed by the RPTWO and the HE in terms of its possible implications for the relative position of the two organizations. They concluded that the Joint Committee was a mistake and should never have been formed because it distanced the Arab workers from the RPTWO and therefore weakened it. The Central Committee of the RPTWO, and especially the HE, decided to make use of the Joint Committee while it still existed, to strengthen the contacts of the RPTWO with the Arab workers, so as to draw them away from the OARW. The value of the Joint Committee for the advancement of the interests of the railway workers was hardly discussed at all.[82] The only Jewish workers to adopt a significantly different position were the members of the Haifa branch. Its Jewish and Arab members worked in the closest proximity at their place of work. The largest and most active branch of the RPTWO, its members did not share the negative view of the Central

Committee. Its representatives, skilled workers employed in the mechanical workshops, consistently claimed that the Joint Committee was essential for advancing the interests of the workers. It was they who pushed through resolutions supporting the reestablishment of the Joint Committee in 1934 after there had been little cooperation for some years. They were clearly acting against the instructions of the central institutions of both the RPTWO and the Histadrut.

The organized Arab railway workers also had very severe reservations. They feared lest their cooperation with the RPTWO, which continued to present itself as the representative of Arab and Jewish workers, be understood to support that claim. This fear was reinforced by the fact that the RPTWO insisted on including one of its Arab members as a delegate to the Joint Committee. The Arab members of the RPTWO were hardly happy with the position in which they found themselves. The solution proposed time and again by the Arab railway workers was similar to their 1924–25 proposals. They called on the workers, Jews and Arabs, to disassociate themselves from the labor movements of their respective national groups, and form a new association of all railway workers that would disregard nationality and religion.[83] The Jewish workers, as before, equivocated and dodged a direct reply.

The Joint Committee disintegrated in 1928 and the political strife of the summer of 1929 put an end to any formal cooperation among Jewish and Arab railway workers. But, as economic prosperity picked up again after 1932, as the cost of living rose and rents leaped, the dissatisfaction and agitation among the workers swelled. The government published a resolution with various improvements in the conditions of work of daily and monthly government employees (known as Circular 11), but drew back from applying it to the railway workers. Haifa, with its large concentration of skilled workers, once again led the way. The reestablishment of the Joint Committee in February 1934 was in direct response to rank-and-file pressure. It ushered in a two-year period of intensive activity—frequent meetings of the Joint Committee, mass assemblies of hundreds of workers, letters and petitions by joint Arab and Jewish delegations to both the General Manager of the PR and the High Commissioner.[84] The large and partially successful strike of the IPC workers, in March 1935, triggered the railway activists into applying further pressure on the railway management, and moderated the response of the administration. The Campbell Committee was appointed in March 1935 to examine the demands of the workers. Its disappointing recommendations, two months later (Communique 18/35),[85] brought about the first spontaneous one-day strike of all workers—

Jewish and Arab—at the mechanical workshops. A special council of representatives of all Arab and Jewish railway workers from all of Palestine was convened one week later. It sent a deputation of four Arab and four Jewish workers, from all railway departments, to the High Commissioner and also petitioned him in writing.[86] The meeting with the High Commissioner, which lasted for four hours, was also attended by the Chief Secretary of the Palestine Government, the General Manager of the PR, and the Deputy Treasurer. Some of the demands of the workers were partially met and other improvements were promised pending further negotiations.[87]

Tension relaxed. A sense of both satisfaction and expectation prevailed. The workers' representatives continued to negotiate in order to realize the promises made to them at the meeting. However, as rank-and-file pressure subsided, the strong ambivalence of the Central Committee of the RPTWO and of the Histadrut Executive toward the Joint Committee surfaced again. They argued that the RPTWO had lost prestige by working only through the Joint Committee, and it had strengthened the OARW. They agreed that it would not be politically correct to officially back out of the Committee, but made it clear that its disintegration would cause little grief. Many of the speakers suggested ways of bypassing it and reestablishing an independent course of action both in relation to the railway management and to the recruiting of Arab members.[88] Only the representatives of the Haifa branch stuck to their commitment to the Joint Committee. They tried to prevent any act that could be construed as a violation of the understandings that had been established in the Joint Committee and would lead to its dispersal. The Haifa representatives, Henigman, Kleinplatz, Helholtz, and Krisher, workers of the mechanical workshops, continued to claim that the Joint Committee had been a necessity in the past, and was still the only hope of getting the management to fulfill at least some of its promises.[89]

Again it seemed that the Histadrut and the RPTWO on the one hand, and the OARW and the PAWS on the other, were pressuring their representatives in the Joint Committee to lay low and to back out. Each side claimed that the other had tried to act on its own in order to increase its status and had thus jeopardized the chances of joint action.[90] Again the Arab activists called for the formation of a separate railway workers' association and put as much pressure as they could on their Jewish colleagues.[91] Once again the Jewish representatives stalled for time.[92] Once again the national conflict took over. The Arab General Strike was declared on the 20th of April 1936. It led to the Arab Rebellion. Formal cooperation came to a halt, leaving behind it personal friendships that did seem to weather the storm.

Two Organizations and Three Strikes, 1939–1947

The years of the Arab Rebellion left no room for formal cooperation. The two national groups pursued their different and conflicting goals. Arab railway workers joined the general strike, though only for short periods of time, and Jewish workers attempted to increase their share in the railway's labor force. Shortly after the Arab Rebellion ended, the Second World War broke out. The cost of living spiraled. Common difficulties again came to the fore. Italian airplanes bombed Palestine, targeting industrial enterprises, oil refineries, and railway junctions. The workers of the mechanical workshops pushed for concerted action in order to improve their security in the face of the Italian bombing, and to ensure a satisfactory cost of living allowance. They also wished to get the management to fulfill the promises they had made to them as far back as 1935.[93]

Neither the Jewish nor the Arab activists were anxious to reestablish the Joint Committee. The years of the Arab Rebellion had increased their mutual suspicion. But grass-roots pressure for concerted action mounted. As early as September 1939, a letter written in the name of all workers of the mechanical workshops was addressed to the General Manager of the PR. It requested the payment of a higher cost of living allowance, a full working week, provision stores for workers, gas masks for all workers, and shellproof places in the workshops area. No answer was forthcoming. They therefore sent a reminder six weeks later.[94] In February 1940, memoranda written in Arabic and Hebrew, and signed by hundreds of workers from the mechanical workshops, called for improved security as well as improved sanitary and medical conditions.[95] The PR's negative reply generated a spurt of activity. Veteran Arab and Jewish activists from Haifa and Lydda met several times during the following months. They formulated an additional memorandum and sent a joint delegation of workers to speak to the management.[96] This delegation included representatives of the different Railway departments, three of whom were Jewish workers active in the RPTWO and four were Arab workers active in the OARW.[97] This ad hoc level of cooperation continued from 1940 to 1942. Together they dispatched numerous memoranda and appointed delegations. Mutual suspicion, bred by past experience, prevented the formation of a new Joint Committee. Instead, for the first time, the two nationally oriented organizations acknowledged each other and cooperated through their respective delegates.

It was the new General Manager of the PR, A. F. Kirby, who initiated the formalization of the workers' representation. He had been an official of the British Railway and active in the trade union movement. Once he assumed his post in April 1942, he was interested in negotiating with a recognized long-term workers' representation, yet this was not to be found. Neither the RPTWO nor the OARW had been formally recognized by the PR or the Palestine Administration. Kirby suggested establishing a committee of departmental representatives, to bypass the informal status of the workers' organizations, but immediately came up against a new political obstacle. How many Arabs and how many Jews would be members of this committee? The Arab activists demanded that it be made up of a majority of Arab members, to reflect the Arab majority in the PR and in all of Palestine. The Jewish activists insisted on parity between Jews and Arabs.[98] To break through this stalemate, which threatened any hope of recognized representation, Kirby proposed a Staff Committee made up of a senior railway officer as chairman, two technical railway officers, the railway welfare officer, and two workers' representatives chosen by the unions. He appealed for cooperation between the two unions, even though neither had been formally recognized by the PR, and proposed that they each appoint a delegate In a letter addressed to the secretaries of the International Union of Railway, Post & Telegraph Employees (the name the RPTWO had adopted in 1931), and the Railway Arab Workers Trade Union (the OARW), he wrote:

> The Staff Committee which I wish to establish opens a permanent and proper channel of responsible representation and consideration of staff matters. It provides for two members chosen by the staff to sit in committee with railway officers and it is my hope that those two members will bring to the Committee the mature considerations of the Workers' Committee. This is in accordance with the best practice and I am hoping that you will use your good offices in establishing a successful employees' committee through the medium of your Unions and so ensure that the two members of the Staff Committee shall be truly representative.[99]

After further negotiation between the two organizations, which were replete with declarations of good will combined with mutual suspicion, they agreed on two representatives. Sa'id Kawas of the mechanical workshops in Haifa was a veteran activist of both the OARW and the PAWS. Ephraim Schwartzman, of the RPTWO, was a locomotive driver stationed in Lydda. In May 1943, the Staff Committee began to meet regularly every month. A. H. Cousens, the Haifa senior official of the government Labor Department, attended the meetings in an advisory capacity.[100] The workers' representatives raised the issues that had been troubling the workers for many years, and attempted to work together. They consulted with each other before meetings and supported each other during the sessions. But they did not report back to a joint committee. They were the acknowledged representatives of their respective organizations. They continued to cooperate with each other not only within the management-initiated Staff Committee but also in joint petitions and delegations.

As before, their achievements were few. Under conditions of full employment and a high cost of living, pressure from the workers mounted. They became more and more agitated. Small incidents triggered mass protests that were not initiated by the labor organizations, and were often against their wishes. On the 23rd of December 1942, the tinsmiths of the mechanical workshops refused to return to work after their lunch break. They were all Arab and were underpaid. The following morning Sa'id Mahmud, the secretary of the Railway Workers' Section of the PAWS, called on all the railway workers to join their strike. The Jewish workers also complied with this request. The strike lasted only one day and the workers returned after they were promised that a delegation of three Arab and three Jewish workers would meet with the Chief Secretary of the Palestine Administration. This meeting took place within a week. The delegates demanded that the workers participate in all discussions concerning their work conditions before the management took any final decisions.[101] As we have seen, this was eventually implemented in the Staff Committee initiated by the new GM.

Another additional strike was declared a year later. In January 1944, the government announced a cut in the cost of living allowance because of a decline in the cost of living index as measured by the government. And this, only a few months after the CoLA had been raised! The Histadrut Executive accepted the government's decision, but the workers, both Jewish and Arab, were vehemently opposed to it. On Wednesday, February 2, an Arab worker was badly wounded at work. No doctor was at hand, and the doctor who was summoned from the nearby Vulcan factory found no adequate medical equipment. The workers were up in arms. Ephraim Krisher, the secretary of the local branch of the RPTWO, suggested to his colleague, Kleinplatz, that they call a demonstration. Krisher, a member of the *Shomer Hatza'ir*, led the left-wing nucleus of the Haifa branch of the RPTWO.[102] He frequently opposed the organization's central institutions, which were dominated by *Mapai*. Within fifteen minutes the work had stopped. Not a worker remained in the workshops. A strike committee of three Arab and two Jewish workers was set up. The workers staged a sit-in and refused to leave the work site. Krisher later reported that all the workers attended a meeting in the large halls of the mechanical workshops. Workers spoke out in Hebrew and Arabic and others translated. The workers were resolute. They decided that they would not leave the place until their demands were met. The management exerted strong pressure on the strike committee, which chose to resign rather than to give in. The representatives of the two workers' associations continued to negotiate. At the grass-roots level the sit-in continued.

> The Arab workers treated the Jewish workers with fraternity and solidarity. The PAWS sent *pitot* and olives, and these were distributed among all the workers. Many of the Arab workers approached each and every Jewish worker to ask if he had had enough to eat. Friday evening [the evening between Thursday and Friday—D.B.] Jewish and Arab workers sat around the bonfires and warmed themselves together—singing songs and telling tales. When finally, under the pressure of the families of the Jewish workers, the HLC consented to send food to the Jewish strikers, large amounts of bread, *halva* and cigarettes arrived and were received with much appreciation . . . Friday, at 12.00, Sami Taha, the secretary of the PAWS, began negotiating with the management, together with Abramov.[103]

By late Friday night the strike was concluded. Aba Houshi strongly opposed the strike. It went against Histadrut policy and, above all, had been declared without his approval and control. Abramov, the secretary of the RPTWO, argued that any strike in the workshops strengthened the PAWS and thus should be opposed. Sami Taha of the PAWS was ambivalent about the grass-roots Arab-Jewish cooperation. Negotiations continued. The labor representatives were affected by the ambivalence of their leaders and opted for a quick end to the strike. Nothing concrete was promised the workers. The workers' representatives agreed to call on the workers to go back to work in return for arbitration by Mr. Cousens of the Labor Department. However, none of the negotiators was ready to go back to the workshops and bring the decision to the workers. This was left to Cousens' Arab secretary.[104]

Krisher, the *Shomer Hatza'ir* secretary of the Haifa branch concluded his report:

> The embarrassing conclusion of the strike notwithstanding, it was a moving experience for the workers. They feel that they have done a great thing. There was complete unity and joint action between the workers of both nationalities. Sitting together after work they cheered the foremen. The slogan "long live Arab-Jewish unity" was

Figure 10. Sami Taha, secretary of
Palestine Arab Worker's Society, 1947.

enthusiastically received. There is disappointment but also hope that
the strike will nevertheless bear some fruit.[105]

The workers won a few concessions. But it took the general strike of
22,000 government employees to bring about the really significant
gains. On the 10th of April 1946, the postal service workers in Tel Aviv
declared a strike. After five days of negotiations, the workers rejected

the agreement arrived at by the Histadrut and the strike spread to include the railway workers, the unclassified civil servants, and other smaller groups of government employees. Of those who participated in the strike about 10,000 were unclassified civil servants, 2,500 of whom were Jews; 7,000 railway workers (of whom 400 were Jewish), 2,000 postal workers (of whom 800 were Jews) and 2,500 workers of the Public Works Department (of whom 600 were Jewish).[106] As with the previous strike, the Histadrut did not initiate or encourage it. Since fewer than half the Jewish strikers were members of the Histadrut, it had little chance of determining the outcome of the strike. It was better positioned to intervene in the case of the PR, where most Jewish workers were union members. A committee of senior officials of the PR and of the Labor Department and representatives of the labor organizations was set up. Sami Taha represented the Arab workers while Abramov represented the Jewish workers. Aba Houshi, who quickly realized that this strike, unlike the earlier one, could not be dissipated, accompanied it with flaming rhetoric:

> I wish to state unequivocally that the unity and solidarity that we have seen these two weeks between thousands of Jewish and Arab workers (more accurately between Arabs and Jews because the Arabs were the overwhelming and determining majority in these areas) was a surprise to many, but not to us. We have always known that there existed the potential for this kind of unity and solidarity between workers, for this is only natural. It is disunity and lack of solidarity among workers which are not natural. And if there was anyone who argued to the contrary . . . well here we have it—the complete unity and solidarity between Jewish and Arab workers.[107]

For the first time, after many years of negotiations, the workers were able to satisfy some of their most basic and persistent demands. These included an increase in the basic wage, an increase in the cost of living allowance, and the payment of compensation for the fall in earnings during the war.[108]

But time was running out. Political tension was mounting as the final decision on Palestine's future drew nearer. During 1946 and 1947, violent clashes spread throughout Palestine. As before, the railways were a major target for sabotage, which was usually aimed at mainlines, bridges, station buildings, and moving trains.[109] Clashes, bombings, and murders spread within Haifa as well. Groups of Arab villagers entered the town and targeted Jews, British, and those Arabs who were considered not totally committed to the Arab national struggle.

Jewish forces attacked as well. At times they retaliated; at others they initiated the attacks. The Jewish underground groups—the *Etzel* and the *Lehi*—struck out on their own.[110] Fear spread, and by December 1947, 15,000 to 20,000 Arabs had fled the town.[111] Work in the mechanical workshops continued. There were no major clashes, but both Jews and Arabs feared attacks by outside forces or small incidents that could easily flare into serious violence. Ephraim Krisher described the relations in the Workshops in an impassioned letter to the HE:

> Even in these days the contact between the Jewish and Arab representatives has not been severed and as in normal times we have continued to appear together before the management of the railways in professional matters and even in security matters. We formulated the security demands together and we appeared together in order to ensure the lives of all the workers. At their initiative the demand was put forward that Jewish workers work in Jewish areas and Arab workers in Arab areas.
>
> We have seen with our own eyes how the leaders of this organization [OARW—D.B.] are standing the test today against a furious and incited mob and even endangering themselves. At the beginning of the riots there were odd clashes between Jewish and Arab workers in the workshops which were resolved by the intervention of the union activists. They did not once support and vindicate the Arab attacker. I understand that the workers council of the Railway workers called a special conference to discuss relationships at work, at which Abu Faris spoke and advocated peaceful relationships between Jewish and Arab workers in the workplace and seriously criticized attacks on peaceful people who are not taking part actively in the riots . . . these leaders, moreover, appeared at their full stature on 30/12/47, the day of the tragedy at the oil refineries and blocked the wild mob, hot to attack their Jewish comrades.[112]

That day the Jewish workers of the Consolidated Refineries Limited were brutally attacked. The attack was instigated as a reprisal against two bombs that members of the *Etzel* underground hurled into a crowd of about 150 Arabs who were standing at the entrance to the refineries. Six Arabs were killed and fifty were wounded. As word of the disaster spread through the grounds and workshops of the refineries, Arab workers attacked, wounded, and killed Jewish workers. Thirty nine Jewish workers were murdered and many more wounded. According to the inquest, many of the Arab workers at the refinery took part in the attack. Some did help Jewish workers escape. None tried to prevent or stop the attack.[113]

The mechanical workshops of the railway were located near the refineries, and before long news and rumors of what was happening reached the workshops. Krisher continued his account:

> When the news of the attack on the Arab workers next to the oil refineries reached the workshops, the agitators shut down all the machines. The union activists tried by all sorts of means to bring the workers back to work. S. Qawwas tried unsuccessfully three times to restart the machines to the chagrin of the workers. Meanwhile there was a commotion amongst the younger workers. They collected all sorts of tools and screws. The gates were closed and there were all the signs that they were about to attack us. Despite this S. Qawwas, Abu Farris and many of the veteran workers made immense efforts to prevent the outbreak of violence. Without a shadow of a doubt we must acknowledge gratefully that it was their great courage that saved us from the fate of the refinery workers on that day.[114]

Krisher ended his letter by appealing for a complete revision of the Histadrut's cooptative and manipulative attitude to the Arab workers and their organizations:

> We must free ourselves from the illusions about the PLL and accept the fact that there are stable Arab Workers' Organizations who have earned their right to exist. To the extent that we succeed in establishing relations of mutual trust, we will bring them closer to us especially if they accept, as indeed appears to be the case, the fact of the division of the land and the establishment of a Jewish state on the Jewish half.[115] Our joint work of many years has proven that this is possible and depends in no small measure on us.[116]

This was not to be. On the 22nd of April 1948, not long after the letter was sent, the *Hagana*, the Jewish armed forces, took control of Haifa. Over 55,000 Arabs fled during the months before and the days immediately after the surrender of the Arab community.[117] Most of the Arab railway workers were probably among them.[118]

TO CONCLUDE

The Palestine Railway was different from all the other places of work. It was the one place in which Jewish and Arab workers were employed, on equal terms, directly under the same management and over a long period of time. It was the one place in which the workers joined together to fight for improved working conditions. Thus the PR can demonstrate both the feasibility of joint action and its limitations. Precisely those conditions that made joint action a viable option, in fact an inevitable one, in the railway, help explain why it was so rare. The conditions of the Palestine Railway did not enable the creation of any form of closure that would have protected the Jewish workers from the competition of cheaper Arab labor, as was the case in the Haifa port. There was no possibility of securing a special niche for Jewish workers, in which relations of labor and levels of reward would approach their expectations and aspirations. Jewish workers, like the Arab workers, were employed by an authority of the colonial government. In the railway "they were all natives." The rank-and-file workers thus all experienced the same conditions and this common experience created the push toward joint organization. It was at the level of rank-and-file workers and activists that mutual help, which transcended national divides, developed. It was at that level that the workers expressed the desire to disengage from politics and "phraseology." This desire was never realized. Its implementation was not even seriously attempted. The farther one moved from the work site, the more salient were criteria of political benefits, considerations of cooptation and manipulation, and the greater was the gap between public rhetoric and petty calculations. And yet, despite the contradictions in which the attempts at cooperation were repeatedly entrapped, and despite their meager achievements, they do provide one of the very few legacies of cooperation between Arab and Jewish workers in Palestine.

Conclusion

This study began by questioning the starting point of much Israeli historiography, by questioning the separateness and isolation of the Jewish community in Palestine, the Jewish *Yishuv*. The close proximity of Jews and Arabs and its impact has been overlooked by most students of the Jewish settlement. It has concerned those studying the Arab-Jewish (or Arab-Israeli) conflict, but appeared quite irrelevant for the understanding of the Jewish society "in itself." The boundaries of the Jewish settlement were accepted as a given. The very separateness of an autonomous, Jewish society, with its distinct identity, interests, and processes of consolidation, was taken as a given. And yet, how autonomous and how separate could the Jewish settlement be, a small minority lacking political sovereignty? Was there not far more interpenetration between the Jewish and Arab communities/societies than previous studies would lead us to assume? Could the Jewish settlement have developed without being deeply affected by the Arab society and economy predominant in Palestine?

The complete focusing on, and into, the Jewish community as if it was secured within clear-cut, impenetrable and unrefuted boundaries, served to reinforce the self-image of the Jewish settlement—the *Yishuv*. Even accepting that boundaries did exist that distinguished the new Jewish community, such a focus did not lead to sufficient understanding of the formation of such boundaries. It could not shed light on the controversies and conflicts concerning boundary formation, as the boundaries themselves were taken for granted. Such a perspective was not geared to examine the impact and the long-term ramifications of such boundaries. They were conveyed as part of the basic order rather than as a negotiated and dynamic social construct.

I intended to open up the issue of the autonomy and separation of the Jewish community by studying the growth of the Jewish community in a mixed town, and its activity within the town economy. I had assumed that a mixed town would provide varied opportunities for mutual relations, which would come to the fore once attention would be directed at them. I further assumed that the economy in general, and the labor market in particular, would be the sphere least easily separated and segregated, and thus most revealing of forms of interaction and cooperation.

The study of Haifa's society and economy modified my expectations. The most salient trend appeared to be the initiation of separation by the Jewish community with regard to the Arab majority. Separate neighborhoods, separate communal institutions, separate economic enterprises, and separate labor organizations were on the increase, overshadowing points of contact and direct interaction. The economy was an integral part of this overall process. Rather than finding numerous expressions of joint economic activity, as I had expected, I seemed to come across a wide-ranging, pervasive attempt at separation. At the same time, the drive for economic separation was not equally shared by all segments of Haifa's population, not even by all segments of the Jewish community. While boundary building was the most salient process, it was certainly not accepted and shared by all. It was above all the project of Jewish organized labor. Arab economic elites did not seek to separate themselves from the economic growth triggered by Jewish colonization. Neither were Jewish economic elites keen on complete separation, as they also benefited from various forms of exchange of resources between Arabs and Jews. While they accepted a fair measure of separation, they had strong reservations toward the total closure demanded by organized Jewish labor. Arab workers did not want to construct boundaries. To the contrary, the expanding economy created hopes for new opportunities of employment. The evolving boundaries between the Arab and Jewish economy and labor market in Haifa were, above all, the vested interest of Jewish labor. The basic pattern that emerged from the study of Haifa's labor market was the overall, pervasive separation and boundary construction between Jews and Arabs which was pushed through by organized Jewish labor. The essence of the construction of boundaries in the economic sphere was to close the Jewish economy to Arab labor so as to protect Jewish workers from the competition of much cheaper Arab workers. The numerous ways in which such closure was pursued, the extent to which it was achieved, and the implications of the dominance of closure in the relations between Jewish and Arab workers, became the heart of the story of the mixed town of Haifa and its labor market.

The Haifa labor market was studied through focusing on a number of large industries: construction and manufacturing industries, the Haifa port, and the Palestine Railways. Each industry was studied according to its economic development and internal differentiation, to the composition of its labor force, and to the ensuing relations between Jewish and Arab workers, the major interest of this study. These aspects were analyzed at the overall level of the industry; they were studied as they fluctuated over time taking into account economic and political events; and they were examined at specific sites and junctures, labor conflicts, and strikes.

Haifa was indeed a major center for both Jewish and Arab workers. Early on in the first years of the twentieth century Haifa won the name of *Um al-Amal*, "Mother of Labor" in Arabic, to which Arab peasants congregated in search of wage labor. Some twenty years later it became known in the new Jewish settlement as 'Haifa *ha-Aduma'*—"Red Haifa," where the strongest and most effective local labor council was consolidating its power. By the end of the 1920s, it had obtained its monopoly over the Jewish labor market, and to no small extent its hegemony over the Jewish community in general. Did this lead to new and different relations between Jewish and Arab workers? Did the proximity of a mixed town, did the common goal of congregating to the coastal city and finding employment, did the very process of labor organization, lead to cooperation?

My central conclusion was that these conditions did not lead to the establishment of new forms of joint action. Much of the time, the opposite took place. The proximity and competition over often scarce employment created clashes of interest rather than foci for joint action. The development of both Jewish and Arab labor was deeply affected by each other's existence, but the most salient outcome was the drive of Jewish labor for organization and separation, for closure, and for the construction of boundaries. Resources, energy, and ingenuity were devoted to achieve that goal, and its implications were immense. To a major extent it ruled out the possibility of joint action between Jews and Arabs, and particularly between Jewish and Arab workers.

The previous chapters presented a detailed discussion of the particular dynamics within the different industries. Construction work was especially susceptible to competition between Jewish and Arab workers, as the latter were well able to do the required work for a much lower wage. As a result the Haifa Labor Council devoted much of its efforts to achieve an outstandingly high level of organization of Jewish construction workers. This was supplemented by widespread and diverse social pressure directed at all levels of Jewish employers. This pressure peaked from time to time with concerted action of Jewish workers to block the entrance of Arab workers to Jewish-owned construction work. The relations were thus ones of competition and conflict, latent or salient hostility, or at best distance and separation. To the extent that separation was achieved, there was little contact and few common interests. To the extent that Arab workers continued to be employed by Jewish houseowners and contractors, there was once again little contact and even less chance of common interests emerging. It was doubtful whether issues of concern to both, such as an eight-hour work day in construction, could be stronger than the competition over places of work, or whether such common interests could compensate for the possible deterioration of labor conditions already obtained by Jewish organized workers.

Manufacturing industry entailed much less direct competition, as the skills required were much more prevalent among Jewish workers, and the industry in general less labor intensive. Thus the closure of Jewish-owned industry was achieved far more easily and less conflictually. Nevertheless, on a number of occasions joint action was called for. In the few Jewish-owned enterprises where Arab workers were employed together with Jewish workers, the necessity for cooperation could emerge. When organized Jewish workers demanded improvement of labor conditions and confronted their employers, all the workers had to be mobilized. For that specific moment cooperation was essential, overshadowing long-term claims of Jewish workers for the monopoly of labor market. Common struggle could very well lead to a genuine sense of solidarity, especially at the grass-roots level. But this did not transform the long-term relations. These were primarily determined by the demand for the closure of the Jewish owned workplace before Arab labor due to the threat of substitution of Arab for Jewish workers. Let us recall two incidents previously discussed. In the Nur match factory, in the years following the strike of the Jewish and Arab workers, the labor force became almost exclusively Arab. In the Mosaica tile factory, following the strike in which both Jewish and Arab workers took part, the labor force became primarily Jewish. The circumstances of the two places differed, as discussed in detail in Chapter 4. But in both cases the expressions of solidarity that developed during the joint strike did not change the basic pattern of relations between Jewish and Arab factory workers.

The Haifa port was, once again, an arena of separation within a mixed context. As a government-owned enterprise, there was no possibility of closing the port to Arab labor. On the contrary, Arab workers were highly suited for the port work. It was the Jewish workers who had to make their way into the Haifa port. They had to find a way to persuade the port authority to employ them, and to do so on conditions of work that would be at least minimally satisfactory for them. In principle, such conditions could be obtained through joint demands of Jewish and Arab workers. And yet that was highly unlikely. The casual nature of much of the work, the exchangeability of the workers, and the competition over opportunity of employment, all made the possibility of improving conditions, via joint action, highly improbable. Instead, most Jewish workers entered the port through the creation of a separate Jewish "niche," via the introduction of Jewish contractors, who reproduced a form of closure within the government-owned port. Such closure was achieved through close cooperation between the HLC, other Histadrut institutions, and the Jewish Agency, which combined to provide the necessary financial, organizational, and political resources necessary to enable the introduction of Jewish contractors who would employ Jewish workers. Once again, cooperation between Jewish and Arab workers could hardly be expected. The one case of cooperation and solidarity discussed in Chapter 5, the joint strike of Arab and Jewish seamen, can serve to reinforce this conclusion rather than to refute it. The strike in which Jewish workers supported the struggle of their Arab comrades took place before the large-scale introduction of Jewish workers occurred. More important, this strike was held in one of the rare cases in which Jewish workers were employed together with Arab workers, by an Arab contractor, and under the same conditions of work. It was under such circumstances, highly exceptional in the split labor market of Haifa (or Palestine in general), that joint action took place.

The Palestine Railway was the one place in which a strikingly different pattern of relations emerged between Arab and Jewish workers. It was the one place where Jewish and Arab workers continuously attempted various forms of cooperation. These attempts varied. Initially an organization composed of half Jewish and half Arab workers came close to offering a radical alternative to the existing, nationally divided, organizations of labor. Later, far more moderate forms of cooperation evolved, also stumbling against numerous obstacles, primarily those of political and national priorities. The PR was the one place in which no form of closure could be introduced or maneuvered by Jewish labor. Thus it was far more difficult for Jewish workers to protect themselves against the low level of wage and work conditions that were paid to

Arab workers. Because they could not create a separate niche in the PR, it was far more difficult to effectively recruit the help of Zionist institutions in improving the conditions of Jewish workers. As a result, Jewish workers employed by the PR concentrated in the skilled occupations, where they worked together with skilled Arab workers. Under those conditions the only way to win improvements was through joint action. The work of the skilled Arab and Jewish railway workers took place in the same location, and over extended periods of time. It was there that a consistent shift in the concern of the Jewish workers could be discerned. It was the one place where the issue of cooperation with the Arab workers became the primary issue of concern while the issue of the introduction of Jewish workers was secondary.

The major response of Jewish workers to the condition of the SLM is not difficult to understand. It was predictable on sociological-theoretical grounds. It was also highly compatible with the overall perspective of the Jewish settlement. Bonacich's theory of the Split Labor Market claimed that the higher priced workers, of a distinct ethnic and national group, would attempt to protect their position in competition with much cheaper labor, by striving to close the labor market to the latter. This strategy was especially appropriate to the conditions of Zionist settlement. The overall Zionist goal was to establish a distinctly separate, and eventually dominant, Jewish national home in Palestine. To that purpose it structured its institutions, directed its financial resources, developed its widespread network of political relations, and articulated its ideology and symbolic apparatus. Economic separation thus was a priority of Jewish labor which reinforced the overall Zionist goal, and was in turn reinforced by it. The concrete ways in which this mutual reinforcement was put into effect were discussed in the above chapters, revealing the numerous ways through which Jewish labor could obtain support in its competition with Arab labor.

The Jewish community of Haifa, and especially organized Jewish labor, was no exception to the general pattern. But in Haifa, probably more than elsewhere in Palestine, there were circumstances in which attempts at closure were not sufficient, or at least not sufficiently effective. Despite the energy, ingenuity and resources devoted by Jewish institutions for ensuring the employment of Jewish workers (aided by the rallying call of *Avoda Ivrit*—Hebrew Labor), Arab workers were still an accessible and visible alternative for Jewish employers, just as they remained the primary labor force for the government employer. These circumstances, and these only, I have argued in previous chapters, led to attempts at joint action and organizational cooperation.

Such attempts at cooperation on the part of organized Jewish labor were, most often, hesitant and intermittent. They were usually tinged with a heavy dose of cooptation. They were often geared as much, if not more, to obtain influence over Arab workers and to divert them from the Arab national labor movements, than to advance the common class interests of the workers of both nationalities. In most cases the attempts at cooperation met with very limited success. Time and again attempts at cooperation, at joint action, failed or met with very short-term success. This was often due, as illustrated in the previous chapters, to obstacles embedded in the overall closure of the Jewish settlement and particularly of the Jewish labor movement. More generally, attempts at all forms of cooperation came up against conflicting national-political priorities, interests, and overall ideological perspectives of both national groups.

The Jewish community of Haifa did not develop alternative ways of relating to the Arab population or, at least, these did not become a salient option. By the term "alternative" I am referring to the conception of, or structuring of, a substantially different pattern of relations. Primarily, one in which the "zero-sum" mutual perspective would be rejected, the perspective according to which any benefit gained by one national group was, by definition, detrimental to the other. Moments of such nonconflicting relations did exist, and in all likelihood they were more common in the mixed context of Haifa than in homogeneously Jewish settlements, but these did not come together to an overall pattern of relations and forms of organization. As such, the dominant pattern, separation combined with elements of cooptation on the part of the Jewish population and its elites, and strong opposition combined with attempts to gain personal benefits on the part of the Arab population and its elites, were evident in all spheres of life.

Nevertheless, while Haifa was not the breeding ground of alternative relations between Jews and Arabs, different voices could and were heard. Cases of cooperation did exist among Jewish and Arab workers, at both an informal personal level and an organizational level. Concerning these, two points should be noted. First, such cases appeared primarily when closure was not an effective, or even possible, option. Second, cooperation was desired, initiated, and/or advanced to a far greater extent at the rank-and-file level, or the closer one got to it, than at the level of labor leadership. Time and again the initiative, even the pressure, for cooperation and for joint action came from the "shop floor." Regrettably it is precisely the level that is least documented. Nevertheless, the indications are clear. Rank-and-file workers were more inclined to cooperate with the workers of the other nationality than were the further removed central labor institutions. This was evident both among railway workers and among the workers of the military camps. The initiative to recruit Arab workers into the organization of railway workers came from the Jewish workers, and not from the full-time functionaries. It was an anonymous worker in a mass meeting of Jewish and Arab workers who called on them all to put aside "philosophies and phraseology" and act together to improve their conditions of work. Initiatives for joint action among railway workers were far more sustained in Haifa, where rank-and-file workers were in the closest day-to-day contact, than in the Tel Aviv-based central institutions. The RPTWO, in general, was far more inclined to joint action than the Histadrut Executive. And so once again, in the army camps of the Second World War,[1] time after time, rank-and-file cooperation between Jews and Arabs working in the camps preceded the initiative of the higher echelons of labor institutions, and triggered them into action they might well have preferred to avoid. My intention is not to claim that rank-and-file workers, especially rank-and-file Jewish workers, developed a different perspective concerning the workers of the other, rival, nationality. I am not contending that class interests, in the case of the workers, transcended national commitments. I see no reason and no grounds to put forward such a claim. I am arguing that during specific moments of need, in which it was clear that only joint action could possibly lead to positive result, rank-and-file workers were far more ready to give priority to daily bread and butter needs, while labor functionaries and leaders tended to continue to give priority to consideration of national interests, relative power, influence, and legitimacy. When and where small steps were taken to transcend national considerations, they were triggered by the rank-and-file workers. Such steps, I would further argue, turned into relatively successful ventures when, and only when, Jewish and Arab labor organizations cooperated as autonomous, equal entities. It was there that a glimmer of genuine cooperation was evident. As discussed above—far too little, far too late.

Class interests could not and did not transcend national interests. In many respects the two were deeply intertwined. Jewish workers strove for separation and closure to advance their class interests as higher priced, organized workers who sought for ways to ensure employment and beneficial returns. In doing so they benefited in numerous ways by the overall Zionist venture. It provided them with a channel for immigrating to Palestine, with a developing economy fueled by national and private funds, with an organizational and institutional infrastructure, and with a community and a sense of identity. There is little reason, either theoretical-sociological or historical, to expect Jewish workers to

reject the strategy of closure embedded in an overall national movement. But the very acceptance of separation had a deep impact, to
which we shall soon return.

The reaction and strategy of Arab workers and Arab labor is more
difficult to define. The theoretical-sociological model adopted so far,
Bonacich's SLM model, did not even contemplate the possibility of action and reaction on the part of the cheaper and weaker groups of
workers, though recent studies have begun examining such possibil-
ities.[2] Historically, Arab workers were far less organized and articulate.
But Arab spokesmen, from the very beginning of the British rule, expressed strong opposition to the attempted monopoly of Jewish workers over employment in the Jewish-owned sector. They rightly considered such labor policy to be closely linked to the Zionist venture in
general. Arab elites opposed Zionist settlement as the creation of a separate and separatist entity, which would benefit its members and them
alone, and as such they opposed all aspects of such separatism. They
opposed labor immigration as causing unemployment among Arab
workers, already short of employment opportunities. They opposed
the Histadrut as the spearhead of the struggle for the exclusion of Arab
workers from employment in Jewish-owned enterprises, and rejected
its explanations and justifications. The Histadrut justified its "Jewish
labor only" policy and claimed that it was a legitimate policy for a socialist labor movement. It emphasized that the Jewish sector was developed by Jewish capital in order to absorb Jewish immigrants and otherwise would not have been developed in the first place. It further
argued that the government sector hardly employed Jewish workers
and that therefore the Jewish sector was their only source of employment. The Histadrut also claimed that the level of pay already obtained
by Jewish workers would no doubt decline if Arab workers were employed, thus justifying the precaution of closure. These arguments
were rejected by Arab speakers. Closure was closure . . . it served, so it
was argued, to increase unemployment among Arab workers who
could, and often did, find employment in the Jewish sector until strong
pressure led to their removal. Too many, rather than too few, Jews were
employed in the government sector, Arab spokesmen claimed, while
the argument of the "legitimate right of Jewish workers to protect their
conditions of labor by ruling out Arab workers" only added insult to
the injury. The arguments put forward by the Histadrut were repeatedly rejected and the Histadrut itself was delegitimized by leaders of
Arab labor on account of its policy.

The strong negative reaction on the part of Arab labor to the strategies of Jewish labor became most evident as the Arab labor organiza-

tions grew and their impact increased. Arab workers were still only able to obtain much lower wages than the Jewish workers. In this respect the split labor market situation did not change. And yet the "cheap workers" themselves underwent change. Ironically, the split labor market was, in itself, one of the major stimulants of change. The visibility of higher priced and well-organized workers was both a source of resentment and a trigger for organization by the Arab workers. The difficulty of cooperation between the labor organizations of both groups of workers can be accounted for primarily by the interplay of national and class considerations. Thus to the extent that national considerations could be "put aside," joint action was likely to develop. This did happen in response to concrete, specific situations, albeit rarely. To the extent that considerations of national power and prestige were paramount, it was the interests of the rank-and-file workers that were pushed aside.

The Histadrut's policy of closure had a significant impact both in the short and the long run. It conflicted with, and contradicted, cooperation between Jews and Arabs, even between those sharing similar class experience and class interests. It was extremely difficult to embark on joint action by Jewish and Arab workers in so separatist a context. It was close to impossible to "implant" cooperation, let alone partnership, onto or into such a separatist milieu. When separation was not possible, Jewish labor leaders reverted to cooptation and manipulation rather than to cooperation and partnership. This was detrimental to the immediate interests of the workers because such means usually failed. Time and again workers attempted joint action as the only way in which they could advance their goals of improving their labor conditions, and time and again their success was highly limited. But, far more important, I would argue, the Histadrut policy, coupled with the general Zionist orientation, had a long-term impact. To this day, fifty years after the Zionist venture achieved its central goal, joint action between Israeli Jews and Palestinian Arabs, initiated by Israeli elites, free of cooptation and/or manipulation, is infrequent, difficult, and highly tenuous.

Glossary

Ahdut ha-Avoda—Workers' party established in Palestine in 1919. Defined itself as Zionist and Socialist. The largest workers' party in the 1920s. United with Hapoel Hatzair to form Mapai.

Hakkibutz Hameuchad—Federation of Kibbutzim founded in 1927. Was affiliated with the largest workers' party, Ahdut ha-Avoda.

Hapoel Hamizrahi—Founded in 1922. Workers' branch of the Mizrahi, the religious Zionist party. Formed a close alliance with Mapai and enjoyed the benefits and services allocated by the Histadrut.

Hapoel Hatzair—Formed in 1905. A workers' party formed in Palestine. Did not consider itself a socialist, class-oriented party. United with Ahdut ha-Avoda in 1930 to form Mapai.

Hashomer Hatzair (The Young Guardsman)—Originally a youth movement established in eastern Europe. An important member of the pioneering immigration to Palestine from Third Aliya 1919 and onwards. Left of center of the Jewish Labor Movement in Palestine. Supported class cooperation between Jewish and Arab workers.

Itzel (Irgun Zva'i Le'umi—National Military Organization)—An underground Jewish paramilitary organization affiliated with the Revisionist movement. Founded in 1931. Did not accept the authority of the Labor Movement–dominated institutions of the Yishuv.

Lehi (Lohamei Herut Yisrael—Fighters for the Freedom of Israel)—Underground paramilitary organization that seceded from the Itzel in 1940. Both Itzel and Lehi adopted an aggressive strategy toward both Arabs and the British forces.

Mapai (Mifleget Poalei Eretz Israel—the Party of the Workers of the Land of Israel)—The largest workers' party in the Yishuv. Estblished in 1930 through the uniting of Ahdut ha-Avoda and Hapoel Hatzair. Was the dominant party in all elected institutions of the Yishuv, and in the World Zionist Organization, from the mid-1930s. Attempted to combine national goals with working-class interests.

Moshava (pl. **Moshavot**)—Private enterprise agricultural settlements. Most of them established in the end of the nineteenth century. Based on plantation and citrus agriculture. Tended to employ Arab workers as seasonal hired labor.

Palestine Office—Representing agency of the WZO in Palestine, established in 1908 and headed by Arthur Ruppin.

PKP—Palestine Communist Party—Known as PKP according to its original name in Yiddish—Palestiner Kumunistishe Partie. Established in 1919. Strongly opposed to Zionist movement, Zionist settlement in Palestine, and to the Histadrut and its Jewish labor policy. During most of the period of British rule, the PKP was illegal. Composed of both Jewish and Arab members. Split into Jewish and Arab sections in 1943.

Po'alei Zion Smol—The left wing of Po'alei Zion, the Workers of Zion. Seceded from Po'alei Zion when it united with unaffiliated workers, in 1919, to form Ahdut ha-Avoda. Was on the left fringe of the Zionist Labor Movement and supported Arab-Jewish joint trade unionism.

Va'ad Le'umi (National Council)—The executive body of the elected institutions of the Yishuv.

Abbreviations

FATULS	Federation of Arab Trade Unions and Labor Societies
GFJL	General Federation of Jewish Labor, the Histadrut
HC	High Commissioner
HE	Histadrut Executive
HLC	Haifa Labor Council
JA	Jewish Agency
OARW	Organization of Arab Railway Workers
PAWS	Palestine Arab Workers' Society
PLL	Palestine Labor League
PKP	Palestine Communist Party
PR	Palestine Railways
RPTWO	Railway, Post and Telegraph Workers' Organization
WTUF	World Trade Union Federation
WZO	World Zionist Organization

Notes

Introduction

1. Ya'acov Davidon, *There Once Was a Haifa* (Haifa: Mai Publication, n.d.) (Hebrew).
2. Quoted by Barnai Ya'acov, *Historiography and Nationalism* (Jerusalem: Magnes Publication, 1995), p. 82 (Hebrew).
3. Ibid., 80–83.
4. Anita Shapira, "Politics and Collective Memory: The Debate over the 'New Historians' in Israel," *History and Memory* 7 (1995):25.
5. Ibid., 25–26.
6. Shlomo Swirsky, "Notes on the Historical Sociology of the *Yishuv*," *Mahbarot le-Mehkar u-le-Bikoret* 2 1979:27 (Hebrew).
7. Ehrlich Avishai, "Israel: Conflict, War and Social Change," in C. Creighton and M. Show (eds.), *The Sociology of War and Peace* (Devonshire: Macmillan Press, 1987), pp. 121–142.
8. Ibid., 129.
9. Uri Ram, *The Changing Agenda of Israeli Sociology* (Albany: SUNY Press, 1995), p. 6; more generally, Ch. 9.
10. Baruch Kimmerling, "The Management of the Jewish-Arab Conflict and Processes of Nation Building in the Mandate Period," *Medina, Mimshal ve-Yekhasim Ben-Le'umi'im* 9 (1976): 35–55 (Hebrew).
11. Baruch Kimmerling, *The Economic Interrelationships between the Arab and Jewish Communities in Mandatory Palestine* (Cambridge: Center for International Studies, MIT, 1979); Kimmerling, *Zionism and Territory: The Socio-territorial Dimensions of Zionist Politics* (Berkeley: Institute of International Studies, University of California, 1983); Kimmerling, *The Israeli State and Society, Boundaries and Frontiers* (Albany: SUNY Press, 1989).
12. Gershon Shafir, *Land, Labor and the Origins of the Israeli-Palestinian Conflict, 1882–1914* (Cambridge: Cambridge University Press, 1989).
13. Michael Shalev, *Labour and the Political Economy in Israel* (Oxford: Oxford University Press, 1992).
14. See Uri Ram, "Memory and Identity: The Sociology of the Historians' Controversy in Israel," *Te'oria u-Bikoret* 8 (1996): 9–32 (Hebrew) as a presentation of the "post-Zionist" perspective, and Jacob Katz, "History and

Historians, New as Well as Old," *Alpayim* 12 (1996): 9–34 (Hebrew), Anita Shapira, "Politics and Collective Memory," as thoughtful, rather than above all polemical, replies.

15. One of the first and most controversial studies that called accepted notions and longtime taboos into question was Benny Morris's study of the origins of the Palestinian refugees during the 1948 war; see Benny Morris, *The Birth of the Palestinian Refugee Problem, 1947–1949* (Tel Aviv: Am Oved, 1991), pp. 65–71 (Hebrew). To mention only a number of important studies that have developed ideas put forward in the above controversy, in addition to Kimmerling, Shafir, and Shalev mentioned above, see Lev Luis Grinberg, "The Strike of the Jewish-Arab Drivers' Organization, 1931, A Contribution to the Critique of the Sociology of the National Conflict in Eretz Israel/Palestine," in Ilan Pappe (ed.), *Jewish-Arab Relations in Mandatory Palestine* (Givat Haviva: Institute for Peace Studies, 1995), pp. 157–78 (Hebrew); Gershon Shafir, "Israel Society: A Counterview," *Israel Studies* 1 (1996): 189–213; Oren Yiftachel, "Power Disparities in the Planning of a Mixed Region: Arabs and Jews in the Galilee, Israel," *Urban Studies* 30 (1993):157–82; Juval Portugali, *Implicate Relations, Society and Space in the Israeli Palestinian Conflict* (Tel Aviv: Hakibbutz Hameuchad, 1996) (Hebrew). A number of journals devoted much room, during the years 1994 to 1997, to articles concerning the new trends in Israeli historiography, among these *Israel Studies, Te'oria u-Bikoret* (Hebrew), *Zmanim* (Hebrew) *Alpayim* (Hebrew), and *History and Memory.*

16. For a recent article by a leading Israeli sociologist, which, I would contend, is primarily a polemical reprisal, see—Eliezer Ben-Rafael, "Critical Versus Non-critical Sociology: An Evaluation," *Israel Studies* 2 (1997):174–93, and his is not the only one. Much of the public debate took place in the daily press, replete with name calling and labeling.

17. Zachary Lockman, *Comrades and Enemies, Arab and Jewish Workers in Palestine, 1906–1948* (Berkeley: University of California Press, 1996). I would also note a more specific study by Lev Grinberg of a joint Arab and Jewish strike, the "Drivers' Strike" of 1931, mentioned above. See Grinberg, "The Strike of the Jewish-Arab Drivers' Organization, 1931," in Pappe (ed.), *Jewish-Arab Relations in Mandatory Palestine.*

18. Beshara Doumani, "Rediscovering Ottoman Palestine: Writing Palestinians into History," *Journal of Palestine Studies* 21 (1992):22.

19. Edna Bonacich, "A Theory of Ethnic Antagonism: The Split Labor Market," *American Sociological Review* 37 (1972):547–59; Bonacich, "The Past, Present and Future of Split Labor Market Theory," *Research in Race and Ethnic Relations* 1 (1979):17–64; Bonacich, "Class Approaches to Ethnicity and Race," *Insurgent Sociologist* 1 (1980): 9–75.

20. Bonacich, "Class Approaches," 65.

21. Bonacich, "Past and Present,"35.

22. Shafir, *Land and Labor;* Shalev, *Labor and the Political Economy.*

23. For some of the major recent works on nationalism see Ernest Gellner, *Encounters with Nationalism* (Oxford: Blackwell, 1994); Eric Hobsbawm,

Nations and Nationalism Since 1780 (Cambridge: Cambridge University Press, 1990); Benedict Anderson, *Imagined Communities, Reflections on the Origin and Spread of Nationalism* (London: Verso, 1983); Anthony Smith, *The Ethnic Origin of Nations* (Oxford: Oxford University Press, 1994).

24. See Ilan Pappe, "Zionism According to the Theories of Nationalism and the Historiographic Method," in *Zionism, A Contemporary Controversy* (The Institute for Ben Gurion's Heritage and the Ben Gurion University Press, Beer Sheba, 1996), pp. 223–61 (Hebrew); Hedva Ben-Israel, "The Study of Nationalism as an Historical Phenomenon," in Reinharz, Shimoni, and Salmon (eds.), *Jewish Nationalism and Politics: New Perspectives* (Jerusalem and Boston: Zalman Shazar Center and the Tauber Institute, Brandeis University, 1996), pp. 57–80; Berlovitz Yaffah, *Inventing a Land, Inventing a People* (Tel Aviv: Hakibbutz Hameuchad, 1996) (Hebrew).

25. Baruch Kimmerling, *Zionism and Economy* (Cambridge: Schenkman, 1983); Kimmerling, *Zionism and Territory.*

26. Agnes Calliste, "The Struggle for Employment Equity by Blacks on American and Canadian Railroads," *Journal of Black Studies* 25 (1995):297–317.

27. Bonacich, "Past, Present and Future," 32–34.

28. Cliff Brown and Terry Boswel, "Strikebreaking or Solidarity in the Great Steel Strike of 1919: A Split Labor Market, Game-Theoretic, and QCA Analysis," *American Journal of Sociology* 100 (1995):1479–1519.

Chapter 1

1. David Horowitz and Rita Hinden, *Economic Survey of Palestine* (Tel Aviv: Economic Research Institute of the Jewish Agency, 1938), p. 22, hereafter, *Economic Survey;* Gad Gilbar, "Trends in the Demographic Development of the Arabs of Palestine, 1870–1948," *Cathedra* 45 (1988): 44–49 (Hebrew). The proportions were reversed for the Jewish community. Eighty-one percent of its growth was due to immigration, and only 19 percent to natural reproduction. Horowitz and Hinden, *Economic Survey,* 22.

2. Gertz, *Statistical Handbook,* 37.

3. "Palestine, Report and General Abstracts of the Census of 1922," in Aaron S. Klieman (ed.), *The Rise of Israel — Practical Zionism, 1920–1939* (New York: Garland Publishing Inc., 1987), p. 39 (hereafter, *Census — 1922*).

4. Abraham Cohen, *Prosperity and Depression in the Economy of the Country* (Merhavia: Hashomer Hatza'ir, 1956) (Hebrew); Nadav Halevi, "The Political Economy of Absorptive Capacity: Growth and Cycles in Jewish Palestine under the British Mandate," *Middle Eastern Studies* 19 (1983): 456–69.

5. *Census — 1922*, Tb. 1–1.

6. Halevi, "The Political Economy of Absorptive Capacity," 458. Taking the census of 1922 as a reference point, Gertz calculated that the rate of growth of the Jewish population from 1922 to 1945 was 706.5 percent. Gertz, *Statistical Handbook,* 46.

7. Gilbar, "Trends in the Demographic Development," 46; Horowitz and Hinden, *Economic Survey,* 21.

8. Gertz, *Statistical Handbook*, 47; for the year 1947 see, Ruth Klinov and Nadav Halevi, *The Economic Development of Israel* (Jerusalem: Academon, 1968), p. 11 (Hebrew).

9. Metzer Jacob and Oded Kaplan, "Jointly but Severally: Arab-Jewish Dualism and Economic Growth in Mandatory Palestine," *The Journal of Economic History* 45 (1985): 329 (hereafter, Metzer and Kaplan, "Jointly but Severally").

10. Horowitz and Hinden, *Economic Survey*, 21.

11. Gilbar, "Trends" 46; Metzer and Kaplan, ibid., 329; Horowitz and Hinden, ibid. 21.

12. During 1920 to 1945, approximately half of all immigrants were listed under the category of "labor." The other half were listed as "capitalists" — immigrants with various levels of private means—and "pupils," "dependents" and "unspecified." Gertz, *Statistical Handbook*, 103.

13. For 1926 see Histadrut, *The Second Census of Hebrew Workers in Palestine* (Tel Aviv: The Histadrut, 1926), Tb. 17 (Hebrew) (hereafter, *Labor Census—1926*), and for 1937 see Histadrut, "Census of Tel Aviv Workers—1937," *Pinkas* (Supplement to *Davar*, January 1938) (1936–38): 11, Tb. B. (hereafter, *Labor Census—1937*). Jewish workers from Middle Eastern and North African countries were on the periphery of the labor market and were underrepresented in the censuses carried out by the Histadrut.

14. According to the census of 1926, one-third had been members of Zionist political parties before immigrating. See *Labor Census—1926*, Tb. 31.

15. *Labor Census—1937*, quoted by Horowitz and Hinden, *Economic Survey*, 185.

16. *Labor Census—1926*, Tb. 2, and *Labor Census—1937*, Tb. 46.

17. *Labor Census—1926*, Tb.1.

18. David Gurevitz (ed.), *Report and Summary of the Census of Hebrew Workers—1930* (Tel Aviv: The Jewish Agency and the Histadrut, 1930) Tb. 63 (hereafter, *Labor Census—1930*).

19. *Labor Census—1937*, Tb. 2. Gertz, *Statistical Handbook*, 106.

20. For a more detailed discussion of the immigration policy in relation to women see Deborah Bernstein, "Daughters of the Nation—Between the Public and the Private Spheres of the *Yishuv*," in Judith Baskin, *Jewish Women in Historical Perspective* (Second edition, Wayne University Press, 1998); Aviva Halamish, *Immigration and Absorption Policy of the Zionist Organization, 1931–1937* (Unpublished Ph.D. Thesis, University of Tel Aviv, Tel Aviv, 1995), pp. 248–53 (Hebrew).

21. *Labor Census—1926*, Tb. 18.

22. 51 percent in 1930, Labor Census—1930, Tb. 64, and 43 percent in 1937, *Labor Census—1937*, Tb. H 1.

23. In 1922, single men and women accounted for 58.5 percent of all workers, in 1930, they accounted for 53.5 percent, and in 1937, for approximately 47 percent. See Histadrut, "Census of Hebrew Workers—1922," in *Pinkas*, 1923, Supplement 8 to *Davar*, Tel Aviv (hereafter, *Labor Census—1922*); *Labor Census—1930*, Tb. 64: *Labor Census—1937*, 13.

24. Gertz, 290.

25. Zeev Tzachor, *The Histadrut—The Formative Period* (no place, no publisher, 1979) (Hebrew); Lev Luis Grinberg, *The Histadrut Above All* (Jerusalem: Nevo Publishing, 1993) (Hebrew). Michael Shalev, *Labour and the Political Economy in Israel* (Oxford: Oxford University Press, 1992).

26. Deborah Bernstein, "From Split Labour Market Strategy to Political Co-optation: The Palestine Labour League," *Middle Eastern Studies* 31 (1995): 755–71.

27. For a detailed analysis of the debt relationships in a rural-urban area, see Beshara Doumani, *Rediscovering Palestine, Merchants and Peasants in Jabal Nablus, 1700–1900* (Berkeley: University of California Press, 1995).

28. For a detailed discussion of the deterioration of the rural sector and its impact on the villagers, see Mahmud Yazbeck, "From *Falahin* to Rebels: The Economic Causes of the Outbreak of the 1936 Rebellion" (mimeo).

29. Sarah Graham-Brown, "The Political Economy of the Jabal Nablus, 1920–48," In Roger Owen (ed.), *Studies in the Economic and Social History of Palestine in the Nineteenth and Twentieth Centuries* (Basingstoke and London: St. Anthony's, 1986), pp. 145–51.

30. Shulamit Carmi and Henry Rosenfeld, "The Origin of the Process of Proletarianization and Urbanization of the Arab Peasants in Palestine," *Annals of the New York Academy of Sciences* 220 (1974): 270–85.

31. Ibid.

32. Gilbar, "Trends in the Demographic Development," 50.

33. Ibid., 51; see also, Lister G. Hopkins, "Population," in Sa'id B. Himadeh (ed.), *Economic Organization of Palestine* (Beirut: American Press, 1938), p. 13.

34. F. M. Gottheil, "Arab Immigration into Pre-State Israel: 1922–1931," *Middle Eastern Studies* 9 (1973):316–18.

35. Joseph Vashitz, *The Arabs of Palestine* (Merhavia: Sifri'at Ha-Po'alim, 1947), p. 153 (Hebrew) (hereafter, Vashitz, *Arabs of Palestine*).

36. Rachel Taqqu, "Peasants into Workmen: Internal Labor Migration and the Arab Village Community Under the Mandate," in Joel Migdal (ed.), *Palestinian Society and Politics* (Princeton: Princeton University Press, 1980), p. 270.

37. Eliahu Agassi, The Arab Worker in Palestine and his Organization During the British Mandate (mimeo, 1947). LA, IV 104–143–20.

38. June 19, 1941. ISA, C.O., 733 441. Tape 75430 2.

39. One of the very few previous works to discuss the disparity of wages between Jewish and Arab workers was the study of Zvi Sussman. An economist, he explained the large gap between Jewish skilled and unskilled workers by the impact of the much cheaper Arab unskilled workers. While he was the first to call attention to the impact of Arab workers on the condition of Jewish workers, his main interest was in the disparities within the Jewish community, see Zvi Sussman, "The Determination of Wages for Unskilled Labor in the Advanced Sector of the Dual Labor Market of Mandatory Palestine," *Economic Development and Cultural Change* 22

(1973): 95–113, Zvi Sussman, *Wage Differentials and Equality within the Histadrut* (Ramat Gan: Massada, 1974) (Hebrew).

40. The currency in Palestine was linked to the pound sterling. Until 1927, the currency used was the Egyptian pound. In that year a Palestine pound was introduced—£P = 100 grush = 1,000 mils. The daily wage was usually given in mils.

41. Report of The Wage Commission—1928, ISA, C.O., 733 152, Item 5. While the report dealt with recommendations for policy concerning the wages of unskilled labor, it reviewed the current status of both unskilled and skilled workers.

42. Colonial Office, Report by His Majesty's Government to the Council of the League of Nations on the Administration of Palestine and Trans-Jordan for the year 1929 (London: His Majesty's Stationery Office, 1930), p. 127.

43. Labor Legislation Report, 6 October, 1932. ISA, C.O., 733/220, Tape 97130/1.

44. Gertz, *Statistical Handbook*, 296.

45. A detailed breakdown of the relative share of agriculture, manufacture and construction in Jewish and Arab sectors is given in Jacob Metzer and Oded Kaplan, *The Jewish and Arab Economies in Mandatory Palestine: Product, Employment and Growth* (Jerusalem: Mossad Bialik, 1990), pp. 88–94. (Hebrew) (hereafter, *The Jewish and Arab Economies*); see also Metzer's comparison of structural features of the Arab economy in mandatory Palestine and in the Occupied Territories since 1967, "The Administered Territories and the Arab Economy of Mandatory Palestine, an historical perspective," *The Economic Quarterly* 35 (1988):129–45 (Hebrew).

46. Metzer and Kaplan, "Jointly but Severally," 328.

47. Halevi, "The Political Economy of Absorptive Capacity," 460; Gertz, *Statistical Handbook*, 375; and Nahum Gross, "The Economic Policy of the Mandatory British Administration in Palestine," *Cathedra* 25 (1982): 169 (Hebrew).

48. Metzer and Kaplan, "Jointly but Severally," 329.

49. Ibid.

50. Ibid., 343.

51. Abraham Cohen, *The Economy of the Arab Sector in Mandatory Palestine* (Givat Haviva: Institute for Arab Studies, 1978), p. 56 (Hebrew).

52. Concerning forms and changes of taxation see Jacob Metzer, "Fiscal Incidence and Resource Transfer Between Jews and Arabs in Mandatory Palestine," *Research in Economic History* 7 (1982): 87–131; Gross, "Economic Policy"; M. F. Abcarius, "Fiscal System," in Sa'id B. Himadeh (ed.), *Economic Organization of Palestine*, pp. 505–56; Government of Palestine, *Survey of Palestine*, Prepared in December 1945 and January 1946 for the information of the Anglo-American Committee of Inquiry (Jerusalem: Government Printer, 1946), Vol. II, pp. 535–53 (hereafter *Survey*).

53. For regular workers, see Government of Palestine, Palestine Royal Commission, *Memoranda Prepared by the Government of Palestine* (London: His Majesty's Stationery Office, 1937), p. 145 (hereafter, *Memoranda*). The casual

workers were usually employed indirectly, via contractors, see *Memoranda,* 140–46; *Survey,* 775–80.

54. Metzer and Kaplan, *The Jewish and Arab Economies,* 13.

55. Metzer and Kaplan, "Jointly but Severally," 340.

56. The major expenditure on goods went to agricultural produce (47 percent). Nineteen percent was spent on transport and trade; 22.5 percent on labor, and 8.7 percent on rent, ibid.

57. About ten percent of Jewish industrial products sold on the Arab market, and about a third to 40 percent of all Arab agricultural produce was sold on the Jewish market, see Survey of Jewish Industry conducted in 1937, quoted by Abramovitz and Gelfat, *The Arab Economy in Palestine and the Countries of the Middle East* (Ein Harod: Hakkibutz Hameuchad, 1944), p. 102 (Hebrew) (hereafter, Abramowitz and Gelfat, *Arab Economy);* a similar direction of flow of capital though with slightly lower estimates is noted by Metzer and Kaplan, "Jointly but Severally," 343.

58. n.d. LA, IV 219–65.

59. Of the money transferred to the wealthy, 4.5 million £P were paid out for the purchase of land, 5 million £P for rent, 1 million £P for tradesmen, and 500,000 £P for industrial produce. Of the money transferred to the middle class, half went for the purchase of land, 4.5 million £P for the purchase of agricultural produce and manure, and another million £P for tradesmen. Of the 8 million £P that Cohen calculated went to the poor, 4 million £P were paid as wages (3 million £P to agricultural and 1 million £P to nonagricultural laborers), 3.2 million £P bought building materials, and another 500,000 £P comprised the wages of Arab workers in Arab-owned factories whose products were purchased by Jews. An additional 300,000 £P were paid as compensation to tenants for loss of land. Finally Cohen claims that another 3 million £P were transferred to Arab land owners living outside Palestine for the purchase of their land—ibid.

60. Jacob Metzer, "Fiscal Incidence and Resource Transfer Between Jews and Arabs in Mandatory Palestine," *Research in Economic History* 7 (1982): 87–131; Gabriel Sheffer, "The Principles of British Pragmatism: Reevaluation of British Policies Towards Palestine in the 1930s," *Cathedra* 29 (1983): 133 (Hebrew).

61. Metzer and Kaplan, *Jewish and Arab Economies,* 81, 116. Arab agricultural produce increased in response to the demand by the Jewish market, Metzer and Kaplan, "Jointly but Severally," 342–43.

62. Abramovitz and Gelfat, *The Arab Economy,* 104.

63. Nemirovsky, "Jewish Immigration and Arab Population," in Sereni and Ashery (eds.), *Jews and Arabs in Palestine* (New York: Hyperion Press, 1976. Reprint from New York: Hechalutz Press, 1936), p. 84.

64. For example, George Mansur, *The Arab Worker under the Palestine Mandate* (Jerusalem: Commercial Press, 1937), pp. 29–32.

65. Ibid., 28–29.

66. Letter of the General Federation of Jewish Labor, the Histadrut, quoted in Colonial Office, Palestine, Report on Immigration, Land Settlement and

Development, by Sir John Hope-Simpson (London: His Majesty's Stationery Office, 1930), p. 128.

67. Detailed discussion of issue of Arab unemployment and its relation to Jewish immigration in Hope-Simpson Report. Presenting the Jewish position, the Arab position, and the British assessment of the situation, the responsibility and recommended course of action. See Hope-Simpson Report, 127–40.

68. See, inter alia, Sa'id B. Himadeh, "Industry," in Himadeh (ed.), *Economic Organization*, 213–300; Horowitz and Hinden, *Economic Survey*, Ch. V; Gertz, *Statistical Handbook*, 206–32.

69. Metzer and Kaplan, *Jewish and Arab Economies*, 73.

70. May Seikaly, *The Arab Community of Haifa, 1918–1936, A Study in Transformation* (London: Tauris, 1995), pp. 81–97 (hereafter, Seikaly, *Haifa*).

71. Yasin Abd el-Kadr, "The Working Class and the Political Movement in Palestine," *Shu'un Palestini'ya* 56 (1976): 106–50 (Arabic).

72. For example, Cohen, *The Arab Economy*, 31–38; Vashitz, *The Arabs in Palestine*, pp. 96–97 .

73. Report of the HLC for the year 1934, written by Aba Houshi, LA, IV 250–27–5–145.

74. 6 October 1924, "Memorandum of Arab Executive to League of Nations," in Gabai M. (ed.), *Palestinians on Palestine, 1890–1948* (Givat Haviva: Institute of Arab Studies, 1986), p. 95 (Hebrew); Additional examples of such fears appeared in the daily press, e.g., *al-Karmil*, 21 May 1921; *Filastin*, 9 December 1927; *al-Karmil*, 6 January 1928.

75. February 1934. Report on a visit to Palestine, January 1934, by Rhys J. Davies, M.P. CZA, A106/7.

76. Edna Bonacich, "A Theory of Ethnic Antagonism: The Split Labor Market," *American Sociological Review* 37 (1972): 547–59.

77. See detailed discussion of impact of economic policy on separatism, and vice versa, in Barbara J. Smith, *The Roots of Separatism in Palestine, British Economic Policy 1920–1929* (London: Tauris & Co. Ltd., 1993) and in Elizur Yuval, *Economic Warfare, The Hundred-Year Economic Confrontation between Jews and Arabs* (Tel Aviv: Kinneret, 1997), pp. 37–108 (Hebrew).

78. Gertz, *Statistical Handbook*, 366–67.

79. Michael Shalev, *Labour and the Political Economy in Israel* (Oxford: Oxford University Press, 1992).

80. Ndabezitha Siyabonga and Stephen Sanderson, "Racial Antagonism and the Origins of Apartheid in the South African Gold Mining Industry, 1886–1924: A Split Labor Market Analysis," *Research in Race and Ethnic Relations* 5 (1986): 241; Edna Bonacich, "Capitalism and Race Relations in South Africa: A Split Labor Market Analysis," *Political Power and Social Theory* 2 (1981): 255.

81. Palestine Royal Commission, Report (London: His Majesty's Printer, 1937), p. 34, Article 2.

82. For example, Weitzman to Under-Secretary of State, Article 15, 9 October 1928. LA, IV 208 -1-128; Shertok for the Executive of the Jewish Agency to

E. Mills, Acting Chief Secratery, 16 July 1933. ISA, C.O., 733/238; Memorandum Submitted to the Palestine Royal Commission on behalf of the Jewish Agency for Palestine (London, 1936), Articles 385–95.

83. Weitzman, ibid.

84. Executive Committee of General Federation of Jewish Labour to High Commissioner, Article (b), 21 June 1931. ISA, C.O., 733 203.

85. J. A. Chancellor to Lord Passfield, Article 5, 23 July 1931. ISA, C.O., 733 203.

86. Ibid., Article 18.

87. Palestine Royal Commission, Report.

88. One of the very few Israeli writers to deal with the Arab position concerning government employment policy is Yuval Elizur in his recent book, *Economic Warfare*.

89. Edna Bonacich, "The Past, Present and Future of Split Labor Market Theory," *Research in Race and Ethnic Relations* 1 (1979): 32–33; For Palestine see Deborah Bernstein, "Strategies of Equalization: Jews and Arabs in the Split Labor Market of Mandatory Palestine," *Ethnic and Racial Studies* 21 (1998):449–75.

90. See Report of the Wage Commission—1928, ISA, C.O., 733 152; Report of the Wages Committee, Under the Chairmanship of His Honour Mr. Justice F. Gordon Smith K.C., Chief Justice of Palestine (Jerusalem: Government Printer, 1943).

91. Bonacich, "The Past, Present and Future," 32–33.

92. Ibid.

93. Shmuel Dotan, *The Reds, The Anti-Zionist Palestine Communist Party* (Kfar Saba: Shavna Hasofer, 1991) (Hebrew).

Chapter 2

1. Ya'acov Davidon, *Once Upon a Haifa* (Haifa: Mai Publication, n.d.), pp. 5–6 (Hebrew).

2. Yossi Ben Artzi, *From Germany to the Holy Land, Templer Settlement in Palestine* (Jerusalem: Yad Yitzhak Ben Zvi, 1996) (Hebrew).

3. Mahmud Yazbeck, *Haifa in the Latter Period of the Ottoman Rule: Selected Issues in the Development of Administration and Society* (Unpublished Ph.D. Thesis, University of Haifa, 1992), p. 313 (Hebrew) (hereafter, *Ottoman Rule*).

4. Alex Carmel, "The German Settlers in Palestine and Their Relation with the Local Arab Population and the Jewish Community," in M. Maoz (ed.), *Studies on Palestine During the Ottoman Period* (Jerusalem: The Magnes Press, 1975), pp. 443–65; Alex Carmel, *The German Settlement in Palestine in the Late Ottoman Period* (Haifa: University of Haifa, 1995) (Hebrew).

5. Joseph Vashitz, *Arab-Jewish Relations at Haifa During the British Mandate* (Giv'at Haviva, Institute for Arab Studies, 1973), Part 1, p. 7 (unpublished ms.) (hereafter, *Arab-Jewish Relations*).

6. See Yazbeck, *Ottoman Rule*, ch. 6; Joseph Vashitz, "Dhawat and Isamiyyun: Two Groups of Arab Community Leaders in Haifa During the British Mandate," *Asian and African Studies* 17 (1983): 95–120.

7. Yazbeck, *Ottoman Rule*, 307–8; May Seikaly, *The Arab Community of Haifa 1918–1936* (London: Tauris, 1995), p. 380 (hereafter, *Haifa*); Se'adia Paz, "The Land of 'Nesher,' Yajur and Khreiba," in Aminadav Ashbal (ed.), *Sixty Years of the PLDC* (Jerusalem: The Restoration Fund, 1970), pp. 50–51 (Hebrew).

8. Yazbeck, *Ottoman Rule*, 286–87.

9. Vashitz, "Dhawat and Isamiyyun," 109.

10. Ibid., 100.

11. Yazbeck, *Ottoman Rule*, p. 276–78; May Seikaly, *The Arab Community of Haifa 1918–1936. A Study in Transformation* (Unpublished D. Phil., University of Oxford, Oxford, 1983), p. 192 (hereafter, *Arab Community*).

12. Joseph Vashitz, *Social Changes in the Arab Community of Haifa during the British Mandate* (Unpublished Ph.D. dissertation, Hebrew University of Jerusalem, 1993), pp. 27–29 (Hebrew) (hereafter, *Social Changes*).

13. Pick Pinhas, "Meissner Pasha—The Pioneer of the Railways in Palestine— The Man, His Railways and Their Fortune," *Cathedra* 10 (1979): 102–28 (Hebrew).

14. Alex Carmel, *The History of Haifa During the Period of the Turks* (Haifa: Haifa University, 1969), pp. 149–59 (Hebrew) (hereafter, *Haifa*).

15. Herbert Gilbert, "Crossroads: Imperial Priorities and Regional Perspectives in the Planning of Haifa, 1918–1939," *Planning Perspectives* 4 (1989):319.

16. Carmel, *Haifa*, 157.

17. al-Tamimi and al-Halabi, two Ottoman officials, noted that Haifa was a small town, unparalleled in its heterogeneity, as quoted by Yazbeck, *Ottoman Rule*, pp. 214–15.

18. According to the census of Montefiori—1839, *The Census of the Jews of Palestine—1839*, According to Montefiori's Manuscript, No. 528 (Jerusalem: The Dinur Center, 1987), pp. 192–99 (Hebrew).

19. Carmel, *Haifa*, 142; Gad Gilbar, "Trends in the Demographic Development of the Arabs of Palestine, 1870–1948," *Cathedra* 45 (1988): 52 (Hebrew).

20. K. I. Silman, *The History and Settlement of Haifa* (Tel Aviv: Omanut, 1931), pp. 25–30 (Hebrew); Carmel, *Haifa*, 142.

21. Herzl, "Altneuland," in Y. Nedava (ed.), *Haifa, Olifant and the Zionist Vision* (Haifa: University of Haifa, n.d.), 48–50 (Hebrew).

22. Quoted by Carmel, *Haifa*, 146–7; see also Arthur Ruppin, *Chapters of My Life* (Tel Aviv: Am Oved, 1947) Vol. II, pp. 153–62 (Hebrew); Aminadav Ashbal, *The Palestine Land Development Corporation* (Jerusalem: The Restoration Fund, 1976), pp. 191–202 (Hebrew) (hereafter, *The PLDC*).

23. Quoted by Carmel, *Haifa*, 148.

24. Yazbeck, *Ottoman Rule*, 351–67.

25. Yehoshua Porath, *The Emergence of the Palestinian-Arab National Movement, 1918–1929* (Tel Aviv: Am Oved, 1976), pp. 19–21 (Hebrew).

26. al-Muktabas, 15 March 1910. Quoted by Yazbeck, *Ottoman Rule*, 367.

27. Ibid.

28. Herbert, "Crossroads," 314.

29. Gilbar, "Trends in the Demographic Development," 52.

30. See Gilbar, "Trends," 52; Eliahu Biletzki, *Creation and Struggle, The Haifa Labor Council, 1921–1981* (Tel Aviv: Am Oved, 1981), pp. 107, 199 (Hebrew) (hereafter, *Creation and Struggle*); Mahmud Yazbeck, *The Arab Immigration to Haifa, 1933–1948* (unpublished M.A. dissertation, University of Haifa, 1986), p. 17 (Hebrew) (hereafter, *Arab Immigration*).

31. Zeev Vilnai, *Haifa, Past and Present* (Tel Aviv: The Hebrew Society for the Study of Eretz Israel, 1936), p. 140 (Hebrew).

32. Ruppin, *Chapters*, 154.

33. Ashbal, *The PLDC*, 192–93.

34. Vashitz, *Social Change*, 105

35. David Hacohen, Relations between Jews and Arabs in Haifa, 18 October 1936. CZA, S25/4178.

36. Vashitz, *Arab-Jewish Relations*, Part II, 14; Vashitz, *Social Changes*, 156–57; Seikaly, *The Arab Community*, 188–192, 347.

37. Seikaly, *Haifa*, p. 212, n. 43; p. 260, n. 29; for a detailed list of murdered members of prestigious Muslim and Christian families and attempted assassinations, see: Letter to Moshe (probably Moshe Shertok), 7 November 1938. Haifa, unsigned. Haganna Archive, 8/2. Hajj Tahr Qaraman and his family were not hurt. Yet he was a leading new entrepreneur of the Arab community and he had extensive dealings with Jews. David Hacohen suggests that, unlike the other notable families, Qaraman contributed generously to the Arab fighting forces. David Hacohen, *My Way* (Tel Aviv: Am Oved, 1979), p. 45 (Hebrew).

38. Yazbeck, *Ottoman Rule*, 361; Abraham Khalfon, "Haifa My Town," in Yoseph Nedava (ed.), *Haifa, Olifant and the Zionist Vision* (Haifa: University of Haifa, 1980), p. 60 (Hebrew).

39. Ha'im Aharonovitz, *Hadar Hacarmel* (Haifa: Va'ad Hadar Hacarmel, 1958), p. 4 (Hebrew); Yazbeck, *Ottoman Rule*, 362–63.

40. Vilnai, *Haifa*, p. 141.

41. For example, in 1926, 1937, 1941; see Yazbeck, *Arab Immigration*, 97, 101, 102.

42. Ben Artzi, *Residential Patterns*, p. 29

43. Silman, *Haifa*, 45.

44. Ibid.; Yossi Katz, "The Establishment and the Beginnings of the Neighborhood of Herzlia—The First Hebrew Neighborhood on the Carmel," *Horizons in Geography* 8 (1983):49–56 (Hebrew).

45. Elias Auerbach, *From the Land of My Father to the Fatherland, The First Jewish Doctor in Haifa* (Jerusalem: Yad Yizhak Ben Zvi and the Leo Beck Institute, 1997) (Hebrew, translated from German) (hereafter, *The First Jewish Doctor*).

46. Aharonovitz, *Hadar Hacarmel*, 29.

47. From letter of the Temporary Committee of Hadar Hacarmel, to the executive of the JNF, Haag, July 1921. Quoted by Aharonovitz, *Hadar Hacarmel*, 44.

48. The development of the neighborhood began with 394 dunam in 1921, increased to 1,278 by 1930, incorporating a number of small Jewish sections on its boundaries, and on to 1,730 dunam by 1940, with the purchase of the

land up the side of the mountain. The population grew from 200 people in 1921, to 2,876 by 1926, to 9,000 by 1932, and to 15,037 and 32,820 by 1934 and 1938, respectively, see ibid., 278.

49. Vilnai, *Haifa*, 116.

50. Ruppin, *Chapters*, 160–61.

51. Biletzki, *Creation and Struggle*, 200–202.

52. Aharonovitz, *Hadar Hacarmel*, 94, for relations within the neighborhood; see also Biletzki, ibid., 93–94.

53. Shim'on Stern, "Hadar Hacarmel—Center of Jewish Life in Haifa," in *Idan* 12 (1989): 41 (Hebrew); Aharonovitz, ibid., 74, 134–35; Ya'acov Davidon, *Once Upon a Haifa*.

54. Aharonovitz, ibid., 196–97.

55. Vilnai, *Haifa*, pp. 116–19.

56. Seikaly, *Arab Community*, 95.

57. Vashitz, *Arab-Jewish Relations*, Part III, 19.

58. Seikaly, *Arab Community*, 51.

59. Quoted by Seikaly, *Arab Community*, 89.

60. Quoted by Vashitz, *Arab-Jewish Relations*, III, 19.

61. Hope-Simpson was sent to Palestine by the British Government to study the economic and social causes of the outburst of violence of August 1929. He claimed that the development of the Jewish settlement had been detrimental to the Arab majority, taking over land and employment, already scarce resources in Palestine. See Colonial Office, Palestine, Report on Immigration, Land Settlement and Development, by Sir John Hope-Simpson C.I.E (London: His Majesty's Stationery Office, 1930); for discussion of the response of Zionist leadership to the Hope-Simpson report, see Yuval Elizur, *Economic Warfare, The Hundred-Year Economic Confrontation between Jews and Arabs* (Tel Aviv: Kinneret, 1997), pp. 67–71 (Hebrew).

62. Ya'acov Goldstein, "The Events of 1929 in Haifa," *Idan* 12 (1989): 171–84 (Hebrew).

63. See annual address of the chairman of the Haifa Chamber of Commerce, Mr. Natansohn, for the years 1932–1935. Haifa Municipal Archive, Haifa Chamber of Commerce—11, Unit—53.

64. Mahmud Yazbeck, "From *Falahin* to Rebels: The Economic Causes of the Outbreak of the 1936 Rebellion" (mimeo); see also Shai Lachman, "Arab Rebellion and Terrorism in Palestine 1929–39: The case of Sheikh Izz al-Din al-Kassam and His Movement," in E. Kedouri and S. Haim (eds.), *Zionism and Arabism in Palestine and Israel* (London: Frank Cass, 1982), p. 77.

65. Ibid.

66. Izz al-Din al-Kassam has remained a venerated figure in Palestine nationalism. Recently, the armed terrorist unit of the Hamas has taken his name.

67. For example, Reports by Aba Houshi, 20 March 1936, CZA, S25/10537; 17 August 1936, LA IV 250-27-2-529.

68. Nader Aboud, *The Palestine Arab Workers' Society, 1925–1947* (unpublished M.A. Dissertation, University of Haifa, 1988), pp. 101–103 (Hebrew) (hereafter, *The Palestine Arab Workers' Society*).

69. For example, Review of events among the Arabs, Haifa, July 1942; Report of an Arab journalist to the Hagana intelligence—21 October 1942; 12 November 1942. Hagana Archive, 8/3.

70. Joseph Vashitz, "Arab-Jewish Relations in Haifa, 1940–1948," in Yoseph Nevo and Y. Nimrod (eds.), *The Arabs and the Zionist Movement and Jewish Settlement, 1946–1950* (Tivon: Oranim, 1987): 21–37 (Hebrew).

71. For example, Documents of January 1945, July 1945, ISA I/Lab/1/45. 260/39.

72. Yazbeck, *Late Ottoman Rule*, pp. 363–64; Silman, *Haifa*; Khalfon, "Haifa, My Town," 62; Shabtai Levi, "From My Memories," in Y. Nedava (ed.), *Haifa, Olifant and the Zionist Vision* (Haifa: University of Haifa, n.d.), pp. 78–174 (Hebrew); Auerbach, *The First Jewish Doctor.*

73. Yazbeck, ibid., 361; Khalfon, ibid., 61.

74. Ibid.

75. Yossi Ben Artzi, *Residential Patterns and Intra Urban Migration of Arabs in Haifa* (Haifa: The University of Haifa and the Jewish-Arab Center, Occasional Papers on the Middle East, No. 1, 1980), p. 24 (Hebrew).

76. Haifa was one of a number of towns with a mixed Jewish-Arab population and mixed local council, see Elyakim Rubinstein, "Jews and Arabs in the Palestine Municipalities (1926–1933), with Special Reference to Jerusalem," *Cathedra* 51 (1989): 122–147 (Hebrew).

77. For information concerning the Shukri family, see Yazbeck, *Ottoman Rule*, 280–81; for more detailed discussion of Haifa municipality, see Vashitz, *Arab-Jewish Relations*, Part I, Ch. 4; Seikaly, *Arab Community*, 320–46, 384–88. For memoirs, see Shabtai Levi, ibid.; David Hacohen, "Jews and Arabs in Haifa Municipality," in *Idan*, pp. 228–40; David Hacohen, *My Way* (Tel Aviv: Am Oved, 1979), pp. 94–106 (Hebrew); Avraham Khalfon, "Working with Hasan Shukri," *Idan*, 241–44.

78. For a detailed report of the Haifa municipality during the first few months of the Arab rebellion, including the harassment of Hasan Shukri, see "Haifa Municipality during the Riots," most probably written by David Hacohen, n.d. CZA, S25/4178.

79. Vashitz, *Jewish-Arab Relations*, Part I, Ch. 4, p.3.

80. Seikaly, *Arab Community*, 329–33.

81. Aharonovitz, *Hadar Hacarmel*, 53.

82. *Kehilat Haifa, 1932–1941* (Haifa: Ott Press, 1942) (Hebrew).

83. Ibid.

84. Seikaly, *Arab Community*, 385.

85. Ibid.

86. Both the organization of Arab workers and the joint work sites will be discussed in detail in the following chapters.

87. The following discussion deals briefly with merchants and contractors. It can be added that Jewish professionals, lawyers, and mainly doctors, had many Arab clients and patients.

88. 29 May 1921. Minutes of first meeting of Hebrew Chamber of Commerce, Haifa. Haifa Municipality Archive, Chamber of Commerce—11, Unit—53.

89. Quoted by Vashitz, *Arab-Jewish Relations*, Part II, 56. The quote is from a debate in the Jewish Chamber of Commerce, which took place on April 16, a few days before the beginning of the clashes between Arabs and Jews and the ensuing Arab strike and boycott.

90. Vashitz, *Arab-Jewish Relations*, Part II, 61–63; Report of owners of Jewish shops in the market and the Arab district, 2 August 1936, CZA, S25/4178.

91. Vashitz, *Arab-Jewish Relations*, Vol. II, p. 31.

92. Ibid., 34.

93. Ibid., 33–34; other examples are given by Vashitz, *Arab-Jewish Relations*, Vol. II, 31–34; Vashitz, *Social Changes*, 75–77.

94. Relation between Jews and Arabs in Haifa, by David Hacohen. 18 October 1936. CZA, S25/4178.

95. The committee was composed mainly of well-known liberals and intellectuals such as Yehuda Magness, Ha'im Margalit Kalverisky, Yaacov T'hon, Michael Asaf of the Labor Movement, and Rabbi Uziel. The demand for moderating economic segregation was frequently raised both by members of the committee and by many of those appearing before it, though not by the leaders of the Labor Movement. Minutes of many of the meetings in CZA, S25/22196; Joseph Vashitz, "Jewish-Arab Relations in Haifa, 1940–1948," p. 25.

96. Elizur, *Economic Warfare*, 117–22; Vashitz, *Arab-Jewish Relations*, Part II, 100–108.

97. Ibid., 108.

98. Aba Houshi Archive, Aba Houshi Collection, Container 5; File 1_61/4.

99. These figures were calculated from the 1943 census of the Arab worker, ibid., complemented by figures from Mahmud Yazbeck, "Arab Immigration to Haifa, 1933–1948: Quantitative Analysis, according to Arab Sources," *Cathedra* 45 (1988): 135 (Hebrew) (hereafter, "Arab Immigration, Quantitative Analysis").

100. A detailed count of Haurani workers, at the height of the 1935 boom conducted by the HLC, reported that there were about 4,000 Haurani workers. This figure indicates that they made up more than 20 percent of the Arab labor force at that time, 28 February 1935. Report from HLC to Labor Department of the Executive of the Jewish Agency. LA, IV 208-1-788B.

101. Joseph Vashitz, "The Immigration of Villagers to Haifa During the Mandate Period: A Process of Urbanization?" *Cathedra* 45 (1988):113–30 (Hebrew) (hereafter, "Immigration of Villagers"); Yazbeck, *Arab Immigration*; Yazbeck, "Arab Immigration, Quantitative Analysis."

102. From Report of Inquest Committee, appointed by the Department of Health, *Filastin*, 1 July 1934.

103. George Mansur, *The Arab Worker under the Palestine Mandate* (Jerusalem: Commercial Press, 1937), p. 14.

104. Vashitz, "Immigration of Villagers," 126.

105. FATULS was established in Haifa in 1942, having split off from the Palestine Arab Workers' Society (PAWS).

106. 31 December 1942. Letter of Federation of Arab Trade Unions and Labor

Societies to Wage Committee. LA, IV 208–1–3721. Original document written in English. The Wage Committee was appointed by the Palestine government in 1942, in light of the sharp increase in the cost of living index during the war. The Committee was called on to make recommendations concerning wages for unskilled labor and cost of living allowance. The report was published in February 1943, Report of the Wages Committee Under the Chairmanship of His Honour Mr. Justice F. Gordon Smith K.C. (Jerusalem: Government Printer, 1943).

107. Eliyahu Agassi, Arabic speaking, of Iraqi origin, became a highly dependable source on the developments among Arab wage labor, and provided the Histadrut Executive with detailed periodic reports, e.g. organization activity among the Arab in Haifa, 1932–1933, IV 104–143–27; The Strike in the Tobacco Factory of Qaramn, Dik and Salti, August 1935. LA, IV 250–1–435; The Arab Worker and His Organization During the British Mandate, 1947, IV 104–143–20.

108. Agassi, Activity among Arab Workers in Haifa. 31 April 1935. LA, IV 250–27–1–435.

109. Nader Aboud, *The Palestine Arab Workers Society*.

110. See Aboud, *The Palestine Arab Workers Society*; also, "Sami Taha, Pioneer Unionist," *Palestine Post*, September 1947, written after his assassination and signed by "A Friend." There are some discrepancies in these and other sources concerning Taha's native village (one source claims that he came from the village of Igzim in the Haifa district) and concerning his year of birth, but there is no disagreement on the basic facts of his career and influence.

111. Vashitz, "Immigration of Villagers," 123.

112. Agassi, Activity among Arab Workers in Haifa. 31 April 1935. LA, IV 250–27–1–435.

113. Aboud, *Palestine Arab Workers Society*.

114. Biletzki, *Creation and Struggle*, 173, 181.

115. Jewish Agency for Palestine, "Report and General Abstracts of the Census of Labour 1930," *Palestine and Near East* 6 (1931): Tb. 63 (hereafter, Labor Census—1930).

116. The Histadrut, "The General Census of the Jewish Workers of Eretz Israel—1937," *Pinkas* (Supplementary to *Davar*, January 1938): Tb. 2 (Hebrew) (hereafter, Labor Census—1937).

117. Biletzki, *Creation and Struggle*, 143, 212–22; The rate of growth in Tel Aviv was 450 percent and that in Jerusalem, 210 percent. Labor Census—1930, Tb. 63, Labor Census—1937, Tb. 2.

118. David De Vries, "The Formation of a Jewish Workers' Movement in Haifa in the 1920s," *Proceedings of the Tenth World Congress of Jewish Studies*, Division B. 1 (1990): 378.

119. David De Vries, "Roots of 'Red Haifa,'" *Idan* 12 (1989): 83–90 (Hebrew).

120. Ibid.

121. Biletzki, *Creation and Struggle*, 108–14; 163–66.

122. For Arab labor we have a few hundred questionnaires for the year 1934,

stating place of work and level of wage for men, women, and children. This survey was conducted by the Palestine Labor League and the HLC. The internal consistency of the answers, and its compatibility with other sources, lends it credibility. LA, IV 250–27–1–433. Hereafter, LA, Questionnaires—No. X. For Jewish labor, a publication of the HLC gives detailed figures of the wages agreed on between the trade unions and employers for different occupations. It distinguishes between the years of prosperity—1933–35, and the years of depression, 1936–39. We should note that the figures state the agreed wages, but not necessarily those actually paid. One can assume that in years of prosperity and increased demand for workers, employers honored the agreed wages. See the Histadrut, *The Histadrut in Haifa 1933–1939* (Haifa: the HLC, 1939) (Hebrew) (hereafter, *Histadrut in Haifa*).

123. *Histadrut in Haifa*, 71.
124. Ibid., 72.
125. Early 1935.
126. Letter of General Manager to PAWS. 27 February 1935. LA, IV 250–27–1–435.
127. Letter of Nesher Workers' Committee to Executive Committee of the Histadrut, 30 October 1935. LA, IV 208–1–1150.
128. LA, Questionnaires, No. 99.
129. Minutes of Hashomer Hatza'ir, Haifa, 11 May 1935. Giv'at Haviva, (4)A 17.90
130. LA, Questionnaires, Nos. 95, 96.
131. *Histadrut in Haifa*, 36–37.
132. LA, Questionnaires, Nos. 30, 33.
133. LA, Questionnaires, Nos. 36, 37.
134. Ibid., No. 135.
135. *Histadrut in Haifa*, 37.
136. LA, Questionnaires, No. 26.
137. LA, Questionnaires, Nos. 81–88.
138. Ibid., 54–65.
139. On the basis of twenty-three workdays per month. Workers often worked fewer days than that.
140. *Histadrut in Haifa*, 12.
141. Ibid., 13.

Chapter 3

1. David Horowitz and Rita Hinden, *Economic Survey of Palestine* (Tel Aviv: Economic Research Institute, 1938), pp. 104–105.
2. As compared by Horowitz and Hinden, *Economic Survey*, 108.
3. Jacob Metzer and Oded Kaplan, *The Jewish and Arab Economies in Mandatory Palestine: Product, Employment and Growth* (Jerusalem: Mossad Bialik, 1990), p. 91, also 88–95 (Hebrew) (hereafter, *Jewish and Arab Economies*).
4. A. Gertz, *Statistical Handbook of Jewish Palestine* (Jerusalem: Department of

Statistics of the Jewish Agency for Palestine, 1947), pp. 102–103, 375 (hereafter, *Statistical Handbook*).

5. Joseph Vashitz, *Jewish-Arab Relations at Haifa Under the British Mandate* (Givat Haviva: Institute for Arab Studies, 1973) Unpublished Manuscript, Vol. II, P. 48, based on government sources.

6. Joseph Vashitz, Social Changes in Haifa's Arab Society under the British Mandate (Unpublished Ph.D. Dissertation, Jerusalem: Hebrew University, 1993), pp. 158–62 (Hebrew) (hereafter, *Social Changes*).

7. Eliahu Biletzki, *Creation and Struggle, the Haifa Labor Council, 1921–1981* (Tel Aviv: Am Oved, 1981), pp. 152–53 (Hebrew) (hereafter, *Creation and Struggle*).

8. The Histadrut, *The Histadrut in Haifa 1933–1939* (Haifa: the HLC, 1939), p. 84 (Hebrew) (hereafter, *Histadrut in Haifa*).

9. Ibid., 93.

10. Report of the HLC for 1931, LA IV-208-1-295E.

11. Biletzki, ibid., 168–80.

12. Aba Houshi, Report to the HLC for the Year 1934, LA, IV 250-27-5-145.

13. Aba Houshi, Report of 1934.

14. Biletzki, *Creation and Struggle*, 173.

15. Colonial Office, Report by His Majesty's Government in the United Kingdom of Great Britain and Northern Ireland to the Council of the League of Nations on the Administration of Palestine and Trans-Jordan for the year 1932 (London: His Majesty's Stationery Office, 1933), pp. 77–78, 80; Likewise, The Report for the Year 1933, pp. 100–101; The Report for the Year 1934, pp. 119–20; The Report for the Year 1935, pp. 119–20.

16. The account is based on a detailed report as documented by the HLC. Unsigned (possibly Agassi). LA, IV 208-1-312. n.d.

17. This position was put forward clearly in the Labor Legislation Report of the Labor Legislation Committee, of October of that year—6 October 1932, ISA, CO. 733 220, Document No. 97130/1. It was also evident in the report of the Wage Commission of 1928, 15 June 1928, Report of the Wage Commission, 1928, ISA, CO. 733 152. Document No. 570204.

18. Haifa: March 1930; C.Z.A, S9/967.

19. Ibid.

20. List of wages in construction, 19 October 1933. LA, IV 208-1-608.

21. *Histadrut in Haifa*, 87; List of Wages in Construction, ibid.

22. See Chap. 2, note 30; LA, IV 250-27-1-433.

23. Survey of Arab Workers, conducted by the HLC, 1935. LA, IV 20-27-1-433, Questionnaires Nos. 101–103.

24. Gertz, *Statistical Handbook*, 298.

25. Ibid., 299.

26. Ibid.

27. Biletzki, *Creation and Struggle*, 118.

28. 14 Kislev, 6582(1922), CZA, S9/1750B.

29. Report of the HLC for the year 1923, p.3, LA, IV 208-1-31A; Biletzki, *Creation and Struggle*, 118.

30. Minutes of the meeting of the HLC, November 1924, LA, IV 250–27–1–617.
31. Letter of HLC to HE, 12 March 1925. LA, IV 208–1–60A.
32. Minutes of the HLC, 16 June 1925. Similar discussion in following meeting, 30 June 1925, LA. IV 250–27–1–617. An urgent letter repeating the same basic facts, and asking for public intervention, was sent some months later to the Executive of the Va'ad Ha-Leumi, 27 October 1925, CZA, S9/842.
33. Minutes of the HLC, 25 December, 1925, LA, IV 205–27–1–662A.
34. 4 October 1932. Haifa Municipal Archive, Document 79. File 589 Unit.
35. Letter of HLC to Mr. Brunstein, 28 September, HMA, File 589.
36. Leaflet distributed to the Jewish community in Haifa by the HLC, 4 September 1934. HMA, File 589.
37. See minutes of four consecutive meetings of the Community Council, 30 August 1934, to 4 September 1934. HMA, ibid.
38. Aba Houshi, Report to Council for year 1934, pp. 20–21, LA, IV 250–27–5–145.
39. *Histadrut in Haifa*, 21–23.
40. *Davar*, 27 August 1934.
41. Ibid.
42. 28 August 1934. HMA, File 589.
43. *Davar*, 28 August 1934.
44. *Davar*, 29 August; 2 September 1934.
45. *Davar*, 30 August 1934
46. Ibid.
47. Foreign labor is the literal translation of the Hebrew term "Avoda Zara." Avoda Zara has the additional meaning of foreign worship, meaning idolatry. The choice of this term was very powerful and evocative. It was clearly understood by the community to which it was directed. 30 August 1934. HMA, File 589.
48. *Davar*, 2 September 1934.
49. Anita Shapira, *Futile Struggle, The Jewish Labour Controversy, 1929–1939* (Tel Aviv: Hakkibutz Hameuchad, 1970), p. 230 (Hebrew) (hereafter, *Futile Struggle*).
50. *Davar*, 1 September 1934.
51. *Davar*, 3 September 1934: and so on in Davar, 5–12 September 1934.
52. *Filastin*, 29 August, 1934.
53. *Filastin*, 30 August, 1934.
54. *Filastin*, 31 August, 1934.
55. Ibid.
56. *Filastin*, 1 September 1934.
57. *Filastin*, 31 August 1934.
58. 5 September, ibid.
59. 11 September, ibid.
60. Leaflet of HLC to Arab workers, 4 September 1934, LA. Missing.
61. *Davar*, 1 October 1934.

62. Quoted by Shapira, *Futile Struggle*, 230.

63. Ibid., 56.

64. Shprintzak was a member of *Ha-Po'el Hatza'ir*, a workers party that united with *Ahdut Ha'-Avoda* to form *Mapai*, the dominant workers' party. *Hapo'el Hatza'ir* was far less militant than *Ahdut Ha'-Avoda* in issues of class conflict, though they were also committed to the ideology and practice of "Hebrew Labor."

65. Shapira, ibid.

66. Ibid.

67. *Davar*, 2 September 1934.

68. For example, *Ha-Yarden*, 3 September 1934; 7 September 1934.

69. Ibid., 4 September 1934.

70. Ibid., 7 September 1934.

71. Ibid.

72. *Davar*, 1 September 1934.

73. Anita Shapira, "The Controversy in Mapai on the use of Violence, 1932–1935," in Shapira (ed.), *Visions in Conflict* (Tel Aviv: Am Oved, 1989), pp. 82–118 (Hebrew).

74. Ibid.

Chapter 4

1. Yossi Beilin, *Roots of Hebrew Industry* (Jerusalem: Keter, 1987), pp. 67–84 (Hebrew) (hereafter, *Hebrew Industry*).

2. Agriculture is not discussed in this book because it was not an urban industry. The ideological glorification of labor was predominantly associated with agricultural work, the labor of the pioneers, the *halutzim*. Construction work followed, well behind.

3. Said Himadeh, *Economic Organization of Palestine* (Beirut: American Press, 1938), pp. 224–29 (hereafter, *Economic Organization*); Abraham Cohen, *The Economy of the Arab Sector in Mandatory Palestine* (Givat Haviva: Institute for Arab Studies, 1978), pp. 28–30 (Hebrew).

4. Baruch Kimmerling and Joel S. Migdal, *Palestinians, the Making of a People* (New York: The Free Press, 1993), pp. 62–63; Joseph Vashitz, *The Arabs in Palestine* (Merhavia: Sifri'at Hapoalim, 1947), p. 95 (Hebrew).

5. Vashitz, ibid.; Barbara Smith, *The Roots of Separatism in Palestine, British Economic Policy, 1919–1929* (London: Tauris, 1993), p. 359 (hereafter, *Roots of Separatism*).

6. Zeev Abramovitz and Y. Gelfat, *The Arab Economy in Palestine and the Countries of the Middle East* (Ein Harod: Hakkibutz Hameuchad, 1944), pp. 59–81 (Hebrew) (hereafter, *The Arab Economy*).

7. As summarized by Beilin, one-third of all enterprises were owned by Jews. They produced 44 percent of the products and employed 44 percent of all workers. Sixty-four percent of all invested capital was invested in these enterprises. Beilin, *Hebrew Industry*, p. 54.

8. Smith, *Roots of Separatism,* p. 358.
9. Jacob Metzer and Oded Kaplan, *The Jewish and Arab Economies in Mandatory Palestine: Product, Employment and Growth* (Jerusalem: Falk Institute, 1990), p. 74 (Hebrew) (hereafter, *Jewish and Arab Economies*).
10. A. Gertz, *Statistical Handbook of Palestine, 1947* (Jerusalem: Jewish Agency, 1947), p. 225 (hereafter, *Statistical Handbook*).
11. Ibid.
12. The Jewish Agency, Memorandum submitted to the Palestine Royal Commission on behalf of the Jewish Agency of Palestine (London: Jewish Agency for Palestine, 1936), pp. 221–29 (hereafter, Memorandum).
13. Mahr al-Sherif, "The Social Dynamic and Development of Arab Workers in Palestine During the British Mandate," *al-Jadid* (Arabic), Budeiri Musa, *The Development of the Workers' Movement in Palestine, 1919–1948* (Jerusalem: Dar al-Kitab, 1979) (Arabic).
14. Barbara J. Smith, *British Economic Policy in Palestine Towards the Development of the Jewish National Home, 1920–1929* (Unpublished D. Phil, University of Oxford, Oxford, 1978), 325–37.
15. May Seikaly, *The Arab Community of Haifa 1918–1936. A Study in Transformation* (Unpublished D. Phil., University of Oxford, Oxford, 1983), p. 103.
16. Memorandum, 220.
17. In this chapter we will be discussing the Jewish- and Arab-owned industry and not the international industries or government concessions that were also located in Haifa—for example, the concession for the production of electricity granted to Pinhas Rutenberg, and the Consolidated Oil Refineries. Government enterprises will be discussed in the following two chapters, which will deal with government transportation enterprises, the Haifa port, and the Palestine Railways.
18. Nahum Gross, "Haifa in the Beginning of Jewish Industrialization in Palestine," *Economic Quarterly* 27 (1980): 308–19 (Hebrew); Gilbert Herbert, "Crossroads: Imperial Priorities and Regional Perspectives in the Planning of Haifa, 1918–1939," *Planning Perspectives* 4 (1989): 313–31.
19. For additional sources concerning Haifa's industrial development, see Gideon Biger, "The Industrial Structure of the Towns of Palestine in the Beginning of the Mandate Period," *Cathedra* 29 (1983): 79–113 (Hebrew); Arnon Sofer, "Distribution of Industry in the Haifa Bay Area," *Studies in the Geography of Eretz Israel* 9 (1976):136–55 (Hebrew).
20. David Gurevitz, *Jewish Industry, Transportation and Commerce,* Report and Statistical Conclusion of the censuses conducted in 1937 (Jerusalem: Publication of the Department of Commerce and Industry of the Jewish Agency, 1939), Tb. 4 (Hebrew) (hereafter, *Jewish Manufacture—1937*).
21. *Jewish Manufacture—1937,* Tb. 16.
22. Joseph Vashitz, *Arab-Jewish Relations at Haifa During the British Mandate.* (Unpublished Manuscript, Giv'at Haviva, Institute for Arab Studies, 1973), Part II, p. 70 (hereafter, *Arab-Jewish Relations*); see also, The Histadrut, *The Histadrut in Haifa, 1933–1939* (Haifa: the HLC, 1939), pp. 72–79 (Hebrew) (hereafter, *Histadrut in Haifa*); Government of Palestine, Palestine Royal

Commission, Memoranda prepared by the Government of Palestine (London: His Majesty's Stationery Office, 1937), pp. 168–73.

23. Beilin, *Hebrew Industry*, 74.

24. *Jewish Manufacture—1937*, Tbs. 3, 13.

25. Ibid., Tb. 13.

26. Memorandum, 169; Himadeh, *Economic Organization*, 225.

27. Shmuel Avitzur, *The History of Industry in Eretz Israel*, In the memory of Nahum Vilbush (Herzelia, 1974) (Hebrew).

28. Ha'im Ahronowitz, *Hadar Hacarmel* (Haifa: Council of Hadar Hacarmel, 1958).

29. Seikaly, *The Arab Community*, 114–15.

30. Beilin, *Hebrew Industry*, 47.

31. Vashitz, *Jewish-Arab Relations*, Part II, 73–74, 76.

32. For a detailed discussion of the soap industry of Nablus, see Beshara Doumani, *Rediscovering Palestine, Merchants and Peasants in Jabal Nablus, 1700–1900* (Berkeley: University of California Press, 1995), pp. 182–232.

33. Abramovitz and Gelfat, *The Arab Economy*, 68.

34. Ibid.

35. Ibid., 71.

36. Doumani, *Rediscovering Palestine*.

37. Vashitz, *Arab-Jewish Relations*, 73.

38. Ibid., 76.

39. Sarah Graham-Brown, "Political Economy of Jabal Nablus, 1920–48," in Roger Owen (ed.), *Studies in the Economic and Social History of Palestine in the Nineteenth and Twentieth Centuries* (Basingstoke and London: St. Anthony's, 1986), p. 140.

40. *Survey*, 454.

41. See Beilin, *Hebrew Industry*, 38–40; Tzadok Eshel, *The Cement and Its Makers: Nesher's Jubilee* (Haifa: Nesher, 1976) (Hebrew) (hereafter, *Nesher*).

42. Eshel, *Nesher*, 12–14, 23, 54–55.

43. David De Vries, *The Labour Movement in Haifa, 1919–1929: A Study in the History of Urban Workers in Mandatory Palestine* (Unpublished Ph.D. dissertation, Tel Aviv University, 1991), pp. 223–31 (Hebrew) (hereafter, *The Labor Movement*).

44. See story of the strike in Nesher in Aharon Kaminker, *The Neighborhood by the Smoke Stacks: Memories of the Nesher Neighborhood* (Haifa, 1978), pp. 52–59; Eshel, *Nesher*, 46–48. Also minutes of the HLC, 24 February 1925, LA, IV 250–27–1–658B.

45. See "Conditions for the return to work in Nesher," 26 February 1925, LA, IV 208–1–60A.

46. De Vries, *The Labour Movement*, 213.

47. Report of meeting of HLC, 16 September 1925, LA, IV 250–27–1–612.

48. HLC, Bulletin, 25 March 1930, p. 4, LA Library; Nesher Labor Council, Report of Activity, April-May 1932, pp. 6–7, LA, IV 208–1–894; Nesher Labor Council to Histadrut Executive, 30 October, 1935, LA, IV 208–1–1150.

49. HLC, Bulletin, ibid.

50. Seikaly, *Arab Community*, 116.

51. *Survey*, 455.

52. Seikaly, *Arab Community*, 110.

53. Quoted by Vashitz, *Jewish-Arab Relations*, Part II, 66–67.

54. Report on Immigration, Land Settlement and Development, by Sir John Hope-Simpson (London: His Majesty's Stationery Office, 1930), p. 109.

55. Seikaly, *Arab Community*, 123.

56. Joseph Vashitz, "Dhawat and Isamiyyun: Two Groups of Arab Community Leaders in Haifa During the British Mandate," *Asian and African Studies* 17 (1983): 115 (hereafter, "Dhawat"); Gelfat and Abramovitz, *Arab Economy*, 76.

57. Vashitz, "Dhawat," 114–15, 117.

58. In 1931, Qaraman replaced Nasrallah al-Khuri who resigned after the family, previously one of largest landowning families in Haifa, went bankrupt. He was elected in 1934 at the next municipal election Vashitz, "Dhawat," 105.

59. Unsigned letter to "Moshe," from Haganna Intelligence, 7 November 1938. HA, 8/2.

60. David Hacohen, *My Way* (Tel Aviv: Am Oved, 1971) (Hebrew), p. 45; Yazbeck has suggested that Qaraman was willing to pay off the rebel bands, while the veteran notables probably considered such behavior beneath their dignity (personal communication).

61. Vashitz, "Dhawat," 114–15. Vashitz's sources are veteran residents of Haifa whom he interviewed in the late 1960s and early 1970s.

62. Ibid.; Seikaly, *Arab Community*, 122.

63. Maspero employed Jewish labor only, Gelfat and Abramovitz, *Arab Economy*, 77.

64. *Survey*, 518.

65. *al-Karmil*, 22 July 1928.

66. Vashitz, "Dhawat," 115.

67. Hacohen, *My Way*, 45. The close relationship between Hacohen and Qaraman was based both on their joint membership in the Municipal Council and their partnership in Even va-Sid.

68. Seikaly, *Arab Community*, 130.

69. Hacohen, *My Way*, 45.

70. Gelfat and Abramovitz, *Arab Economy*, 78.

71. From Survey of HLC, 1935, LA IV 250–27–1–433.

72. Censuses were conducted by the HLC in 1941 and 1943; see Census of Arab Workers in Haifa, July 1941, LA, IV 250–27–5–131; and "The Arab Worker in Haifa, December 1943," AHA, The Aba Houshi Collection, Container 5.

73. For 1932, see Report of Agassi to the Histadrut Executive, June 1932, CZA, S25/3120; for 1935 see Questionnaires of HLC, Questionnaire No. 30, LA, IV 250–27–1–433.

74. LA, IV 250–27–5–131.

75. The Arab Worker in Haifa—1943, AHA, Aba Houshi Collection, Container 5.

76. Government of Palestine, Department of Statistics, *Wage Census — 1943* (Jerusalem, Government Printer, 1943), Tb. 6.

77. For increase of cost of living, as measured by the cost of living index of the government, see Gertz, *Statistical Handbook*, 318–20, or according to the rise in price of food products in the Arab market, see David Horowitz, "The Arab Economy in Times of War," *Hameshek Hashitufi* 21 (1943): 52–53 (Hebrew).

78. Report of Agassi, 1932, CZA, S25/3120.

79. Ibid.

80. *Davar*, 21 May 1928.

81. *al-Karmil*, 27 May 1928.

82. *Davar*, 5 June 1928.

83. *Davar*, 28 January 1930.

84. Colonial Office, Report by His Majesty's Government to the Council of the League of Nations on the Administration of Palestine and Trans-Jordan for the Year 1930, London, 1931; Likewise for the years 1931 to 1935; Agassi, Action among Arab Workers in Haifa, 31 April 1935. LA, IV 250–27–1–435.

85. Agassi, "The Strike in the Tobacco Factory of Qaraman, Dik and Salti" — Haifa, 15 September 1935. AHA, Aba Houshi Collection, Container 51.

86. al-Hajj Ibrahim made his fortune in trade and soon became one of the leading merchants in Haifa. He was elected Chairman of the Haifa Chamber of Commerce in 1927, a position of economic and political influence that he held for many years. He was elected to the Municipal Council in 1934; see Seikaly, *Arab Community*, 375, 387; Report of the Political Department of the Jewish Agency, "Rashid Hajj Ibrahim," May 1946. CZA, S25/4022.

87. Five hundred workers according to *Davar*, 29 August 1935, and 250 according to *Filastin*, 28 August 1935.

88. *Davar*, 8 September 1935.

89. Agassi, Report of the Strike at Qaraman, Dik and Salti, Haifa, December 1936. 8 March 1937. LA, IV 205–7.

90. Ibid.

91. Minutes of Meeting of the Acre Workers' Committee, 19 May 1927. LA, IV 208–1–58.

92. Minutes of Histadrut Executive, 11 May, 1927. LA, Library; Agreement between Gershon and Meir Weitzman and Y. Apter, representative of workers, n.d. probably June 1927, LA, IV 208–1–58.

93. *Davar*, 23 February 1927, 17 May 1927; Sheik Ahmad Shukeiri of Acre, who gave his support to the strike, *Davar* 8 March 1927, was one of the leaders of the northern-based opposition to the Mufti Hajj Amin al-Husseini and his leadership of the Arab national movement.

94. Letter from Acre Workers' Committee to Histadrut Executive, 12 July 1927, LA, IV 208–1–58.

95. *Davar*, 18 July 1929.

96. Acre Workers' Committee to Histadrut Executive, 15 October 1929 and 30 October 1929, LA, IV 208–1–191.

97. Report on strike of Arab Nur workers, 1938, LA, IV 104–22.

98. Diary of secretary of PLL in Acre, 1945–46, LA, IV 219–38, Notebook 3.

99. Deborah Bernstein, "Jews and Arabs in the Nesher Cement Works," *Cathedra* 78 (1995): 82–107 (Hebrew).

100. Letter of Aba Houshi to Histadrut Executive, 14 July 1930, LA, IV 208–1–186.

101. It should be remembered that at the time Jewish unskilled workers in Nesher were earning approximately 350 mils per day.

102. Sentence of Arbitration, 22 June 1933, LA, IV 208–1–608.

103. Agassi, Action among Arab Workers in Haifa, 1932–1933, p. 4, LA, IV 250–27–1–435.

104. Ibid.

105. Letter of Zvi Grinberg and Aba Houshi to Histadrut Executive. August 1933. LA, IV 208–1–894.

106. Report of Workers' Committee of Mosaica to Histadrut Executive, 9 October 1935. GH, (3)17.90b.

107. The workers of *Hashomer Hatzair* were based in Haifa while awaiting their settlement on a *kibbutz*.

108. See Deborah Bernstein, "From Split Labour Market Strategy to Political Co-optation: The Palestine Labour League," *Middle Eastern Studies* 31 (1995): 755–71.

109. Ibid.

110. Meetings of Arab workers of Volfman with Aba Houshi and Alfia of the PLL, October-November 1935, LA, IV 205–4.

Chapter 5

1. For the British debate concerning the best location of the deep-water harbor and the strategic and economic benefits of Haifa, see Gilbert Herbert, "Crossroads: Imperial Priorities and Regional Perspectives in the Planning of Haifa, 1918–1939," *Planning Perspectives* 4 (1989):323; Shimon Stern, "The Dispute Concerning the Construction of Haifa Port During the British Mandate," *Cathedra* 21 (1981):171–74 (Hebrew); Gabriel Sheffer, "The Principles of British Pragmatism: Reevaluation of British Policies Towards Palestine in the 1930s," *Cathedra* 29 (1983):117–21 (Hebrew).

2. A. Gertz, *Statistical Handbook of Palestine 1947* (Jerusalem: Department of Statistics, The Jewish Agency for Palestine, 1947), pp. 240–42 (hereafter, *Statistical Handbook*).

3. Ibid.

4. Palestine Royal Commission, Memorandum Prepared by the Government of Palestine (London: H.M. Stationery Office, 1937), p. 166.

5. Husni Sawwaf, "Transportation and Communication," in Said Himadeh, *Economic Organization of Palestine* (Beirut: American Press, 1938), p. 336.

6. Herbert, "Crossroads," 323

7. "Rendel, Palmer and Tritton," the company which planned the port and oversaw its construction, in their report of 1935, quoted by Stern, "The Dispute," 183.

8. Gertz, *Statistical Handbook*, 280.
9. Rachela Makover, *Government and Administration of Palestine, 1917–1925* (Jerusalem: Yad Yitzhak Ben Zvi, 1988), p. 158 (Hebrew).
10. For March 1934, see LA, IV 250–27–2–322. For further details of 1935 see LA, IV 208–1–755.
11. LA, IV 250–27–2–322.
12. Report from Dr. Vidra of the Sea Department to the Labor Department of the Jewish Agency, 27 December 1936, CZA, S9/1135.
13. 19 April 1934. LA, IV 250–27–2–322
14. David De Vries, *The Labour Movement in Haifa, 1919–1929: A Study in the History of Urban Workers in Mandatory Palestine* (Unpublished Ph.D. dissertation, Tel Aviv University, 1991), pp. 37–38 (Hebrew).
15. Letter of Weitzman to Under-Secretary of State for the Colonies 9 October 1928. LA, IV 208–1–128; Similar letter sent to the High Commissioner a month earlier, 11 September 1928, LA, IV 203–15.
16. Gertz, *Statistical Handbook*, 46–47.
17. Jacob Metzer, "Fiscal Incidence and Resource Transfer Between Jews and Arabs in Mandatory Palestine," *Research in Economic History* 7 (1982):95.
18. There are no firm statistics to support this claim. Fifty percent was the Jewish estimate, as seen in the above letter.
19. For example, *al-Karmil*, 9.12.27; 8.1.28; 16.1.30; 5.8.31.
20. *al-Karmil*, 8.1.28.
21. For detailed discussion of the East Africa and Palestine Loan, see Barbara J. Smith, *British Economic Policy in Palestine Towards the Development of the Jewish National Home, 1920–1929* (Unpublished D. Phil, University of Oxford, Oxford, 1978), pp. 40–55.
22. For example, *al-Karmil*, 28.11.26.
23. *al-Karmil*, 17 April 1927.
24. For example, *al-Karmil*, 8 June 1929; 27 February 1930.
25. Gertz includes the tonnage unloaded and loaded in the Haifa port in 1927, which was significantly lower than that given for 1930. Gertz, *Statistical Abstract*, 280.
26. Gertz, ibid., 184, 248–49.
27. Gertz, *Statistical Handbook*, 181.
28. Jacob Metzer, *The Divided Economy of Mandatory Palestine* (Cambridge, Cambridge University Press, 1998), pp. 145–48.
29. Ibid. 179.
30. For comparison of the number of workers in the busy season as compared to the off-season, for the years 1934 to 1938, see 21 July 1938. LA, IV 250–27–2–322.
31. There are no figures for the percentage of Jewish workers, but various comments of the HLC indicate that it was very small.
32. Yitzhak Rokah was born in Jaffa to a well-known Jewish family. He worked in the cultivation of citrus and naval transportation and was appointed as the manager of Pardess, established by his father. In 1933, he resigned from Pardess and established a new company, Syndicate of the

Jaffa Oranges, which became the second large organization of citrus grow-ers. Shmuel Tolkovski was a member of the Tel Aviv city council, estab-lished and ran a company for the export of citrus, and from 1934 was the general manager of the Palestine Citrus Bureau. See A. Tidhar, *Encyclopedia of the Pioneers and the Builders of the Yishuv* (Tel Aviv, 1947), Vol. 4, pp. 1572–73; Vol. 6, p. 2446 (Hebrew).

33. Aba Houshi to The Citrus Center, 10 August, 18 October 1932, LA, IV 250–27–1–295.

34. The certificates for the Saloniki port workers came from the "labor sched-ule," immigration certificates intended for workers who had places of work waiting for them. For the different categories of immigration, see Gertz, *Sta-tistical Handbook*, 93–94. For Aba Houshi's visits to Saloniki, see, e.g., HLC to Histadrut Executive, 18 September 1933, LA IV 208–1–615; HLC to Exec-utive of Jewish Agency, 15 November 1933, IV 208–1–608; see Z. Studny, "The Salonikis (Memories)," *Me'asef* 8 (1976): 153–56 (Hebrew). They were soon recognized as excellent workers by both Arab and Jewish contractors. By the citrus export season of 1933/34, they accounted for about two-thirds of the Jewish workers in the port—78 out of the 110 Jewish porters and all 22 Jewish stevedores. A count of the workers in the Haifa port, 6–11 March 1934; 19 April 1934. LA, IV 250–27–2–322; for a detailed account of place of work within the port of Saloniki immigrants, see letter of Aba Houshi to Histadrut Executive, 16 September 1934. LA, IV 208–1–615.

35. Eliezer Lipton, Mordechai Eldar, and Theodor Ben Nahum.

36. David Hacohen of Solel Boneh and Aba Houshi of the HLC.

37. See partnership contract, 15 April 1934, and accompanying letter of Aba Houshi to Histadrut Executive, 8 August 1934. LA, IV 208–1–615.

38. The Port Works, unsigned but probably written by Aba Houshi, 1939. LA, IV 250–27–2–244.

39. Ibid.

40. Aba Houshi, Report on events in Haifa, 20 May, 22 May 1936. LA, IV 250–27–2–119A

41. Ibid.; also, Aba Houshi, The Strike in Haifa and the Work in the Port, 3 No-vember 1936. CZA, S25/10537.

42. Ibid.

43. The Port Works, unsigned but probably written by Aba Houshi, 1939. LA, IV 250–27–2–244.

44. Ibid.

45. Labor Exchange to Sea Department of the JA. 20 December 1938. LA, IV 250–27–2–325.

46. The trade unions undertook to provide their members with work in accor-dance with their level of skill. Due to the deep depression, they were not able to provide such employment; members therefore sought work through the Labour Exchange of the HLC in its Port Department,

47. A description of the experience of a group of *Kibbutz* workers appeared in the *kibbutz* pamphlet, see A Letter to Our Members, 27 December 1937. Archive of Kibbutz Kfar Masarik.

48. Labor Exchange to Sea Department of the JA. 20 December 1938. LA, IV 250–27–2–325.

49. Ibid.

50. HLC to Political Department of the Executive of the Jewish Agency, 30 December 1931. CZA, S8/2734.

51. For details of number of workers in customs porterage, see: for busy season of 1933/34–19 April 1934. LA, IV 250–27–2–322; for 1935/36—Meirovitz to Greenbaum, 15 December 1936, CZA, S9/1102; for the season of 1936/37—Letter of Vidra, Sea Dept. of the JA, to Meirovitz of Merkaz Ha'avoda, 23 December 1936. CZA, S9/1135; Vidra to Meirovitz, 3 February 1937. Ibid.

52. Aba Houshi to Stead, 25 September 1933. LA, IV 208–1–608.

53. For similar complaints see Aba Houshi to Histadrut Executive, 2 July 1934. LA, IV 208–1–608; Meirovitz to Shertok, 5 September 1936. CZA, S9/1135.

54. D. Remez to Stead, 29 March 1936. LA, IV 104–49–1–76

55. Chief Secretary to Executive of JA, 9 April 1936. CZA, S9/1135.

56. Shertok to Stead, 5 January 1937. CZA, S9/1135.

57. Letter of Vidra to Shertok, 7 December 1936. CZA, S9/1135

58. Vidra to Shertok, 9 December 1936. CZA, S9/1121.

59. Ibid.

60. F. O. Rogers, Report on Work of Jewish Porters in the Port of Haifa. 18 June 1937. ISA, CO 733/328. Tape No. 421.

61. The Port Works, unsigned but probably written by Aba Houshi, 1939. LA, IV 250–27–2–244

62. Rogers, Report, Item 3. June 1937. Ibid.

63. Ibid. Item 6.

64. Ibid. Item 7.

65. Wauchope to Ormsby-Gore, 17 January 1938. ISA, CO, 733/328. Tape No. 421.

66. Ibid. Item 12.

67. Report on the Employment of Jewish Labour on Porterage Work at Haifa Port, 23 December 1937. Item 3. Ibid.

68. Ibid. Item 13.

69. Ibid. Item 15.

70. Ibid. Items 8, 16.

71. Rogers, ibid. Item 11.

72. Ibid. Item 17.

73. For example, Letter of Customs' porters to the Labor Exchange of the Haifa Port, HLC. 28 August 1939, and answer of Solel Boneh to HLC, 5 September 1939. LA, IV 250–27–2–322; letters of the workers' committee of the Solel Boneh workers in the Haifa port to the executive of the HLC, 20 February 1941, 22 April 1941. LA, IV 250–27–5–79.

74. "Solel Boneh" to HLC, 9 January 1942, LA, IV 250–27–5–79; Vidra to Greenbaum, 10 January 1943. CZA, S9/1132.

75. Hileli Aryeh, "Potash," in *Kfar Masarik—25 Years* (Kfar Masarik, 1958), p. 135 (Hebrew).

76. The description of the seamen's strike is based on two detailed descriptions—"The Organization of the Arab Worker in the Port." Report to the Kibbutz Ha'artzi. Summer 1932. Givat Haviva, (3)B17.90; Lina Dar, "Jewish-Arab Joint Organization in the Haifa Port, 1932," *Me'asef* 14 (1988): 45–79 (Hebrew) (hereafter, "Joint Organization").

77. Dar, "Joint Organization," 63.

78. Dar, "Joint Organization," 64.

79. Aba Houshi to Histadrut Executive, 29 July 1932. LA, IV 208–1–321.

80. Ibid.

81. Ibid.

82. Aba Houshi to Histadrut Executive, 1933 (no exact date), CZA, S25/3120.

83. The international oil companies presented similar labor problems.

Chapter 6

1. For overall reviews of transportation in Palestine during the British mandatory period see Husni Sawaf, "Transportation and Communication," in Himadeh Said (ed.), *Economic Organization of Palestine* (Beirut: American Press, 1938), pp. 301–42 (hereafter, Sawaf, "Transportation and Communication"); Shalom Reichman, "The Evolution of Land Transportation in Palestine, 1920–1947," *Jerusalem Studies in Geography* 2 (1971): 55–90 (Hebrew); Shmuel Avitsur, "Seventy Years to the Railway in Eretz Israel," in The Department of Geography of the Kibbutz Movement, *The Development of the Trains in Eretz Israel* (Mimeo, 1987), pp. 62–71 (Hebrew).

2. Pick W. Pinhas, "Meissner Pasha—The Pioneer of Railways in Palestine, The Man, His Railways and Their Fortunes," *Cathedra* 10 (1979): 102–28 (Hebrew).

3. Ibid., 111.

4. Palestine Royal Commission. Memoranda Prepared by the Government of Palestine (London: His Majesty's Stationery Office, 1937), p. 160.

5. Sawaf, "Transportation and Communication," 326; for a detailed breakdown of the Railway finances between 1929–1946/47 see Government of Palestine, Palestine Railways and Operated Lines for the Year 1946/47 (Palestine, 1947), p. 128.

6. Sawaf, "Transportation and Communication," 322–23.

7. Government of Palestine, Palestine Railways. Report of the General Manager on the Administration of the Palestine Railways and Operated Lines For the Year 1938/39 (Palestine, 1939).

8. Ibid.

9. Report of the General Manager 1946/47, 128.

10. Ibid.

11. Report of General Manager for the Year 1946/47, 12–14; 128.

12. Government of Palestine, Palestine Railways. Report of The General Manager on the Administration of the Palestine Railways and Operated Lines, For the Year 1931, p. 51; for the year 1938/39, p. 122; for the year 1946/47, p. 131.

13. For example, Ben Zvi to Abramov, 7 March 1937. LA, IV 250–27–2–201; Dr. B. Joseph to Meirovitz, 27 November 1938. CZA, S11/81; Meeting of Aba Houshi and Kirbi, 28 March 1947. LA, IV 250–27–3–32.
14. Grobman, A Short Review of the Development and the Professional, Organizational and Constructive Activity of the RPTWO, 1936. HLC Archive (no filing number); Interview of Yehezkiel Abramov, 9 April 1972. Oral Documentation, LA, No. 126.
15. Organization of Railway Workers of Palestine to Sir Herbert Samuel, 8 August 1920. LA, IV 237–34A.
16. Abramov, ibid.; Grobman, ibid.
17. Meirovitz to Kaplan and Shertok, 14 August 1936. CZA, S9/1135; Secretary of RPTWO and Secretary of Labor Bureau of HLC to Executive of Jewish Agency, 31 August 1936. LA, IV 210–142; Meirovitz to Shertok, 5 September 1936. CZA, S11/83; Meirovitz to B. Joseph, 13 April 1937. CZA, S9/1122.
18. Abramov to Histadrut Executive, 19 April, 1937. LA, IV 208-1-1325.
19. Report of General Manager 1931, 50; RPTWO, Jewish and Arab Workers in the PR. 11 October 1935. LA, IV 208–1–515A; Abramov to Histadrut Executive, ibid.
20. For the occupational distribution of workers see Survey of Railway, Post and Telegraph Workers, n.d., received by Histadrut Executive 18 January 1937. LA, IV 201–3–228; Report of the Central Committee, RPTWO, August 1939. LA, IV 237–20C, p. 5.
21. Grobman to Zionist Executive and National Council, 15 November 1929, LA, IV 208–1–172.
22. Ibid.
23. Ibid.
24. Ibid.
25. Abramov to Histadrut Executive, ibid.
26. Ibid.
27. Ibid.
28. RPTWO, Report of Central Committee to the Eighth Convention, 4–5 August 1939. LA, IV 237–20C
29. Minutes of the Histadrut Executive, 10 April 1946. p. 6. LA, Library.
30. Interview with Ephraim Shwartzman, 20 March 1972. LA, Oral History, No. 7.
31. Bonacich Edna, "A Theory of Ethnic Antagonism: The Split Labor Market," *American Sociological Review* 37 (1972): 547–59.
32. *Al Ha-Mishmar*, RPTWO, 24 July 1928. LA, 280–1–20; *Hedim*, RPTWO, 27 February 1930, LA, 208–1–320; Memorandum of the Joint Committee of the Railway Workers in Haifa to the HC, 17 July 1934, ISA, Doc. 375, File R/36/34.
33. RPTWO, Report of the Central Committee, 4–5 August 1939, p. 12, LA, IV 237–20C.
34. RPTWO to GM, 11 June 1942. LA, IV 208–1–2471.
35. Ibid.

36. General Manager to Controller of Manpower, 22 September 1942. ISA, Doc. 371, File R/36/34

37. RPTWO to Center of Labor, 23 June 1929. LA, IV 104–49–238; Abramov to Histadrut Executive, 19 April 1937. LA, IV 208–1–1325.

38. As of 1929, ibid.; 19 April 1937, ibid.

39. Ibid.

40. Survey of Railway Workers, 18 January 1937. LA, IV 288–3–201.

41. RPTWO, 11 June 1942. LA, IV 208–1–2471.

42. Government of Palestine, Office of Statistics. *Statistical Abstract of Palestine, 1942* (Jerusalem: Government Printer, 1942) p. 127.

43. For example, *Hedim*, RPTWO, 27 February 1930, LA, IV 208–1–320; Joint Committee of the Railway Workers to the HC, 17 July 1934, ISA, Doc. 375, File R/36/34; Central Committee of RPTWO to General Manager, 11 June 1942. LA, IV 208–1–2471.

44. Ibid.

45. Report of Central Committee, 4–5 August 1939. LA, IV 237–20C.

46. Notice of General Manger to Railway Workers, 15 January 1943. LA, IV 250–27–3–32.

47. *Al Ha-Mishmar*, RPTWO, 24 July 1928. LA, IV 280–1–20.

48. For example, Report to RPTWO Convention, 1 May 1931, p. 16–17. LA, IV 237–20B.

49. Ibid.

50. Ibid.

51. November 1922; December-January 1923/24. LA—Library.

52. April 1925, ibid.

53. July 1925, ibid.

54. RPTWO, 24 July 1928. LA, 280–1–20.

55. RPTWO, 27 February 1930.

56. *Ha-Katar*, December-January 1923/24, pp. 20–21.

57. Ibid.

58. A Jewish worker who spoke in the assembly of railway workers, 20 August 1934. LA, IV 250–27–2–201.

59. Organization of Railway Workers to HC, 8 August 1920. LA, IV 237–34A.

60. Grobman, A Short Review of the Development and the Professional, Organizational and Constructive Activity of the RPTWO, 1936. HLC Archive (no filing number).

61. "The Organization of Railway Workers," n.d. LA, IV 237–1.

62. For example, Meeting of Ben Gurion and Hoz with Chief Secretary on dismissal of railway workers, 28 April 1922. LA, IV 237–34B; Meeting of Ben Zvi and Ben Gurion with Chief Secretary, 10 March 1925. LA, IV 237–34E; Meeting of representatives of RPTWO and of HE with GM of PR and Anthony of the CO, 29 September 1925. LA, IV 203–11.

63. The PKP was a vehemently anti-Zionist party, while *Poalei Zion—Smol*, the left wing of *Poalei Zion*, was affiliated with the Zionist movement, but called for joint class struggle and class organization with the Arab workers.

64. The issue was debated in the Fifth Convention of the RPTWO, December

1923. All the representatives of the HE supported the formation of national units, while all spokesmen for the RPTWO rejected it. See *Ha-Katar*, December-January 1923/24, pp. 9–12.

65. Grobman to Histadrut Executive, 30 November 1924. LA, IV 208–1–14.

66. Ibid.

67. Avraham Khalfon was an Arabic-speaking Sephardi Jew who served as a translator for the RPTWO and for the HLC, and later became the first Jewish secretary of the Haifa municipal council.

68. From *al-Nafir*, 22 November 1924. Translated at the time into Hebrew and written in Grobman's handwriting. LA, IV 208–1–14. The original newspaper is not available.

69. See A Railway Worker—J.D., "The Reasons Which Forced the Arab Workers to Establish an Independent Organization in Haifa," Musa Budeiri, *The Development of the Workers' Movement in Palestine, 1919–1948* (Jerusalem: dar al-Kitab, 1979), pp. 98–99 (Arabic); see also Zachary Lockman, *Comrades and Enemies, Arab and Jewish Workers in Palestine, 1906–1948* (Berkeley: University of California Press, 1996), 143.

70. A railway worker, "Must the workers withdraw from the organization of railway workers," Budeire, ibid., 91–92 .

71. M. or—a railway worker, "More and more, the association of railway workers." Ibid., 102.

72. Resolutions of the General Council of the RPTWO, Haifa, 9/1/25. LA, IV 237–1.

73. HE to Chief Secretary, 24 May 1926. LA, IV 237–32; E. Vahl, "Joint Organization," Pamphlet, devoted to the 6th Conference of RPTWO, June 1927, p. 15. LA, Library.

74. Acting Chief Secretary to GFJL, 29 July 1926, LA, IV 237–36A; Railway: Recognition of Union of Railway, Post and Telegraph Workers, 1931. ISA, CO733/205. Doc. No. 87186.

75. For a detailed report of the severely difficult condition of the RPTWO, see "Memorandum," Central Committee of RPTWO to HE, 1926 (no exact date), LA. IV 250–27–1–2020.

76. Deborah Bernstein, "From Split Labour Market Strategy to Political Co-optation: The Palestine Labour League," *Middle Eastern Studies* 31 (1995): 755–71.

77. The Sixth Convention of the RPTWO, Haifa, 29–31 July 1927. Supplement to *Davar*, September 1927.

78. Platform of Joint Committee 1928, no exact date. LA, IV 250–27–1–2019.

79. Meeting of 12 February 1928. In Review of Activity of Central Committee, RPTWO, 15 February 1928. LA, ibid.

80. For example, ibid.; Meeting of 28 February 1928. Review of Central Committee, 29 February 1928. LA, ibid.

81. For example, Grobman to Jerusalem Branch, RPTWO, 8 April 1928. LA, IV 237–3.

82. The strong emphasis on issues relating to the relative strength of the RPTWO, the strong ambivalence in regard to the very existence of the

Joint Committee and the desire to bypass it, are evident in most meetings of the RPTWO Central Committee whenever the subject came up. This was especially true when representatives of the HE were present. See Meeting of the Arab Committee of the Histadrut Executive with representatives of the Central Committee of the RPTWO, 19 October 1934. LA, IV 250–27–1–435; 25 November 1935. LA, IV 28–1–815c; 15 March 1936. LA, IV 208–1–815a.

83. Leaflet of ten Arab railway workers to members of the RPTWO and to railway workers in the PAWS, 7 June 1928. LA, IV 208–1–143A. Document translated into Hebrew from Arabic.

84. For example, From Joint Committee to HC, 9 May 1934. LA, IV 237–34; Joint Committee to HC, 17 July 1934. ISA, R/36/34. Doc. No. 375.

85. Formal Announcement 18/35, 17 May 1935. ISA, Doc. No. 375. File No. R/36/34.

86. General Council of Railway Workers to HC, 30 May 1935. LA, IV 237–34A-G.

87. Official Communique 29/35. ISA, R/36/34. Doc. No. 375; also "Outline of the points raised by the HC in his meeting with the delegates of the PR workers," 17 June 1935. LA, IV 208–1–815A.

88. For example, Meeting of the Central Committee of the RPTWO, 3 September 1935, LA. IV 208–1–815a; Extended Central Committee of RPTWO, 25 November 1935. LA, IV 208–1–815c.

89. Ibid.

90. General Statement of the Arab Organization of Railway Workers, On the Decision to Disband the Joint Committee, February 1936. LA, IV 208–1–815C (Arabic); Secretariat of RPTWO, 1st and 2nd of March 1936, LA, IV 2081–815a, 815c.

91. For example, Minutes of meeting of Arab and Jewish railway workers, 9 April 1936. LA, IV 237–24.

92. For example, Plenary meeting of Central Committee of RPTWO, 18 April 1936. LA, IV 208–1–815A.

93. Report of Central Committee of RPTWO, 16.6.40–7.8.40, LA, IV 208–1–2109; Report of meeting of delegation of workers with General Manager, 27 August 1940. LA, IV 208–1–2109.

94. Workers of the Qishon Workshops to the GM, n.d., LA, IV 208–1–2109.

95. 11 February 1940; 18 February 1940. LA, IV 208–1–2109.

96. Report of Central Committee of RPTWO, 18 June 1940. LA, ibid.

97. Report of the meeting of the workers' delegation with the General Manager, 27 August 1940. LA, 208–1–2109.

98. Report of Abramov concerning renewed contact with Arab representatives, 4 February 1943. LA IV 219–14. The issue of parity had become one of the points of contention between Jews and Arabs in Palestine. The Arabs demanded that the composition of any joint body reflect the relative proportion of each national group in the population of Palestine, while the Jews insisted on equal representation.

99. Letter of General Manager of PR to International Union of Railway and

Post & Telegraph Employees and the Railway Arab Workers Trade Union, 30 January 1943. LA, IV 208–1–3660.

100. For brief report of first five sessions, see Report sent to members of the Central Committee and the local branches, 7 January 1944. LA, IV 208–1–3660.

101. Report by Abramov, 4 February 1943, LA, IV 219–14. Abramov was the secretary of the RPTWO.

102. Concerning the *Shomer Hatza'ir* in Haifa, see Mordechai Lahav, "The Ha-Shomer Ha-Tza'ir Faction in Haifa, 1934–1937," *Me'asef* 15 (1985): 143–57 (Hebrew).

103. On the Strike in the railway workshops, the *Shomer Hatza'ir*, and the Socialist League, Haifa. 10 February 1944. Giv'at Haviva, (4) 15.90. The left-wing *Shomer Hatza'ir* and its affiliated Socialist League were the dominant force in the Haifa branch of the RPTWO. The sercretariat of the branch was composed of two members of the *Shomer Hatza'ir*, one of whom was the secretary, two members of *Mapai* and one communist; thus *Mapai*, the party in total control of the HLC, was in the minority.

104. The Strike in the Railway Workshops in Haifa. Unsigned but most probably written by Aba Houshi. 23 February 1944. LA, IV 208–1–3660. This report differs in many specific points, and in its overall tone, from the report of the *Shomer Hatza'ir* quoted above.

105. On the Strike in the Railway Workshops, the *Shomer Hatza'ir*, and the Socialist League, Haifa. 10 February 1944. Giv'at Haviva, (4) 15.90.

106. Nemirovsky, Minutes of the debate in the Histadrut Executive, 24 April 1946. Minutes of the Histadrut Executive, Vol. 80, LA—Library.

107. Ibid.

108. For a detailed breakdown of demands and achievements, see *Ba-Ma'avak*, RPTWO. 14 April 1946. LA, Library, IV 237–1946.

109. Report of the General Manager for 1946/47, pp. 11–14.

110. See Glossary.

111. Tamir Goren, "Why Did the Arab Population Leave Haifa?" *Cathedra* 80 (1996): 175–208 (Hebrew); Benny Morris, *The Birth of the Palestinian Refugee Problem, 1947–1949* (Tel Aviv: Am Oved, 1991), pp. 65–71 (Hebrew).

112. Krisher to HE, 5 February 1948. LA, IV 250–27–1–32.

113. David Korn, *The Massacre in the Refineries* (Ramat Efal: Yad Tabenkin, 1987) (Hebrew).

114. Krisher to HE, ibid.

115. This was stated based on the assumption that Sami Taha had changed his basic attitude to the Jewish settlement in Palestine, and that his associates carried on that line after his assassination in September 1947, three months previous to the writing of this letter.

116. Ibid.

117. Goren, "Why Did the Arab Population"; Morris, *The Birth of the Refugee Problem*, 106–34.

118. Interview with Y. Abramov, 1972. LA. Oral History. Abramov mentioned that Said Qawwas had become a teacher in a vocational school in Damascus. Qawwas was originally from Syria. It is interesting to note that Abra-

mov had this information, though the interview does not enlighten us as to how and when he received it.

Conclusion

1. In this study I was not able to elaborate on the joint strikes of the Jewish and Arab army camps workers during the Second World War; see Deborah Bernstein, "From Split Labour Market Strategy to Political Co-optation: The Palestine Labour League," *Middle Eastern Studies* 31 (1995):755–71.
2. Agnes Calliste, "The Struggle for Employment Equity by Blacks on American and Canadian Railroads," *Journal of Black Studies* 25 (1995):297–317; Cliff Brown and Terry Boswel, "Strikebreaking or Solidarity in the Great Steel Strike of 1919: A Split Labor Market, Game-Theoretic, and QCA Analysis," *American Journal of Sociology* 100 (1995):1479–1519.

Bibliography

Archives

Labor Archive (LA)
    Histadrut Executive—IV 208
    Haifa Labor Council—IV 250–27
    RPTWO—IV 237
    Department for the Affairs of the Arab Worker—IV 219
    Department of Public Works—IV 210
    Private collections—IV 104
        Eliahu Agassi
        Yitzhak Ben Zvi
Central Zionist Archive (CZA)
    Political Department—S/25
    Labor Department—S/9
    Sea Department—S/11
Israel State Archive (ISA)
    C.O., 733
Givat Haviva (GH)
Aba Houshi Archive (AHA)
Haifa Municipal Archive (HMA)
Haganna Archive
Archive of Kfar Massarik

Unpublished Theses and Manuscripts

Aboud, Nader, *The Palestinian Arab Labour Movement Association, 1925–1947* (Unpublished M.A. Thesis, University of Haifa, Haifa, 1988) (Hebrew).

Agmon, Iris, *Women and Society: Muslim Women, the Shar'i Court and the Society of Jaffa and Haifa under Late Ottoman Rule (1900–1914)* (Unpublished Ph.D. Thesis, Hebrew University of Jerusalem, Jerusalem, 1994) (Hebrew).

Bar-Yishay Zacks, Hanna, *Female Labor Force Participation in a Developing Economy, Pre-State Israel as a Case Study* (Unpublished Ph.D. Thesis, University of Minnesota, 1991).

De Vries, David, *The Labour Movement in Haifa, 1919–1929: A Study in the History of Urban Workers in Mandatory Palestine* (Unpublished Ph.D. Dissertation, Tel Aviv University, 1991) (Hebrew).

Finegold, Julian L., *British Economic Policy in Palestine 1920–1948* (Unpublished Ph.D. Dissertation, London School of Economics, London, 1978).

Halamish, Aviva, *Immigration and Absorption Policy of the Zionist Organization, 1931–1937* (Unpublished Ph.D. Thesis, University of Tel Aviv, Tel Aviv, 1995) (Hebrew).

Rosen, Adi, *A Common Trade Union for Jewish and Arab Workers in Palestine in the Twenties* (Unpublished M.A. Thesis, University of Haifa, Haifa, 1987) (Hebrew).

Rosen, Giora, *The Histadrut Trade Union in the Period of the Second World War, 1939–1945* (Unpublished M.A. Thesis, Tel Aviv University, Tel Aviv, 1974) (Hebrew).

Seikaly, May, *The Arab Community of Haifa 1918–1936. A Study in Transformation* (Unpublished D. Phil., University of Oxford, Oxford, 1983).

Smith, Barbara J., *British Economic Policy in Palestine Towards the Development of the Jewish National Home, 1920–1929* (Unpublished D. Phil, University of Oxford, Oxford, 1978).

Stern, Shimon, *The Development of the Urban Layout of Haifa, 1918–1947* (Unpublished Ph.D. Thesis, Hebrew University, Jerusalem, 1974).

Tadmor, Yoav, *The Palestine Labor League, 1940–1947* (Unpublished M.A. Thesis, Tel Aviv University, Tel Aviv, 1981) (Hebrew).

Taqqu, Rochelle, *Arab Labor in Mandatory Palestine* (Unpublished Ph.D. Dissertation. Columbia University, New York, 1977).

Vashitz, Joseph, *Jewish-Arab Relations at Haifa under the British Mandate* (Institute for Arab Studies, Givat Haviva, 1973) (Unpublished ms.).

———, *Social Changes in Haifa's Arab Society Under the British Mandate* (Unpublished Ph.D. Dissertation, Hebrew University of Jerusalem, Jerusalem, 1993).

Yazbeck, Mahmud, *The Arab Immigration to Haifa, 1933–1948* (Unpublished M.A. Thesis, University of Haifa, 1986) (Hebrew).

———, *Haifa in the Latter Period of the Ottoman Rule: Selected Issues in the Development of Administration and Society* (Unpublished Ph.D. Thesis, University of Haifa, 1992) (Hebrew).

Reports and Censuses

Be'eri, Eliezer, *The Arab Worker in the State of Israel* (1948) (unpublished mimeo) (Hebrew).

Census of the Jews of Palestine—1839, According to Montefiori's Manuscript, No. 528 (Jerusalem: The Dinur Center, 1987) (Hebrew).

Colonial Office, Report by His Majesty's Government in the United Kingdom of Great Britain and Northern Ireland to the Council of the League of Nations on the Administration of Palestine and Trans-Jordan For the Year 1920/21 (London: His Majesty's Stationery Office, 1922). Likewise for the years 1922–1939.

Colonial Office. Palestine, Report on Immigration, Land Settlement and Development, By Sir John Hope-Simpson C.I.E (London: His Majesty's Stationery Office, 1930).

Government of Palestine, Report of the Wages Commission, 1928. ISA, CO. 733 152.

Government of Palestine, Palestine Royal Commission, Memoranda Prepared by the Government of Palestine (London: His Majesty's Stationery Office, 1937).

Government of Palestine, Report of the Wages Committee. Under the Chairmanship of His Honour Mr. Justice F. Gordon Smith K. C., Chief Justice of Palestine (Jerusalem: The Government Printer, 1943).

Government of Palestine, A Survey of Palestine, Prepared in December 1945 and January 1946 for the information of the Anglo-American Committee of Inquiry. Vol. 1, 2. (Jerusalem: The Government Printer, 1946).

Government of Palestine. Notes compiled for the information of the United Nations Special Committee on Palestine (Supplement to Survey of Palestine) (Jerusalem: The Government Printer, 1947).

Government of Palestine. Department of Labour, Annual Report for the Year 1942 (Jerusalem: Printing and Stationery Office, 1943). Likewise—Annual Report for 1944; 1946.

Government of Palestine. Department of Labour, Department of Labour Bulletin, for the years 1942–1947 (Jerusalem: Printing and Stationery Office).

Government of Palestine. Office of Statistics. Statistical Abstract of Palestine 1936 (Jerusalem: The Government Printer, 1937).

Government of Palestine. Department of Statistics, Wage Rates Statistics Bulletin 1937 (January 1937).

Government of Palestine. Office of Statistics. Statistical Abstract of Palestine 1942. (Jerusalem, 1943).

Government of Palestine. Department of Statistics. Statistical Abstract of Palestine 1943 (Jerusalem, 1944).

Government of Palestine. Department of Statistics. Special Bulletin, No. 13. Wage Census, 1943, 1944.

Government of Palestine. Palestine Railways & Operated Lines. Report of the General Manager on the Administration of the Railways, For the year ended 31 December 1931. Jerusalem, 1931.

Government of Palestine. Palestine Railway. Report of the General Manager on the Administration of the Palestine Railways and Operated Lines and on the Ports of Palestine, for the Year 1946/47. Haifa, 1947.

Gurevitz, David, *Jewish Industry, Transportation and Commerce*, Report and Statistical Conclusion of the censuses conducted in 1937 (Jerusalem: Publication of the Department of Commerce and Industry of the Jewish Agency, 1939) (Hebrew).

The Histadrut, *The Histadrut in Haifa 1933–1939* (Haifa: the HLC, 1939) (Hebrew).

The Histadrut, "The General Census of the Jewish Workers of Eretz Israel—1937," *Pinkas* (Supplementary to *Davar*, January 1938) (Hebrew).

Jewish Agency for Palestine, "Report and General Abstracts of the Census of Labour 1930," *Palestine and Near East* 6 (1931): xi-78.

Jewish Agency for Palestine, "Report and General Abstracts of the Census of Industry and Handicrafts," *Palestine and Near East* 6 (1931): 348–98.

Jewish Agency for Palestine, Memorandum submitted to the Palestine Royal Commission on behalf of the Jewish Agency of Palestine (London: Jewish Agency for Palestine, 1936).

Klieman, Aaron S., ed., "Palestine, Report and General Abstracts of the Census of 1922," in *The Rise of Israel—Practical Zionism, 1920–1939* (New York: Garland Publishing Inc., 1987).

Palestine Royal Commission, Report (London: His Majesty's Printer, 1937).

Periodicals

Davar
Filastin
al-Karmil

Books and Articles

Abd al-Kadr, Yasin, "The Working Class and the Political Movement in Palestine," *Shu'un Palestini'ya* 56 (1976):106–50 (Arabic).

Abramovitz, Zeev, "Social-Economic Structure of Arab Palestine," in Sereni Enzo and R. E. Ashery, *Jews and Arabs in Palestine, Studies in a National and Colonial Problem* (New York: Hyperion Press Inc., 1976) (Reprint of publication from 1936, Hechalutz Press, NY), pp. 29–49.

Abramovitz, Zeev, and Yitzhak Gelfat, *The Arab Economy in Palestine and in the Middle East* (Ein Harod: Hakibbutz Hameuchad Publication, 1944) (Hebrew).

Aharonovitz, Haim, *Hadar Hacarmel* (Haifa: Va'ad Hadar Hacarmel, 1958) (Hebrew).

Anderson, Benedict, *Imagined Communities, Reflections on the Origin and Spread of Nationalism* (London: Verso, 1983).

Arlosoroff, Chaim, "Economic Background of the Arab Question," in Sereni and Ashery, *Jews and Arabs in Palestine*, pp. 3–29.

Arnon-Ohana, Yuval, "The Isteqlal Party—The Beginning of Palestinian Arab Radicalism," *Cathedra* 12 (1979): 91–110 (Hebrew).

Ashbal, Aminadav, *Sixty Years of The Palestine Land Development Corporation* (Jerusalem: The Restoration Fund, 1970) (Hebrew).

———, *The Palestine Land Development Corporation* (Jerusalem: The Restoration Fund, 1976) (Hebrew).

Assaf, Michael, *The Relations between Jews and Arabs in Palestine, 1860–1948* (Tel Aviv: Tarbut and Hinuh, 1970) (Hebrew).

Avitsur, Shmuel, "Seventy Years of Railways in Palestine," in The Geography Department of the Kibbutz Movement (ed.), *The Development of the Railway in Palestine* (Tel Aviv: 1980), pp. 62–71 (Hebrew).

———, *The History of Industry in Eretz Israel*, In the memory of Nahum Vilbush (Herzelia, 1974) (Hebrew).

Avi-Yona, Mordechai (ed.), *A Flask of Oil, The Twentieth Anniversary of 'Shemen'* (Haifa: 'Shemen', 1945) (Hebrew).

Avizohar, Meir and Ya'acov Shavit, "A Ceiling to the Standard of Living: On the Absence of a Norm for a Maximum Standard of Living as Part of an Egalitarian Policy," *Social Security* 16 (1978): 40–52 (Hebrew).

Avniel, B., *Labor Problems in Eretz Israel* (Jerusalem: Reuben Mass Publication, 1941) (Hebrew).

Baer, Gabriel, "The Arab Worker and His Organizational Awakening," *Be'ayot* 1 (1944):188–92 (Hebrew).

———, "The Arab Labor Movement," *Be'ayot* 1 (1944):230–38 (Hebrew).

———, "The Question of the Cooperation Between Jewish and Arab Workers," *Be'ayot* 2 (1945): 253–63 (Hebrew).

Barnai, Jacob, *Historiography and Nationalism, Trends in the Research of Palestine and Its Jewish Yishuv (634–1881)* (Jerusalem: Magnes Press, The Hebrew University, 1995) (Hebrew).

Bashear, Suliman, *Communism in the Arab World, 1918–1928* (London: Ithaca Press. 1980).

Beilin, Yossi, *Roots of Israeli Industry* (Jerusalem: Keter Publications, 1987) (Hebrew).

Ben Artzi, Yossi, *Residential Patterns and Intra Urban Migration of Arabs in Haifa* (Haifa: The University of Haifa and the Jewish-Arab Center, Occasional Papers on the Middle East, No. 1, 1980) (Hebrew).

———, "The Uniqueness of Haifa and its Development during the Mandate Period," *Idan* 12 (1989):27–37 (Hebrew).

———, *From Germany to the Holy Land, Templer Settlement in Palestine* (Jerusalem: Yad Yitzhak Ben Zvi, 1996) (Hebrew).

Ben-Israel, Hedva, "The Study of Nationalism as an Historical Phenomenon," in J. Reinharz, G. Shimoni and Y. Salmon (eds.), *Jewish Nationalism and Politics: New Perspectives* (Jerusalem and Boston: Zalman Shazar Center and the Tauber Institute, Brandeis University, 1996), pp. 57–80.

Ben Porath, Amir, *Between Class and Nation, The Formation of the Jewish Working Class in the Period before Israel's Statehood* (New York: Westview Press, 1986).

Ben-Rafael, Eliezer, "Critical Versus Non-critical Sociology: An Evaluation," *Israel Studies* 2 (1997): 174–93.

Berlovitz, Yaffah, *Inventing a Land, Inventing a People* (Tel Aviv: Hakibbutz Hameuchad, 1996) (Hebrew).

Bernstein, Deborah, *Struggle for Equality, Jewish Women in Prestate Israeli Society* (New York: Praeger, 1987).

———, "From Split Labour Market Strategy to Political Co-optation: The Palestine Labour League," *Middle Eastern Studies* 31 (1995):755–71.

———, "Jews and Arabs in the Nesher Cement Works," *Cathedra* 78 (1995): 82–107 (Hebrew).

———, "Expanding the Split Labor Market Theory: Between and Within Sectors of the Split Labor Market of Mandatory Palestine," *Comparative Studies in Society and History* 38 (1996):243–66.

———, "Strategies of Equalization: Jews and Arabs in the Split Labor Market of Mandatory Palestine," *Ethnic and Racial Studies* 21 (1998):449–75.

———, "Daughters of the Nation—Between the Public and the Private Spheres of the *Yishuv*," in Judith Baskin, *Jewish Women in Historical Perspective* (Second edition, Wayne University Press, 1998), pp. 287–331.

Biger, Gideon, *Crown Colony or National Homeland?* (Jerusalem: Yad Yizhak Ben-Zvi Publication, 1983) (Hebrew).

———, "The Industrial Structure of Eretz Israel in the 1920s," *Cathedra* 29 (1983): 79–113 (Hebrew).

———, "The Strategic View of Haifa in the Eyes of the British Rule," *Idan* 12 (1989): 59–68 (Hebrew).

Biletzki, Eliahu, *Creation and Struggle, the Haifa Labor Council 1921–1981* (Tel Aviv: Am Oved: 1981) (Hebrew).

Bonacich, Edna, "A Theory of Ethnic Antagonism: The Split Labor Market," *American Sociological Review* 37 (1972): 547–59.

———, "Abolition, the Extension of Slavery and the Position of Free Blacks: A Study of Split Labor Markets in the United States, 1830–1863," *American Journal of Sociology* 81 (1975): 601–28.

———, "Advanced Capitalism and Black/White Race Relations in the United States: A Split Labor Market Interpretation," *American Sociological Review* 41 (1976): 34–51.

———, "The Past, Present and Future of Split Labor Market Theory," *Research in Race and Ethnic Relations* 1 (1979): 17–64.

———, "Class Approaches to Ethnicity and Race," *Insurgent Sociologist* 10 (1980): 59–75.

———, "Capitalism and Race Relations in South Africa: A Split Labor Market Analysis," *Political Power and Social Theory* 2 (1981): 239–77, 337–43.

Boswell, Terry E., "A Split Labor Market Analysis of Discrimination Against Chinese Immigrants, 1850–1882," *American Sociological Review* 51 (1986): 352–71.

Brown, Cliff, and Terry Boswell, "Strikebreaking or Solidarity in the Great Steel Strike of 1919: A Split Labor Market, Game Theoretic and QCA Analysis," *American Journal of Sociology* 100 (1995): 1479–1519.

Budeiri, Musa, *The Palestine Communist Party 1919–1948, Arab and Jew in the Struggle for Internationalism* (London: Ithaca Press, 1979).

———, *The Development of the Workers' Movement in Palestine, 1919–1948* (Jerusalem: Dar al-Kitab, 1979) (Arabic).

Burawoy, Michael, "The Capitalist State in South Africa: Marxist and Sociological Perspectives," *Political Power and Social Theory* 2 (1981): 279–336.

Calliste, Agnes, "The Struggle for Employment Equity by Blacks on American and Canadian Railroads," *Journal of Black Studies* 25 (1995): 297–317.

Carmel, Alex, *The History of Haifa during the Ottoman Period* (Haifa: University of Haifa, 1969) (Hebrew).

———, "The German Settlers in Palestine and their Relations with the Local Arab Population and the Jewish Community," in M. Maoz, ed., *Studies on Palestine During the Ottoman Period* (Jerusalem: The Magnes Press, 1975), pp. 443–65.

———, *The German Settlement in Palestine in the Late Ottoman Period* (Haifa: University of Haifa, 1995) (Hebrew).

Carmi, Shulamit, and Henry Rosenfeld, "The Origins of the Process of Proletarianization and Urbanization of the Arab Peasants in Palestine," *Annals of the New York Academy of Sciences* 220 (1974): 270–85.

Cohen, Abraham, *Prosperity and Depression in the Economy of Eretz Israel* (Merhavia: Ha-Shomer Ha-Tza'ir, 1956) (Hebrew).

———, *The Economy of the Arab Sector in Palestine during the Mandate Period* (Giv'at Haviva: The Institute for Arab Studies, 1978) (Hebrew).

Cohen, Aharon, *The Arab Labor Movement* (Tel Aviv: The Publication of the Department for the Affairs of the Arab Worker of the Histadrut Executive, 1947) (Hebrew).

Corzine, J., L. Huff-Curzine and J. Creech, "The Tenant Labor Market and Lynching in the South: A Test of Split Labor Market Theory," *Sociological Inquiry* 58 (1988): 261–78.

Dar, Lina, "The Experiment of Jewish-Arab Trade Union in the Haifa Port, 1932," *Me'asef* 14 (1988): 45–79 (Hebrew).

Davidon, Ya'acov, *There Once Was a Haifa* (Haifa: Mai Publication, n.d.) (Hebrew).

De Vries, David, "The Roots of 'Red Haifa,'" *Idan* 12 (1989): 79–94 (Hebrew).

———, "The Formation of a Jewish Workers' Movement in Haifa in the 1920s," *Proceedings of the Tenth World Congress of Jewish Studies,* Division B. Vol. 1 (1990): 378 (Hebrew).

———, "Struggles Over Power and Authority Among Industrial Workers of

Eretz Israel: The Workers of 'Nesher' in the Twenties," *Yahadut Zmanenu* 8 (1993): 177–215 (Hebrew).
———, "Proletarianization and National Segregation: Haifa in the 1920s," *Middle Eastern Studies* 30 (1994): 860–82.
Dothan, Shmuel, "The Beginning of Jewish National Communism in Palestine," *Zionism* 2 (1971): 208–36 (Hebrew).
———, *Reds, The Communist Party in Palestine* (Kfar Saba: Shva Ha-Sofer Publishers, 1991).
Doumani, Beshara, "Rediscovering Ottoman Palestine: Writing Palestinians into History," *Journal of Palestine Studies* 21 (1992): 5–28.
———, *Rediscovering Palestine: Merchants and Peasants in Jabal Nablus, 1700–1900* (Berkeley: University of California Press, 1995).
Ehrlich, Avishai, "Israel: Conflict, War and Social Change," in C. Creighton and M. Show (eds.), *The Sociology of War and Peace* (Devonshire: Macmillan, 1987), pp. 121–42.
Eisenberg, Ovadia, *The Hebrew Community Council of Haifa—1938* (Haifa: Community Council, 1940) (Hebrew).
Elizur, Yuval, *Economic Warfare, The Hundred-Year Economic Confrontation between Jews and Arabs* (Tel Aviv: Kinneret, 1997) (Hebrew).
Esco Foundation for Palestine, *Palestine, A Study of Jewish, Arab and British Policies* (New Haven: Yale University Press, 1947).
Eshel, Tzadok, *The Cement and Its Creators, The Fiftieth Anniversary of 'Nesher'* (Haifa: 'Nesher', 1976) (Hebrew).
———, *The Port of Haifa—From Manual Labor to Advanced Technology* (Haifa: Publication of The Port Authority, 1984) (Hebrew).
Farah, Bulous, *From the Ottomans to the Jewish State* (Acre: al-Sout, 1985) (Arabic).
Firestone, Yaacov, "Crop-Sharing Economics in Mandatory Palestine," in Kedouri and Haim, eds., *Palestine and Israel in 19th and 20th Centuries*, pp. 153–195.
Frances, Baseden Howell, "A Split Labor Market: Mexican Farm Workers in the Southwest," *Sociological Inquiry* 52 (1982): 132–140.
Ganin, Zvi, *Kiryat Ha'im Arlosorov, An Experiment in Urban Eutopia, 1933–1938* (Tel Aviv: Va'ad Kiryat Ha'im, 1984) (Hebrew).
Gat, Ben-Zion, *The Jewish Settlement in Eretz Israel, 1840–1881* (Jerusalem: Yad Yizhak Ben Zvi, 1974) (Hebrew).
Gellner, Ernest, *Encounters with Nationalism* (Oxford: Blackwell, 1994).
Gertz, A., *Statistical Handbook of Jewish Palestine* (Jerusalem: Department of Statistics of the Jewish Agency for Palestine, 1947).
Gilbar, Gad, "Trends in the Demographic Development of the Arabs of Palestine, 1870–1948," *Cathedra* 45 (1988): 43–56 (Hebrew).
Goldstein, Ya'acov, "The Events of 1929 in Haifa," *Idan* 12 (1989): 171–84 (Hebrew).
Goren, Tamir, "Why Did the Arab Population Leave Haifa?" *Cathedra* 80 (1996): 175–208.
Gottheil, Fred, "Arab Immigration into Pre-State Israel," in Kedouri and Haim, eds., *Palestine and Israel in the 19th and 20th Centuries*, pp. 143–53.
Gozansky, Tamar, *Formation of Capitalism in Palestine* (Haifa: University Publishing Projects Ltd., 1986) (Hebrew).
Graham-Brown, Sarah, "The Political Economy of the Jabal Nablus, 1920–48," in Roger Owen (ed.), *Studies in the Economic and Social History of Palestine in*

the Nineteenth and Twentieth Centuries (Basingstoke and London: St. Anthony's, 1986), pp. 88–176.

Grinberg, Lev Luis, *The Histadrut Above All* (Jerusalem: Nevo Publishing, 1993) (Hebrew).

———, "The Strike of the Jewish-Arab Drivers' Organization, 1931, A Contribution to the Critique of the Sociology of the National Conflict in Eretz Israel/Palestine," in Ilan Pappe (ed.), *Jewish-Arab Relations in Mandatory Palestine* (Givat Haviva: Institute for Peace Studies, 1995), pp. 157–78. (Hebrew).

Gross, Nachum, "Haifa at the Beginning of the Industrialization in Palestine," *The Economic Quarterly* (1980): 308–19 (Hebrew).

———, "The Economic Policy of the Government of Palestine During the Mandate Period," *Cathedra* 24/25 (1982): 153–80; 135–68 (Hebrew).

Gross, N. and Y. Metzer, "Palestine in World War II: Some Economic Aspects," in G. Mills and H. Rockoff, eds., *The Sinews of War: Essays on the Economic History of World War II* (Ames: Iowa State University Press. Reprinted by The Maurice Falk Institute for Economic Research in Israel, Research Paper 207, Jerusalem: Falk Institute, 1993).

Hacohen, David, *My Way* (Tel Aviv: Am Oved, 1979) (Hebrew).

Haifa Chamber of Commerce, *Haifa—The City of the Future* (Haifa: Chamber of Commerce, 1932) (Hebrew).

———, *Haifa—What Has Been Done? For the 40th Anniversary, 1921–1961* (Haifa: Chamber of Commerce, 1961) (Hebrew).

Haifa Community Council, *The Community of Haifa in the Decade of 1931–1941* (Haifa: The Community Council of Haifa, 1942) (Hebrew).

Halevi, Nadav, *The Economic Development of the Jewish Community in Palestine, 1917–1947* (Jerusalem: The Maurice Falk Institute for Economic Research, 1979) (Hebrew).

———, "The Political Economy of Absorptive Capacity: Growth and Cycles in Jewish Palestine under the British Mandate," *Middle Eastern Studies* 19 (1983): 456–69.

Herbert, Gilbert, "Crossroads: Imperial Priorities and Regional Perspectives in the Planning of Haifa, 1918–1939," *Planning Perspectives* 4 (1989): 313–31.

Himadeh, Sa'id, *Economic Organization of Palestine* (Beirut: American Press, 1938).

Hobsbawm, Eric, *Nations and Nationalism Since 1780* (Cambridge: Cambridge University Press, 1990).

Horowitz, Dan, "Before the State: Communal Politics in Palestine Under the Mandate," in Kimmerling, ed., *Israeli State and Society*, pp. 28–65.

Horowitz, Dan, and Moshe Lissak. *The Origins of the Israeli Polity* (Tel Aviv: Am Oved, 1977) (Hebrew).

Horowitz, David, and Rita Hinden, *Economic Survey of Palestine* (Tel Aviv: Economic Research Institute of the Jewish Agency for Palestine, 1938).

Kaminker, Aharon, *The Neighborhood by the Smoke Stacks, Memories of the Neighborhood of Nesher* (Haifa, 1978) (Hebrew).

Kark, Ruth, *Jaffa, 1799–1919* (Jerusalem: Yad Yitzhak Ben Zvi, 1985) (Hebrew).

Katz, Jacob, "History and Historians, New and Old," *Alpayim* 12 (1996): 9–34 (Hebrew).

Kedourie, Elie, and Sylvia G. Haim (eds.), *Palestine and Israel in the 19th and 20th Centuries* (London: Frank Cass, 1982).

———, *Zionism and Arabism in Palestine and Israel* (London: Frank Cass, 1982).

Kehilat Haifa, 1932–1941 (Haifa: Ott Press, 1942) (Hebrew).

Khalfon, Avraham, "Haifa, My Town," in Y. Nedava (ed.), *Haifa, Olifant and the Zionist Vision* (Haifa: University of Haifa, n.d.) (Hebrew).

Kimmerling, Baruch, "The Arab-Jewish Conflict and the Processes of National Building During the Mandate Period," *Medina, Mimshal ve-Yekhasim Ben-Le'umi'im* 9 (1976): 35–55 (Hebrew).

——, *The Economic Interrelationships between the Arab and Jewish Communities in Mandatory Palestine* (Cambridge, Mass.: Center for International Studies, 1979).

——, *Zionism and Territory: The Socioterritorial Dimensions of Zionist Politics* (Berkeley: Institute of International Studies, University of California, 1983).

——, *Zionism and Economy* (Cambridge: Schenkman, 1983).

—— (ed.) *The Israeli State and Society, Boundaries and Frontiers* (Albany: SUNY Press, 1989).

——, "Boundaries and Frontiers of the Israeli Control System: Analytical Conclusions," In Kimmerling (ed.), *The Israeli State and Society*, pp. 265–84.

——, "Academic History Caught in the Cross-Fire: The Case of Israeli-Jewish Historiography," *History and Memory* 7 (1995): 41–65.

——, and Joel S. Migdal, *Palestinians, The Making of a People* (New York: Free Press, 1993).

Kirsh, Ephraim, *Fabricating Israeli History: The New Historians* (London: Frank Cass, 1997).

Klieman, Aaron S. *The Rise of Israel*, Vol. 15, Practical Zionism, 1920–1939 (New York: Garland Publishing Inc., 1987).

——, *The Rise of Israel*, Vol. 18. The Turn Towards Violence, 1920–1929 (New York: Garland Publishing Inc., 1987).

Klein, Itzhak, *The Arabs in Haifa Under the British Mandate, A Political, Economic and Social Survey* (Haifa: University of Haifa, The Jewish-Arab Center, Institute of Middle Eastern Studies, 1983) (Hebrew).

Krisher, Ephra'im, "Joint Organization (Memories)," *Me'asef* (1972): 160–170 (Hebrew)

Lachman, Shai, "Arab Rebellion and Terrorism in Palestine 1929–39: The Case of Sheikh Izz al-Din al-Qassam and His Movement," in Kedourie and Haim, *Arabism and Zionism*, pp. 52–99.

Lahav, Mordechai, "The *Ha-Shomer Ha-Tza'ir* Faction in Haifa, 1934–1937," *Me'asef* 15 (1985): 143–57 (Hebrew).

Lamdan, Yossef, "The Arabs and Zionism, 1882–1914," in Kolat, Israel (ed.), *The History of the Jewish Settlement in Eretz Israel Since the First Aliya—The Ottoman Period*, Part I. (Jerusalem: Mossad Bialik, 1976), pp. 215–54 (Hebrew).

Levi, Shabati, "From My Memories," in Y. Nedava (ed.), *Haifa, Olifant and the Zionist Vision* (Haifa: University of Haifa, n.d.), pp. 78–174 (Hebrew).

Livne, Zvi, *The Story of Ha'apala* (Tel Aviv: Tarbut ve-Hinuh, 1960) (Hebrew).

Lockman, Zachary, "Railway Workers and Relational History: Arabs and Jews in British-Ruled Palestine," *Comparative Studies in Society and History* 35 (1993): 601–27.

——, *Comrades and Enemies, Arab and Jewish Workers in Palestine, 1906–1948* (Berkeley: University of California Press, 1996).

Makabe, Tomoko, "The Theory of the Split Labor Market: A Comparison of the Japanese Experience in Brazil and Canada," *Social Forces* 59 (1981): 786–809.

Mansur, George, *The Arab Worker under the Palestine Mandate* (Jerusalem: Commercial Press, 1937).

———, "Evidence of Mr. George Mansur Before the Palestine Royal Commission" in Klieman (ed.), *The Rise of Israel*, Vol. 22., 340–43.

Margalit, Elkana, *The Anatomy of the Left, Po'alei Zion Smol in Eretz Israel, 1919–1946* (Tel Aviv: I. L. Peretz, 1976) (Hebrew).

Marks, Carole, "Split Labor Markets and Black-White Relations, 1865–1920," *Phylon* 42 (1981): 293–308.

Memories of Se'adia Paz (Haifa: Family publication, 1963) (Hebrew).

Metzer, Jacob, "Fiscal Incidence and Resource Transfer Between Jews and Arabs in Mandatory Palestine," *Research in Economic History* 7 (1982): 87–131.

———, "The Administered Territories and the Arab Economy of Mandatory Palestine, an historical perspective," *The Economic Quarterly* 35 (1988): 129–45 (Hebrew).

Metzer, Jacob, and Oded Kaplan, "Jointly by Severally: Arab-Jewish Dualism and Economic Growth in Mandatory Palestine," *The Journal of Economic History* 45 (1985): 327–45.

———, *The Jewish and Arab Economies in Mandatory Palestine: Product, Employment and Growth* (Jerusalem: Falk Institute for Economic Research in Israel, 1990) (Hebrew).

Migdal, Joel, *Palestinian Society and Politics* (Princeton: Princeton University Press, 1980).

Miller, Ylana, "Administrative Policy in Rural Palestine: The Impact of British Norms on Arab Community Life: 1920–1948," in Migdal, *Palestinians*, 124–45.

Miller, N. Ylana, *Government and Society in Rural Palestine 1920–1948* (Austin, Texas: University of Texas Press, 1985).

Mogannam, Matiel, *The Arab Woman and the Palestine Problem* (London: Herbert Joseph Ltd. 1937).

Morris, Benny, *The Birth of the Palestinian Refugee Problem, 1947–1949* (Tel Aviv: Am Oved, 1991), pp. 65–71 (Hebrew).

Nassar, Fat'hi, *The History of the Palestinian Arab Workers' Movement 1922–1946* (Tarablus: 1985) (Arabic).

Nedava, Yoseph (ed.), *Haifa, Olifant and the Zionist Vision* (Haifa: University of Haifa, 1980) (Hebrew).

Owen, Roger, "Economic Development in Mandatory Palestine: 1918–1948," in Abed George, *The Palestinian Economy* (London and New York: Routledge, 1988), pp. 13–35.

Pappe, Ilan, "Critique and Agenda: The Post-Zionist Scholars in Israel," *History and Memory* 7 (1995): 66–90.

———, "A New Agenda for the 'New History,'" *Te'oria u-Bikoret* 8 (1996): 123–37 (Hebrew).

———, "Zionism According to the Theories of Nationalism and the Historiographic Method," in *Zionism, A Contemporary Controversy* (The Institute for Ben Gurion's Heritage and the Ben Gurion University Press, Beer Sheba, 1996), pp. 223–61 (Hebrew).

Peled, Yoav, and Gershon Shafir, "Split Labor Market and the State: The Effects of Modernization on Jewish Industrial Workers in Tsarist Russia," *American Journal of Sociology* 92 (1987): 1435–60.

Porath, Yehoshua, "Revolution and Terror in the Palestinian Communist Party, 1929–1939," *Ha-Mizrah Ha-Hadash* 18 (1968): 255–67 (Hebrew).

———, "The National Liberation League—1943–1948," *Asian and African Studies* 4 (1968): 1–23.

———, "Social Aspects of the Emergence of the Palestinian National Movement," in Menahem Milson (ed.), *Society and Political Structure in the Arab World* (New York: Humanities Press, 1973), pp. 93–144.

———, *The Emergence of the Palestinian-Arab National Movement, 1918–1929* (Tel Aviv: Am Oved, 1976) (Hebrew).

———, *From Riots to Rebellion, The Palestinian-Arab National Movement, 1929–1939* (Tel Aviv: Am Oved, 1978) (Hebrew).

Portugali, Juval, *Implicate Relations, Society and Space in the Israeli Palestinian Conflict* (Tel Aviv: Hakibbutz Hameuchad, 1996) (Hebrew).

Ram, Uri, *The Changing Agenda of Israeli Sociology* (Albany: SUNY Press, 1995).

———, "Memory and Identity: The Sociology of the Historians' Controversy in Israel," *Te'oria u-Bikoret* 8 (1996): 9–32 (Hebrew).

Reichman, Shalom, *From Foothold to Settled Territory, The Jewish Settlement, 1918–1948* (Jerusalem: Yad Yitzhak Ben-Zvi, 1979) (Hebrew).

Repetor, Berl, *Relentlessly* (Tel Aviv: Hakibbutz Hameuchad, 1973) (Hebrew).

Rubinstein, Elyakim, "Jews and Arabs in the Palestine Municipalities (1926–1933), with Special Reference to Jerusalem," *Cathedra* 51 (1989): 122–47 (Hebrew).

Rubenstein, Sondra, *The Communist Movement in Palestine and Israel, 1919–1984* (Boulder: Westview Press, 1985).

Sawwaf, Husni, "Transportation and Communication," in Said Himadeh, *Economic Organization of Palestine*, pp. 301–42.

Sereni, Enzo, and R. E. Ashery, *Jews and Arabs in Palestine, Studies in a National and Colonial Problem* (New York: Hyperion Press, Inc. 1976) (Reprint of publication from 1936, Hechalutz Press, NY).

Shafir, Gershon, *Land, Labor and the Origins of the Israeli-Palestinian Conflict, 1882–1914* (Cambridge: Cambridge University Press, 1989).

———, "Israel Society: A Counterview," *Israel Studies* 1 (1996): 189–213.

Shalev, Michael, *Labour and the Political Economy in Israel* (Oxford: Oxford University Press, 1992).

Shapira, Anita, "The Left of Gdud Ha-Avoda and the PKP until 1928," *Zionism* (1971): 148–68 (Hebrew).

———, *The Futile Struggle, The Jewish Labour Controversy, 1929–1939* (Tel Aviv: Hakibbutz Hameuchad, 1977) (Hebrew).

———, "The Controversy in Mapai over the Use of Violence, 1931–1935," in A. Shapira (ed.), *Visions in Conflict* (Tel Aviv: Am Oved, 1990), pp. 82–117 (Hebrew).

———, *Land and Power* (Tel Aviv: Am Oved, 1992) (Hebrew).

———, "Politics and Collective Memory: The Debate over the 'New Historians' in Israel," *History and Memory* 7 (1995): 9–40.

Sheffer, Gabriel, "The Principles of British Pragmatism: Reevaluation of British Policies Towards Palestine in the 1930s," *Cathedra* 29 (1983):113–45 (Hebrew).

Silman, K. I., *Haifa, History and Development* (Tel Aviv: Omanut, 1931) (Hebrew).

Siyabonga, W. Ndabezitha, and Stephen K. Sanderson, "Racial Antagonism and the Origins of Apartheid in the South African Gold Mining Industry,

1886–1924: A Split Labor Market Analysis," *Research in Race and Ethnic Relations* 5 (1986): 231.

Smith, Anthony, *The Ethnic Origin of Nations* (Oxford: Oxford University Press, 1994).

Smith, Barbara J., *The Roots of Separatism in Palestine, British Economic Policy 1920–1929* (London: Tauris & Co. Ltd., 1993).

Sofer, Arnon, "The Distribution of Industry in the Haifa Bay Area," *Research in the Geography of Eretz Israel* 9 (1976): 136–55 (Hebrew).

Stern, Shimon, "The Dispute Concerning the Construction of Haifa Port During the British Mandate," *Cathedra* 21 (1981): 171–86 (Hebrew).

———, "Hadar Hacarmel—Center of Jewish Life in Haifa," *Idan* 12 (1989): 41 (Hebrew).

Studny, Ze'ev, "The Pioneers of the Class Struggle in the Arab Workers' Movement," *Me'asef* 5 (1973): 196–205 (Hebrew).

———, "The Strike of the 'Nesher' Workers," *Me'asef* 6 (1974): 166–75 (Hebrew).

———, "The Salonikis (Memories)," *Me'asef* 8 (1976): 153–56 (Hebrew).

Sussman, Zvi, "The Determination of Wages for Unskilled Labor in the Advanced Sector of the Dual Labor Market of Mandatory Palestine, *Economic Development and Cultural Change* 22 (1973): 95–113.

———, *Wage Differentials and Equality within the Histadrut* (Ramat Gan: Massada, 1974) (Hebrew).

Swirski, Shlomo, "Comments on the Historical Sociology of the Period of the Yishuv," *Mahbarot le-Mehkar u-le-Bikoret* 2 (1980): 3–29 (Hebrew).

Taqqu, Rochelle. "Peasants into Workmen: Internal Labor Migration and the Arab Village Community under the Mandate," Migdal, *Palestinians*, pp. 261–85.

Teveth, Shabtai, *Ben Gurion and the Palestinian Arabs* (Jerusalem: Schoken, 1985) (Hebrew).

Tidhar, A., *Encyclopedia of the Pioneers and the Builders of the Yishuv* (Tel Aviv, 1947), Vol. 4, pp. 1572–73; Vol. 6, p. 2446 (Hebrew).

Tzachor, Zeev, *The Histadrut—The Formative Period* (no place, no publisher, 1979) (Hebrew).

Vashitz, Joseph, *The Arabs in Eretz Israel* (Merhavia: Sifri'at Ha-Poalim, 1947) (Hebrew).

———, "Dhawat and Isamiyyun: Two Groups of Arab Community Leaders in Haifa During the British Mandate," *Asian and African Studies* 17 (1983): 95–120.

———, "Arab-Jewish Relations in Haifa, 1940–1948," in Nevo Yoseph and Yoram Nimrod (eds.), *The Arabs and the Zionist Movement and Jewish Settlement, 1946–1950* (Tivon: Oranim, 1987), pp. 21–37 (Hebrew).

———, "The Immigration of Villagers to Haifa During the Mandate Period: A Process of Urbanization?" *Cathedra* 45 (1988): 113–30 (Hebrew).

Vilnai, Ze'ev, *Haifa—Past and Future* (Tel Aviv: The Hebrew Society for the Study of Eretz Israel, 1936) (Hebrew).

Yazbeck, Mahmud, "The Arab Immigration to Haifa, 1933–1948: A Quantitative Analysis Based on Arab Sources," *Cathedra* 45 (1988): 132–46 (Hebrew).

———, "From *Falahin* to Rebels: The Economic Causes of the Outbreak of the 1936 Rebellion" (forthcoming).

Yiftachel, Oren, "Power Disparities in the Planning of a Mixed Region: Arabs and Jews in the Galilee, Israel," *Urban Studies* 30 (1993): 157–82.

Subject Index

Name Index